Exploring History All Around

by
Vivienne Evans

*Photographs and maps
by
Lewis Evans*

First published May 2002
by
The Book Castle
12 Church Street
Dunstable
Bedfordshire LU5 4RU

ISBN 1 903747 07 4

Designed by Priory Graphics, Flitwick, Bedfordshire
Printed by Antony Rowe, Chippenham, Wiltshire

CONTENTS

Acknowledgments

This year I am completing thirty years of lecturing about Local History and Heritage, one of the most popular subjects being 'Villages'. Twenty years ago Paul Bowes of The Book Castle attended one of these courses and asked me to write a book (History All Around) which would encourage more people to go out and explore for themselves. It proved a great success and this seemed a good time to write an entirely new version.

So many things have happened in these twenty years. My regular lectures at St Albans Abbey have given me the opportunity to make a detailed study of monastic history and my membership of the National Churches Tourism Group has given me the encouragement to study the history and heritage of our churches. In addition to this my membership of Bedfordshire Heartlands Tourism Association and my friendship with John Pilgrim and BBC Three Counties Radio have given me a wonderful further excuse to go out myself to research and explore a large part of the three counties.

Apart from the seven Routes and their Highlights each chapter starts with a piece of Historical Background. These have been carefully researched but cover such a wide area that mistakes may have crept in, for which I apologise. However I have tried to point out the sources which I have used and hope that others will continue with the research. I have also referred to numerous helpful books and have credited with thanks the many locally produced books and booklets. One of the most encouraging changes which have occurred is the number of history and heritage societies which are now established across the area.

I have been lucky to have so many friends and colleagues who have helped with the research and the production of this book without whose generous support it would not have been possible, but as always I must particularly thank my family and Paul Bowes for their encouragement and enormous support at every stage. We advise people following the routes to take a detailed map with them but Lou's Route-Maps will provide a helpful overview as will the beautiful pictures which he has taken. In addition I would like to thank the following for the use of additional photographs: Marie Kerr (M.K.), Mandy James (M.J.), English Heritage Photographic Library (E.H.), Omer Roucoux (O.R.), Whipsnade Wild Animal Park (W.W.A.P.), South Beds District Council (S.B.D.C.), Buckinghamshire County Council (Bucks C.C.), Mead Open Farm (M.O.F.), Bedfordshire Times and Citizen (B.T.C.), Paul Woodcraft (P.W.), Friends of Luton Museum (F.L.M.)

Foreword
by John Pilgrim, Three Counties Radio

I have spent a number of most revealing and fascinating years wandering around Bedfordshire, Buckinghamshire and Hertfordshire with my trusty tape recorder on behalf of local radio. Many of the places I have visited and the people I have met are preserved in my "Out and About" books, and in the first I paid a special tribute to the advice and support I have always received, whenever required, from "Viv". She has joined me on my travels on numerous occasions - adding her boundless enthusiasm to mine always creates a memorable day, no matter what the weather!

It is a privilege therefore to contribute a foreword to her latest book, which echoes my own endeavours to encourage everyone to explore the heritage around us. What a wealth of historical insight and knowledge she shares with us here. Add her immensely approachable style and it is easy to appreciate why she has been an inspiration to so many over the past thirty years.

Bedfordshire folk should be proud of this Sussex-born lady and glad that she adopted their county, working tirelessly with her husband Lou to explain and promote its many hidden treasures. Her style of broadcasting, lecturing and writing is so infectious and so well-informed. I commend "Exploring History All Around" as a certain joy to all who pick it up.

John and Vivienne in front of a misty Edlesborough Church

Map Symbols

―――― Route

▬ ▬ ▬ ▬ Alternative Route

――― Part of Junction not on Route

◉ Roundabout

▬··▬··▬··▬··· Railway

☐ **Start Town**

● Village or Town en route

☐ *Woburn Abbey*   Building

⛪ Church

🗼 Windmill

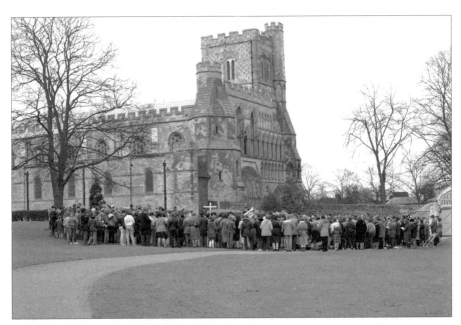

Good Friday 'Pilgrims' outside The Priory Church Dunstable

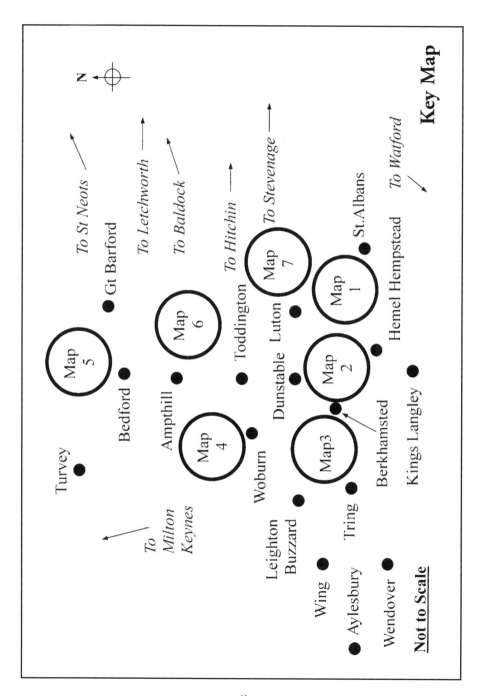

Key Map

Not to Scale

vii

Redbournbury Watermill (M.K.)

Children and animals enjoying each others' company at Woodside Animal Farm (M.K.)

CHAPTER 1 • *ROUTE 1*

The Influence of The Religious Houses

St Albans • Redbourn • (Flamstead) • Markyate • Kensworth
Studham • Whipsnade • Dunstable • (Caddington) • (Luton)
East Hyde • Batford • (Harpenden)
Wheathampstead • Sandridge • St Albans

Introduction

This Route is approximately 25 miles long and much of it is on main roads but there is an optional scenic route which adds a further 11 miles.

It starts in the historically important cathedral city of St Albans where, in addition to the abbey, there are two main museums, an attractive, lakeside park (with ducks), walking trails and numerous other attractions which are of interest to visitors.

On and just off the route there are attractive villages and interesting churches. Just off the A5, south of Redbourn, is the 18th century Redbournbury Watermill which sells organic, stoneground flour. It is in a beautiful setting on the River Ver and there is a riverside walk. Redbourn also has its own museum. On the B4540 between the A5 and Slip End, is Woodside Animal Farm where many animals and birds can be seen and fed.

The optional scenic route passes near to both Whipsnade Tree 'Cathedral', made up of different species of trees and shrubs, and Whipsnade Wild Animal Park. It passes right by Dunstable Downs visitor centre and picnic area. (The above three attractions are described more fully in Chapter 3.)

The Historical Background to this route concerns religious houses. Very few people realise just how many such houses there were in Bedfordshire and West Hertfordshire or that other religious houses, from different parts of England and abroad, also owned land in this area.

1

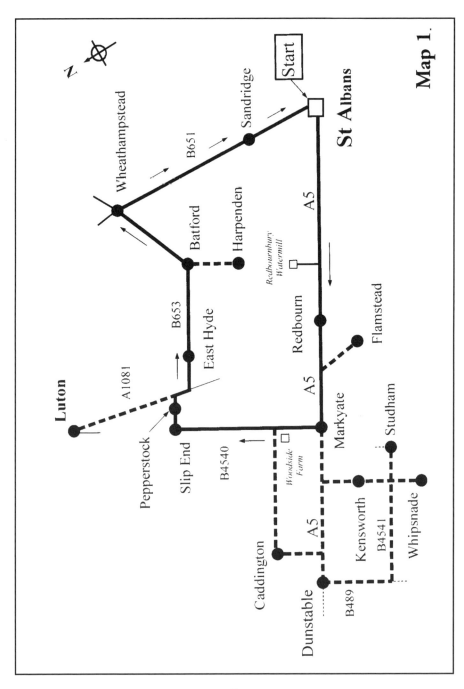

Map 1.

The aim is to use surviving information from different places on the route to demonstrate just how powerful they were and the enormous influence that they had over the people in the villages and towns over which they had control.

There are fewer Historical Highlights to be seen but the thirty-plus miles of roads and the towns and villages, farms and churches were nearly all owned by religious houses and the connections are pointed out in the script.

Historical Background

The Benedictine Monasteries

Sometime around the year 500AD a young Italian called Benedict left his comfortable home and family in Nursia (Umbria) and his wealthy friends in Rome and went to live a solitary life of contemplation at Subiaco. Other young men followed him and, after various experiments with communal living, he settled at Monte Casino and worked out the Rule, which is the backbone of that used by his followers today.

This was not the first attempt by an individual or small group to withdraw to an isolated area in order to enjoy long, uninterrupted periods of prayer and contemplation. However, earlier attempts had often involved searching out very inhospitable sites. In practice, this could mean that so much time was spent in protecting their house and struggling to procure food that there was little time left for prayer.

Benedict made use of previous Rules but felt strongly that the chosen sites should be reasonably sheltered and that the soil should be sufficiently fertile for the group to grow their own food and still have plenty of time for prayer and study. He could see no spiritual benefit in living in harsh conditions or in being short of food. Well before 530AD he was ready to start his first 'monastery' at Monte Casino, which was about forty miles from Rome.

He was also responsible for several other scattered groups and taught them to 'seek God together as a community' and to live in the strength of common prayer and common life. The brothers in each house were to obey their own 'father', the abbot, but Benedict's Rule, a long list of advisory clauses, was there to help them. The abbot was God's representative in the group, so it was necessary for the other members to obey him but Benedict suggested that before making major decisions he should consult with the other senior members. Good discipline was insisted upon, to respect human personality and the individual capabilities of the members.

3

Men who joined his groups were to be unmarried and chaste and the clause concerning poverty covered the fact that all land and possessions were to be shared by the community. There were many other clauses but one that would cause great problems in the future was that the stranger at the gate should be welcomed - as though it was Christ himself who stood there. This worked well at their isolated sites in Italy, where both guests and the occasional traveller were made extremely welcome. However, in the centuries to come, when the movement spread right across Europe, sites were often offered to the movement which were alongside busy roads, or even on important crossroads. Once this happened, the number of travellers made it impossible for the members of the community to grow sufficient food to feed themselves and their visitors. Even the home farms run by lay brothers, or paid workers, were not able to produce enough.

Benedict intended that the monks following his Rule should divide their day into regular periods of communal worship, private prayer, study and physical work. The latter would be in the house, workshops, gardens or farm. They were expected to build their own churches and to keep them extremely simple. Another problem which monasteries faced in later centuries was that the large number of visitors necessitated the provision (and consequential expense) of much larger churches.

Christianity Comes to England

About thirty-four years after the death of St Benedict, the Lombards sacked Monte Casino.* However, the monks escaped and fled to Rome; they built a new monastery and it was from there that Pope Gregory chose St Augustine to carry the message of Christianity across the seas to England. They were welcomed there by the King of Kent and given land at Canterbury.

During the period when the pagan Saxons settled across this part of England, the Romano - British form of Christian worship had more or less died out. However, it continued in Ireland and from there was carried to Iona and, at a later date, to Northumbria. So the original British form of worship was established in the north of England and the Roman/Benedictine form in the south. Travelling back to England from two such different routes, there were small differences in their forms of worship. These were ironed out at a great conference held at Whitby. From then on, the main pattern of dogma and worship was that which had been introduced by the Benedictines.

It was rebuilt and a new community established there in 717

4

After St Augustine's was founded in Canterbury in 597, the movement moved quickly into East Anglia, where Ely and Crowland were early examples, and into the west and south-west, where Glastonbury, Pershore and Bath were soon followed by Evesham and Worcester.

The Abbey at St Albans

As noted below, there is evidence that the Roman town of Verulamium continued for many years after the departure of the Roman legions and that the tomb of St Alban was protected and used as a site of pilgrimage during the unsettled years when the country was occupied by the pagan Saxons. It seems likely that as soon as this part of England became Christian, a group of monks lived on the site to protect and honour the tomb and to welcome pilgrims.

King Offa (757-795) was a devout Christian king and wanted to honour England's first martyr. He founded a Benedictine monastery on the site and over the centuries it became one of England's leading monasteries. Pilgrims from all over the country visited the shrine, while its position on such a busy crossroads brought numerous travellers requesting hospitality.

There were no set charges for this type of accommodation, but visitors were expected to move on quite quickly and leave a generous gift. However many of the pilgrims who visited the shrine (and also a percentage of the travellers) were sick or disabled and remained, hoping for a cure. Large monasteries had so many of this type of visitor that, at their own expense, they provided at least one 'hospital' for lepers and other sick people. This cost a great deal of money and in addition as the years went by, they had to provide an infirmary for their own sick and elderly members.

In the case of St Albans, it was a royal foundation and over the centuries there were many royal visits. Other monasteries were founded by local, wealthy patrons and, generations later, members of the family would use 'their' monastery as a hotel, retirement home or even a place to stay when they were short of money and being chased by their creditors!

These events, which began long before the Norman Conquest, created a situation very different from that envisaged by St Benedict. It was obviously impossible for a group of twenty or thirty monks to maintain buildings and provide food for hundreds of visitors and still to enjoy daily periods of communal worship and private prayer.

Easter Monday Pilgrimage outside St Albans Abbey

The Abbey Gatehouse St Albans

The Abbeys as Landowners

In each case the original patron provided a generous package of scattered land and houses, to provide income. The tenants of these pieces of land worked them (as they had previously) and paid rents to the monastery. These foundation gifts were seldom sufficient to support a house in the years to come and later gifts were essential. People who regularly travelled on a certain route would often make a gift of a house, shop, mill or even farm, as a way of making compensation for all the hospitality that they had enjoyed. Also, as noted in the chapter on churches, throughout the Middle Ages there was a strong and general desire to provide prayers for relatives who had recently died. Poorer people would provide sacks of grain to the abbey kitchen, or to the infirmary, or they might provide a small sum of money out of a rent from a garden, which they had let out to a tenant. Richer people gave (or let rent-free) a complete property which they owned.

When researching the history of a building (including churches), it is sometimes surprising to find that it was once owned by a religious house at the other end of the country, or even overseas. Donors did not necessarily give to their local monastery but to their favourite one, or the one with which they had a family connection. Because of this, King Edward the Confessor gave Wheathampstead Church (near St Albans) to his foundation at Westminster and the Earl of Gloucester gave Houghton Regis (near Dunstable) to St Albans Abbey.

The Managers

Because, even within a small house, there were many different responsibilities, St Benedict recommended the appointment of a prior to assist the abbot and a cellarer to be responsible for all aspects of food production and preparation. It was also advised that one monk should take special care of the novices. Once the houses became larger, an extended team of officials was necessary. The cellarer became the head of a team of monks, each with specific responsibilities: the sacristan looked after any aspect of repair or building work, while the kitchener (with a team to help him) took over the preparation and serving of food. In later centuries, in a very large house like St Albans, the cellarer usually lived in his own house, having his own offices, income and team of five or more officials responsible to him. These included a pittancer, who was responsible for the 'pittances' or little treats which were enjoyed on the Saints' Day or other holidays.

If a large abbey had daughter houses, the prior stood in the position of abbot, but in the motherhouse, the prior continued as abbot's assistant and acted as his representative when the abbot was away travelling on behalf of the king, Pope, or Archbishop of Canterbury. To help him with his duties, the prior had a precentor who was responsible for everything connected with services, musical settings, shrines, the library and the copying of books.

Their Care of Parish Churches

Loosely connected with the precentor was a dean who was responsible for all the parish churches owned by the monastery. The original patrons who built the churches provided them with land; they also arranged for their tenants and workers to give a tithe (a tenth of all that they grew) to help to support the church. When their descendants gave these churches to religious houses, the monasteries received both the church land and the tithes. Not all monks were ordained but at first, some, of those who were, rode around taking services. In the early 13th century, the monasteries were persuaded to provide a house near the church for their resident vicar. Most of the church land and the great tithes remained with the monasteries.

The Role of Hospitality

The of ficers responsible for hospitality (a very important part of abbey life) were loosely linked with the cellarer. However, the guests were so varied that it was necessary to use a range of different officers, each with separate skills. Because the abbot was expected to entertain royal parties, the Archbishop of Canterbury, bishops, judges and many other important people, he lived in his own separate house. This was often luxuriously appointed and included his own office, kitchen and chapel, together with his own personal staff and income.

Sick travellers stayed in the hospital on the town boundary; lepers, in particular, were not allowed to enter the town centre. The remaining travellers were divided between the hosteller and the almoner. Their job descriptions clarify the differences between the two jobs, but it is not clear who directed travellers towards the two separate buildings. The hosteller must be a suitable choice to converse with all manner of guests of both sexes, so he must be well brought up.

'He is that by which the house is judged. He must supply food and drink as required, clean cloths, towels, cups and silver spoons, mattresses, sheets, blankets, pillows, quilts, a clean bowl for washing, a candle and a good fire.'

The almoner should be kind, compassionate, God-fearing, discreet and careful. He must look after pilgrims, beggars and lepers that came to his house and in the town and he must visit the old, lame, bed-ridden and blind. His job was to clothe, feed and comfort, but he must not receive those who are sick without first asking the prior.[1]

Lay Brothers and Officials

So many people donated gifts of land to help support the hostel and hospital that estate managers, accountants and sometimes even lawyers were appointed to accurately record all of the property. These officers were usually lay people, as were many of the workers.

Even before monasteries had accepted the need to hire 'contract' professional workers or to take full-time paid employees, lay brothers had been enrolled. These were less educated men than the choir monks but were anxious to help to support the monastery and in return would be supported by a modified form of the Rule.

By the middle of the 13th century, the abbots of the major Benedictine monasteries were, in their different roles, as powerful as the bishops, judges and senior diplomats. The senior monks (known as obedientaries) had, in their own way, as much power as today's major wholesalers, estate agents (in the original, managerial sense) or hoteliers.

From all this it can be seen that the English monasteries were very different from those which were originally founded by St Benedict. In well-run houses, the regular pattern of worship was continued and the monks had time to study. However, this was only possible because the senior 'officers' (obedientaries) were, for a number of years, given leave to live separate lives from the rest of the community.

The Reformed Orders

All the changes noted above took place at different speeds in different countries. As early as 900 there were already many men who entered a monastery in response to an overwhelming sense of vocation, only to be sadly disillusioned by the noise and bustle of the business community within their house.

1 Willis Clark, J. The observations in use in the Augustinian Priory of St Giles and St Andrew in Cambridgeshire, 1897

The Order of Cluniac Monks

In 909, Benedictine monks at Cluny broke away from the main movement to start a 'reformed' movement. Wherever possible they chose quiet sites away from main roads and centres of population, so that they could devote more time to communal worship and private prayer. The new movement spread very rapidly but, despite their choice of sites, both the piety of their worship, the beauty of their music and the respect with which people regarded their prayers all led them back into worldly situations. They soon wanted bigger and more beautiful churches, accommodation for the travellers who visited them and income to support all these things.

Some of the best-known houses in England were: Lewes, Castle Acre and Thetford, but the only local house of any size was Tickford Priory* near Newport Pagnall.

The Order of Cistercian Monks

Nearly two hundred years went by until, in 1098, a group of Benedictines at Citeaux started another reformed movement. They were anxious to gain more time for worship, prayer and study but were also eager to follow the section of St Benedictine's Rule concerning physical work. Their churches would be small and very plain and although visitors would not be turned away, only deserted sites, well away from main roads, would be accepted. They did not intend to take responsibility for parish churches and any farms that were donated would be let to tenants or run as independent Grange farms by lay brothers or other workers.

The best-known houses in England are probably Rievaulx and Fountains, both of which were patronised by Bedfordshire landowners working in Yorkshire. In 1135, Walter Espec gave (Old) Warden to Rievaulx Abbey and ten years later Hugh de Bolbec gave Woburn to Fountains Abbey. Both sites were sheltered, suitable for mixed farming and were in areas of very low population. As a result, both of these senior Cistercian houses opened daughter-houses in Bedfordshire.

The Augustinian Canons

The Order of 'Regular' Canons was based on a Rule suggested by St Augustine of Hippo early in the 5th century; it arrived in England sometime late in the

---

Unfortunately there is no comprehensive definition for 'Priory', many abbeys had daughter-houses, known as priories but many small (independent) religious houses were also known as priories

10th century. Dunstable Priory was the first house in this part of England and, together with Missenden, was probably the most important and best known. Augustinian houses were never very large and were comparatively inexpensive to establish. Every brother was an ordained priest and quite often their only work was to pray for the King and the families of their patron. As a result, between the early 12th and 13th centuries, this was the fastest-growing Order in England.

Houses like Ashridge and Dunstable became extremely popular, were comparatively wealthy and enjoyed continual royal patronage. Other smaller houses, like Caldwell (south of Bedford), Newnham (east of Bedford) and Bushmead (north of the village of Colmworth) were less wealthy but had far fewer expenses. Apart from the value of their prayers, Augustinian houses were often founded to care for important relics eg Walsingham (Norfolk) and Ashridge (Herts) or to run hospitals eg St Bartholemews (London) or to provide accommodation for travellers eg Dunstable. Gifts of land, houses, businesses and churches poured in to help these excellent causes. Soon the Augustinians found themselves in the same position as the Benedictines; Dunstable Priory owned land in seven counties, including at least eight parish churches. Although vicarages were provided for the churches and most of the land was let out to tenants, the Priory kept control over these different communities. By 1540, well over forty different religious houses elsewhere owned land in Bedfordshire. These were as far apart as Gloucestershire, Lincolnshire and Surrey and although some of the holdings were quite small, others were very large indeed. Geographically, more than half of the land from Bedford to the southern county boundary must have been owned by one or other of these different houses. This situation was not so extreme in Hertfordshire and Buckinghamshire but religious houses did own a great deal of land in both counties.

The Dissolution of the Monasteries

There was no single Act of Parliament that closed all the religious houses, only an Act which resulted in the closure of most of the smaller houses. As one by one, the rest of them 'surrendered' to the Crown, the monks and nuns received small pensions and set out to find a new role in private life.

Crown inspectors witnessed the removal of the roof, the glass and the lead. The latter, including the bells, was broken up and carted on wagons to the Tower of London. Any precious metals or jewels* were removed to the king's personal collection. After this, the stone and other building materials were put up for sale.

*The altar at Ashridge was set with pearls, rubies and diamonds

11

No doubt many were sold but the king's commissioners bought in anything that was a convenient distance from their estates and local people helped themselves.

What Happened to the Books, Music and Charters?

No doubt some of these were sent off to the king's libraries and to those of the new universities but the majority were lost. Many of those which have survived were, some years later, purchased by collectors; some eventually made their way to the British Museum and to other major collections.

Because of this, the surviving documents are quite random and when studying the social history of religious houses, we have to combine snippets of information from many different sources.

Historical Highlights/Route

ST ALBANS

St Albans is a very special cathedral city; it has the shrine of the first Christian saint in Britain and can claim twenty centuries of continuous occupation. As the different periods of occupation are, to a certain extent, on separate sites, they are of great interest to historians and archaeologists.

The Cathedral and Abbey Church is today the motherhouse of its diocese and also one of the greatest tourist attractions in this part of England. However, in its monastic days, not only would the Abbot have been responsible for numerous churches and host to thousands of pilgrims, but he would also have had complete control over the town of St Albans and the villages owned by the abbey.

It was Ulsinus, the 6th Abbot, who is thought to have designed the present city, around 948AD. He arranged for a church to be built at each of the three entrances to the city (St Michael's, St Peter's and St Stephen's) and for an area in the centre of the city to be laid out as a market place. The shops in the middle of the present market developed from market stalls, many of the buildings in this area being very old and dating back to the early days of the abbey.

From the town there are still two main entrances into the abbey precincts. The Sumpter Gate is opposite The White Hart inn on Holywell Hill and was the entrance for pack-ponies and the short-legged heavy horses, known as 'sumpters', which brought provisions into the store-rooms. The Wax Gate, opposite the Clock Tower, was the entrance where pilgrims would buy their candles, on the way into the shrine. In those days England was a Roman Catholic country and candles were an important part of worship.

A Brief History of Verulamium and the Founding of the Abbey

The Coming of the Romans

The first people to build anything like a town in this area were the Catuvellauni. When they moved from Wheathamstead, they had a settlement to the west of Verulamium called Verulamio - 'above the marshes'. This was in the area of Prae Woods (see below). By 20 BC their leader, Tasciovanus, was minting gold and silver coins and trading with the continent. Between 1930 and 1934, Sir Mortimer Wheeler excavated part of the site and the finds, pictures and scenes portraying life in the settlement can be seen in the Verulamium Museum.

When the Romans attacked the Catuvellauni in 43AD, it was at their main settlement at Colchester and it is thought that Verulamio was unharmed. The Roman soldiers built a watch-tower by the River Ver and soon they were conscripting the local people to erect 'Roman-style' buildings alongside their old settlement. A row of timber-framed shops have been excavated including a bronze-smith, a carpenter's shop and a wine shop. By 50AD there was a flourishing town of 'Romanised' Britons living there, but in 61AD Boudicca and her rebelling forces burnt down many of the buildings. The town was rebuilt but there was probably an accidental fire about 155AD and the town had to be rebuilt once again. At first it must have been difficult for the Catuvellauni to adjust to the Roman way of life and the strict laws. Nevertheless the town was a success and soon it was acting as a market for farmers from miles around. Trade increased and merchants visited from all over the Roman Empire. No doubt some of them opened businesses in the city, encouraging even more comings and goings. The Romans classified the town as a municipium, a truly 'Roman' town; the only one in Britain.

Saint Alban

At first the residents were heathen and worshipped many gods and there would have been different temples around the city. However with so many travellers, Christians sometimes slipped in and out of the town. When the Emperor Septimus Severus (193-211AD) came to Britain, he ordered that all Christians should be executed. The story is that at some time around 209AD, a certain resident called Alban received a fugitive priest into his house. He took the priest's clothes, surrendered himself to the authorities, refused to sacrifice to the pagan gods and was condemned to death. He was taken from the town, across a stream to an arena and from there, 500 paces up a gentle hill, to where he was executed. So the pre-Roman town was on the flat land to one side of Verulamium and the probable burial site of St Alban was on a hill on the other side. When, shortly afterwards, the Roman Empire became Christian, a shrine was built over the grave. About 480AD, St Germanus, Bishop of Auxerre, visited Alban's tomb and is said to have placed other martyrs' relics in the tomb.

Verulamium prospered and when Roman legions left England, the town continued to serve the local area. Saxon mercenaries came into the district to keep the peace, while keeping out raiders and invaders. When, in some areas, the mercenaries revolted, there was burning and looting but there is no evidence of damage around Verulamium. In fact there is archaeological evidence that c450AD, the aqueduct was still working and that piped water flowed into the town. When at last the roads became unsafe for country people to bring fresh food to the town, the residents were eventually forced to leave. The town was left deserted and gradually the buildings crumbled and fell. It is not known whether a few people stayed nearby to guard the shrine, but when the Saxons became Christian in the early 7th century, a community developed on the hill. Before 731AD, Bede wrote of the church of 'wonderful workmanship' which had been built on the site and that 'to this day sick people are healed'.[1]

King Offa Founds a Monastery

In 793AD, the Christian king, Offa, founded a Benedictine monastery on the site. The tradition is that he had the earth grave opened and the bones moved into a shrine within the religious house.[2]

The Manor of Kingsbury

During the Danish raids, King Alfred (and locally his son and daughter) defended various sites where administration could be carried on, business conducted and people could shelter from the raiders. As part of this programme, the township of Kingsbury was built on a hill to the northwest of St Albans. The abbots were jealous of Kingsbury and when the danger was over, they gradually gained control of the property. Part of its income came from a very large fish-pool that stretched from the ford at St Michael's to the Holywell Bridge.

1 Sherley-Price, L. (trans) Bede, A History of the English Church and People
2 Runcie, R (ed). Cathedral and City

The monks drained most of the pool, keeping a much smaller fish stream for themselves. One bank remains to provide the name Fishpool Street.

The Norman Abbey

Lanfranc, the first Norman Abbot, rebuilt the Abbey using stone, brick and tile from Verulamium. The abbots were very powerful and the Abbey was involved in many national events.[1]

Magna Carta

It was at the Abbey, in 1213, that the lay barons, church leaders, the reeve (estate foreman) and four men from each town on the royal estates met and used a charter of liberties, worked out for Henry I, to produce what was to become the Magna Carta. During the struggle, the barons invited the King of France to come to take over the kingdom. The Dauphin brought troops to England and, in December 1217, they were quartered in St Albans; by 1259 the road near their camp became known as French Row.

The Black Death

The terrible infection of 1348, known as the Black Death, was responsible for the death of the Abbot and more than half of the monks. It also killed (or seriously weakened) hundreds of the men and women who worked the scattered abbey estates. During the early 1350s, things gradually returned to normal but it became increasingly difficult to take on workers who would accept the strict tenancy and work conditions laid down by the Abbey steward. To enable the land to be cleaned and ploughed, other landlords had to allow many of their labourers to exchange work rents for money payments but the Abbey tenants and workers were still very strictly controlled.

Problems Between Tenants and their Landlords

The abbots of St Albans (and some of the priors of Dunstable Priory) were extremely well-educated and experienced men. Because of their skills in diplomacy, various kings, popes and bishops used them to carry out inspections, enquiries and tricky pieces of political negotiation. Yet when it came to local affairs, they did not seem to have the vision to comprehend the changing times in which they lived or to be able to manage their own townspeople or tenants.

1 Roberts, E. The Hill of the Martyr. This book is a definitive, but easy-to-read study of the abbey building and its history

15

During the late 13th and 14th centuries, the feudal system was breaking down but religious houses tried to keep their workers tied to the land, refusing to accept money rents instead of work services. In Dunstable, during the years 1220 to 1230, the burgesses (businessmen), several of whom were international merchants, quarrelled bitterly with the prior. He dominated the townspeople, not allowing them any responsibility for running their own market or town and fining them heavily if they refused to attend his court. In 1274 the Abbey tenants banded together and refused to pay to use the Abbey fulling mills to cleanse and thicken their wool. They were soon defeated, just as they were when they tried again in the 1330s. To add insult to injury, the Abbey steward had the stones from their hand mills carried back to the Abbey and set in the parlour floor. The townspeople sued the abbot for trespass but even though some of them took the case to Westminster, they failed and were imprisoned. Once again they had to pay for the enforced privilege of using the Abbey mills.

Although the farm-workers gradually obtained their freedom, the tenants were still extremely restricted. During the 14th century, the Abbey cellarer was returning through Luton, from a visit to Hexton, when he was spotted by one of their richer tenants, Philip of Limbury. Rather foolishly, he encouraged his servant to catch hold of the bailiff and put him in the stocks! He was arrested, of course, and made to pay compensation. From time to time the businessmen of St Albans must have longed to put the abbot in the stocks, especially when he prevented them from electing their own MP. The quarrels continued, gradually becoming more bitter on each side.

The 'Peasants' Revolt

Understandably, when in 1381, they heard about a wider revolt, the burgesses of St Albans rushed off to London to meet other dissatisfied businessmen and ten ants. After the meeting at Smithfield, they headed peacefully back home where the news of royal support had already arrived. It was market day and hundreds of people were at the Abbey gates, waiting for the travellers to return. A group from Dunstable heard the news and hurried home to storm the gates of the Priory, to demand a charter of freedom for themselves. As always with large crowds, some elements got out of control and in St Albans, the Abbey gaol was forced open and the prisoners released. Meanwhile one group broke into the park and freed the animals, while others took rabbits from the warren and, as a symbol of their freedom, tied one to the gate.

The Abbot agreed to such requests as the right for farmers to fish in their own streams, snare rabbits in their own fields and have freedom to graze their livestock on the common. Several other small towns and villages, such as Barnet, Redbourn and Rickmansworth, who were represented at the Abbey gates also benefitted. The businessmen of St Albans were given a charter enabling them to administer their own town and market. A similar charter was received in Dunstable.

The horrific end to this bid for freedom was recorded by the Abbey chronicler and has been published in various books. Dr Elsie Toms, in 'The Story of St Albans', has described how King Richard followed the group out of London and arrived in St Albans with a band of armed soldiers. They broke up the excited crowd, restored the charters to the Abbey and arrested the ringleaders. The Moot Hall was used for a show trial of both the local and some of the national leaders. Three men were hung, drawn and quartered, many others were imprisoned. Not surprisingly, the bitterness remained for many years both in the town and out in the villages.

In Dunstable, the revolt was led by Thomas Hobbs, the landlord of the Swan Inn (better known as the Red Lion), which, until 1963, stood on the corner of Church Street. Following events in St Albans, the Prior took back his charter but did not exact the terrible penalties that were meted out by the Abbot of St Albans. More than fifty years later, the then Abbot of St Albans had a man from Watford arrested for daring to set up a barley mill; he was forced to destroy it.

The Battles of St Albans

During the 15th century civil war, there were two battles in or near the city. On May 22 1455, the Yorkist army was camped behind the houses of Holywell Hill and St Peter's Street; where the Lancastrians had barricaded the Market Place and the poor, muddled King Henry VI stood alone amongst the confusion. The Earl of Warwick pulled down houses and led the soldiers through. They broke away some of the barricades and caught the Lancastrians unprepared. The king received a neck wound from an arrow and was taken into a baker's cottage until the Duke of York came and escorted him into the Abbey. The Duke of Somerset was besieged in a house near the Castle Inn, which once stood on what is now the corner of Victoria Street and St Peter's Street; he died trying to fight his way out. According to the Abbey chronicler, they buried forty men in their graveyard and many more in St Peter's churchyard. Sir John Wenlock of Someries, Luton was among the many wounded in the battle. The town suffered a great deal of damage but the Abbot bribed the soldiers with food and wine so that the Abbey itself was not touched. The second battle, on 17 February 1461, was just north of the city. It was won by the Lancastrians but their army was completely out of control and sacked the city. This was the last time that there was any serious fighting around St Albans but it was some years before it recovered.

The Closing Years

During the 16th century, the Abbots of St Albans began to lose their power over the town and increasingly the business people took over the management of their own affairs. To the horror of the monks, when Abbot Ramryge died, in 1519, Cardinal Wolsey was appointed as absentee abbot. This was not as a result of an internal ballot but by the order of Thomas Cromwell, chief advisor to Henry VIII. Following Wolsey's disgrace Prior Robert Catton became Abbot and, long before the official closure, was able to transfer Abbey property to his and Cromwell's friends.

The Dissolution of the Abbey

In 1537, Catton was found to be such a bad manager that he was given a pension and forced to retire. The last Abbot, Richard Boreman, inherited a house that was almost bankrupt. He struggled on until December 1539, then he surrendered his house and the thirty-eight monks each received a pension.

The Old Inns

From its earliest days, the Abbey had to provide accommodation for travellers and it is thought that they had stables for up to 300 horses. However, by the early 15th century, they could not accommodate all the pilgrims and other travellers, so they licensed private 'hospices' or hotels. These would have been run by secular tenants under licence to the Abbey. Originally the guests would have walked across to the Abbey for mass, but in 1483, Abbot Wallingford allowed the landlord of The George and Dragon (in what became George Street) to open his own chapel.[1]

After the closing of the Abbey, the town burgesses were ready to develop their town and the potential travel and tourist industry.

The Small Nunneries

Connected with the important Benedictine monastery for men there were two small nunneries.

1 For details of the old inns see Corbett, J. A History of St Albans

The Nunnery at Sopwell

At one time, Sopwell Lane continued somewhat further than today and led to a small nunnery. A prioress and twelve nuns, representing Christ and the twelve apostles, lived and worked there under the supervision of the Abbot or his representatives. These ladies came from sheltered, genteel homes and must, at times, have found the strict routine very difficult. During the late 1330s, the Abbot suspected that they were getting very slack and ordered an inspection. As a result, he offered some guidelines to tighten up their routine. No nun was to leave the dormitory without permission but once the sub-prioress rang the bell, they were to file down to the church and take part in the early mass, which was intended to be at the break of day. Psalms would be sung for the Blessed Virgin Mary, St Alban and all the saints. Once it was over, they were to sit in the cloister, 'occupied with their private devotions' until the next communal service. This second service of Prime, the first great Mass of the day, was compulsory for all but the sick. After Prime, it was compulsory for all the nuns to attend Chapter. At this meeting, only the prioress, sub-prioress and any offenders who were being questioned, were allowed to talk. If anyone disobeyed the prioress and spoke without permission, or spoke during the grand silence, they were to be put on bread and water. If they refused to accept this, the prioress was free to use much harsher punishments.

Once Chapter was over, the nuns were to split up and go to their various approved forms of work. Only after this would they receive their first and, at some times of the year, only meal of the day. The rest of the day would be divided into periods of work, prayer and communal worship, but as soon as the curfew bell was heard, over at the Abbey, both the parlour and the garden doors were to be closed. They were not to be re-opened before Prime.

St Mary de Pré and the Leper Hospital

The Abbey had a leper hospital for men, on the road leading south out of St Albans near the present Pré Hotel. In 1194, Abbot Warin founded a refuge for leprous nuns. It relied heavily on the Abbey for its support and when, during the early 1200s, it fell into debt, the Abbot diverted some rent money from land in Cambridgeshire, paid for the sisters' clothes and provided clothes, discarded by the monks, to be adapted for the lepers. Meat and ale were to be sent from the Abbey kitchens and

ROUTE
The Route leaves St Albans on the A5 heading towards Dunstable and passes the Pré Restaurant, which represents the site of the nunnery.

from every oven full of loaves baked for the Abbot, two were sent to the nunnery. Even the horses were catered for; two of them were to receive free food from the Abbey granary. The house was rebuilt around 1254, for thirteen nuns and for two or three residential brothers who would manage their affairs and care for male guests.

By the mid 14th century, lepers no longer walked the roads of England and the nuns were caring for travellers and for two paying guests. This made the priory more financially secure. From their 14th century account books, we can see that they must have had a large home farm. They employed four ploughmen and a carter, a shepherd, a cowherd, a swineherd and two dairymaids. Two tanners prepared the hides for shoemaking and the house had its own clerk, chaplain and barber. The agricultural wage was three shillings (15p) per week (plus a cottage?). The barber received two shillings (10p) and the carter five shillings (25p). These wages were being paid just before the frightening loss of life caused by The Black Death. By 1352, there had been a rise and a 'bonus' of a weekly bushel of wheat.

By the mid 14th century, the Rule had been greatly relaxed and they regularly purchased meat, fish (herring and salmon), milk, cheese, butter and eggs plus salt, spices and olive oil. They were even allowed to buy coal for their fires. At the feast of the Blessed Virgin Mary on December 16th, they enjoyed roast ox and goose and at each of the great feasts they received 60 flagons of ale and 'pittances' - special treats, such as spices and candied fruits. Each year before Christmas (15th-17th December) they had their own three-day fair and on Christmas Day they hired harpers and other musicians. At New Year and at Twelfth Night, they had an entertainment called 'Wassail' and on Palm Sunday they decorated their church with flowers and pussy willow. They were allowed to join in the May Day games and as early as the 15th century, long before the days of Guy Fawkes, they enjoyed toast and ale on various bonfire nights.[1]

From all this we can see that the better-class Benedictine nunneries of the 15th century were very different from those of the 13th.

ROUTE

Further along, the entrance to Redbournbury Watermill is on the right, just after the Spritza winebar. Redbourn has a bypass but the position of the village is clearly marked. (St Mary's Church and the museum stand on the common, to the left of the High Street.)

1 VCH Herts Vol 3

REDBOURN

St Albans Abbey already owned part of the village before the Norman Conquest and around 1100, they built St Mary's Church. Inside there are many interesting features, including a stained-glass window, depicting St Amphibalus, to remind us of the connection with the Abbey.

The Grave of St Amphibalus

There is a legend that St Alban appeared one night at the bedside of a citizen called Robert. Alban said that he had been converted to Christianity by a man called Amphibalus and that he wanted to make known where this man was buried. He guided Robert to Redbourn where he pointed out the grave. Then they returned to St Albans where the saint vanished. The Abbot of St Albans heard about this visitation and asked Robert to show his monks the site of the grave. In c1178, the site was excavated and several bodies were uncovered. (Possibly Saxon burials?) The bones were carried back with great honour to the Abbey and the shrine of St Alban was brought out to meet the procession. The bones of St Alban were carried into the Abbey, where his shrine can be seen today.

News of the exciting excavations had spread around the neighbourhood and crowds came out to watch. The chronicler at the Abbey recorded with glee how a hard-headed Dunstable entrepreneur had got his come-uppance. He reported that Algar, a Dunstable brewer, had turned up with a barrel of beer, which he was selling for a good profit, but when a sick traveller begged for a drink 'for the love of the martyr, whose discovery was hourly expected', he refused. In fact, Algar was most annoyed and shouted out for all to hear that he had not come for the sake of the martyr but to make money! Then, to everyone's amazement, both bungs burst out of the barrel and the beer flowed onto the ground. To the fury of the vendor, not only the beggar but also everyone standing around rushed forward to get a free drink.

The Redbourn Priory

A chapel and small monastic cell was then built on Redbourn Heath where monks could come to recuperate from illness. Part of their site remains as rough pasture, opposite The Chequers, but many of their stone foundations are under the Georgian building in the High Street. There is a room in the town museum devoted to the Priory and the pieces of masonry which have been uncovered.

Another story concerning this cell concerned an incident during the fight for

Magna Carta. The Dauphin and a troop of French soldiers were in the neighbourhood during May 1217. It is said that one of the soldiers stole a silver-gilt cross containing a very important relic - a piece of the Holy Cross. Once outside he fell down in a fit and his friends had to bind his hands while they rode to Flamstead Church. Once there, the cross fell from his clothes and was returned to the chapel at Redbourn. In the 14th century the cell and chapel were regularly used as a country retreat where small groups of monks could have a break from the strict discipline of the Abbey. However, they were not to relax too much; they were not to visit friends nearby, keep dogs or go hunting!

FLAMSTEAD

The Problems of a Small Nunnery - St Giles in the Wood

Just north of Redbourn, lying back from the main road, is the parish of Flamstead. Around 1120, a descendant of the Norman, Tosny family who received the village after the Conquest, founded a small, independent Benedictine nunnery. It was not richly endowed and the patrons moved away. Whereas the nunnery of St Mary de Pré illustrates life in a well-patronised nunnery, Flamstead illustrates life in one that was neglected.

ROUTE
Flamstead lies to the left of the A5 but because it is on high ground, St Leonard's Church can be seen from the main road.

Despite occasional gifts from local landowners, the nuns became increasingly poor. On more than one occasion they were forced to beg for food and wrote to the Pope for help. Once, when their livestock had died and they could not even plough their fields, the Pope appealed for local landowners to help them. As a result, they received further gifts of land and gradually began to recover. However, in response to an enquiry in 1530, it was disclosed that their numbers had dropped back to seven and to support themselves they were running a small boarding school. The bishop was very shocked to find that the children were sleeping in the nun's dormitory. Because they were such a small house, they were caught up in the first wave of closures and appear to have left their house during March 1537. The prioress received a pension of £6 per year and the other nuns either returned home or moved to bigger, more prosperous nunneries. At that time, the Flamstead house was in a good state of repair. There was a small hall-parlour, which was very poorly furnished and two other more comfortable rooms. There was a kitchen and a buttery, where wine or ale was stored and their farm was once more well-stocked. They had 6 horses, 7 cows, 2 young heifers, 7 pigs and

38 sheep and lambs. Forty-five acres of their Flamstead farm were sown with wheat. Their chapel was surprisingly well-equipped with a full range of silver vessels.

Unlike the well-endowed nuns at St Mary de Pré, they could not afford to employ much labour and had to do much of their own work. However, the nunnery must have provided a reasonably comfortable home for many ladies from the local towns and villages, but they cannot have had time to fit in the three-hourly services plus periods of private prayer and study.

ROUTE
Markyate also has a bypass and the route stays on this, turning right off the A5, towards Caddington and Luton. (For details of the 6 mile scenic diversion, via Dunstable, please turn to the end of the section.)

MARKYATE

During the monastic period there were occasionally long-serving monks who preferred to live a life of prayer and meditation away from their busy monastery. They had to be near enough to the monastery to collect supplies and for them to make regular visits to attend mass, so Markyate was a convenient place. In the 12th century, the most famous hermit was called Roger; he was a friend of both the Abbot of St Albans and the Archbishop of York.

Christina of Markyate

In Huntingdonshire lived a family called Autti. They were a devout family who, from time to time, made a pilgrimage to St Albans Abbey. A daughter, Christina, was born just before 1100 and when she was about fourteen, she was so influenced by the ceremony at the shrine that she made a personal vow of celibacy. The vow was never taken seriously by her parents, who went ahead with their plans for her to marry their neighbour, Ralph Flambard. We can only try to piece together the events of the next few years, but despite her desperate attempts to stick to her vow, she eventually gave in. However, immediately after the wedding, she escaped and fled to Markyate. After some time of living in hid ing, she begged Roger, the senior hermit, to take her vow seriously and help her to live a life of prayer and meditation. He arranged for her to have her own cell and supported her against all criticism.

Markyate Priory

After some time Roger persuaded the Archbishop of York to annul the marriage and eventually it was possible for her to become a nun. She became friends with

Abbot Geoffrey de Gorham of St Albans and he helped her to start a small priory near her cell, on land belonging to St Paul's Cathedral.

The priory was consecrated in 1145, with Christina as the first prioress. One of her sisters joined her and one of her brothers became a monk at St Albans. Christina died in 1155 but the priory continued until it was dissolved in 1537.

Under the patronage of St Albans Abbey, Markyate Priory was much more prosperous than that at Flamstead. The rent lists, drawn up on behalf of the king, shows how valuable and varied were their estates. Their land at Lewsey (Leagrave area) is commemorated by Nunnery Road. There were several other Bedfordshire estates and rectories. In addition they owned the rectory at Watford and three in Warwickshire. The last prioress, Joan Southe, had bought Ashes Dower, a valuable manor at Bicester (Oxon) but travellers may have donated much of the land.

By the time that they left Markyate there were already three inns or beer houses on the Caddington side of the village, The Porpoise, Bull and Crown plus The Ball on the other side of the road.

The New Owners of the Priory

Once closed, the nunnery building and estates belonged to the Crown. In 1539 the priory and home farm were sold to Humphrey Bourchier. He began to convert it into a private house. The next owner was the Ferrers family of St Albans.

The Story of the Wicked Lady

The story of Kathleen Ferrers has nothing to do with nunneries but is very well known. Although mainly legend, it illustrates the vulnerability of some teenage girls. The unhappy Christina (above) ran away to find a respected hermit; in different circumstances, she might have gone to a nunnery, where before the Dissolution, many unmarried or widowed ladies found a secure home. This security was not available in the 17th century and many girls were exploited by their families.

The Ferrers family prospered and a later member became 'Sir John' Ferrers. In this story it is not always possible to separate history from legend but Sir John's son and heir married Kathleen Wardour and their daughter, Kathleen, was born in 1639. The next year, both Sir John and his son died and the baby girl inherited everything. Her mother may then have married Sir Simon Fanshaw of Ware, in Hertfordshire, because when she died, he became executor of the young

Kathleen, who went to live with his family at Ware. When she was twelve years old, she was taken to church and married to Sir Simon's sixteen-year-old nephew, Thomas. He was so deeply in debt that he had been threatened with prison but after the ceremony he became owner of all her money and estates. In 1655, the Markyate estate was sold to three London businessmen.

Until 1658, a Lady Beal befriended Kathleen, but when she died, Kathleen returned to Markyate, where she lived with the housekeeper. The area had always been notorious for highwaymen and it is said that soon after her arrival, Kathleen saw a gentleman farmer caught trying to rob an army baggage wagon; he was killed on the spot and nailed to a tree. Then the attacks by highwaymen became more frequent and a reward was offered. Two young men riding across Nomansland Common, near Wheathamstead, shot a highwayman, rode into the next town, and reported wounding him. A search party looked for his body without success.

The next morning Kathleen was not in her room and her bed had not been slept in. At the end of the passage, the housekeeper found a door open in a place she had never seen a door before. She went through and found a flight of steps; she started to go down and half way found Kathleen's body, soaked in blood, wearing highwayman's clothes. The story was hushed up and the passage door blocked. It is said that many years later, local workmen refused to touch the door and it was eventually opened up by a firm of London builders. From the outside a chimney hides the stairs.

THE ROUTE TO DUNSTABLE

The next Priory is Dunstable, a few miles up the A5 but there is an optional pleasant country drive via Kensworth and the Dunstable Downs. There were no monasteries along this loop but the land was owned by various religious houses.

Kensworth land, village and church were owned by the canons of St Paul's, London but Dunstable Priory also had an interest and there were several disputes.[1]

1 Evans, V. Dunstable with the Priory 1100 to 1550

THE ADDITIONAL SCENIC ROUTE

This does not leave the A5 at Markyate but continues on until it is approaching the Packhorse and then turns left beside the public house, onto the B4540. This road will pass through Kensworth village. (If visiting St Mary's Church, as soon as you leave the Packhorse, watch out for a right-hand turn via Kensworth Lynch.)

The main route is heading through Kensworth to Whipsnade 'crossroads'. This is now a roundabout and the route turns right onto the

Kensworth Church

Studham Church

Studham and Whipsnade churches were given to the canons of Dunstable Priory although the first reference, c1060, to Studham church is when the widow of a Saxon landowner, Ulf, gave land to St Albans Abbey.

Totternhoe and Eaton Bray churches, viewed from Dunstable Downs, also went to Augustinian canons; the former to Dunstable Priory and the latter to Merton.

DUNSTABLE

Henry I founded the Augustinian Priory sometime after his visit to the town in 1109. This was the occasion when he gave permission for the newly settled Augustinians to build a house at Holy Trinity, Aldgate. The same two canons from Colchester came on, at a later date, to oversee the building at Dunstable. One of them, called Bernard, stayed on to become first prior.

The Augustinian Priory of St Peter

Neither the date when Henry invited the businessmen to settle in his new town, nor the date when the canons arrived, is known. However, to have had sufficient buildings finished and enough canons in residence to be able to put the new town into their hands, in 1131, building must have started well before 1120. All Augustinians (and other religious) were expected to pray for the souls of their founders and Henry expected the Dunstable canons to do so, but many Augustinians were also expected to provide hospitality for travellers. For about four centuries, a period of time which can be compared with looking back from the present to the death of Queen Elizabeth I, the canons offered hospitality to all travellers passing through the town. As Dunstable stood on the crossing of what is today the A5 and the A505, it meant that they were burdened with an enormous responsibility.

B4541 for Dunstable, via Dunstable Downs. (If visiting Whipsnade Church, on the left of the village green, the Tree Cathedral on the right of the green or Whipsnade Wild Animal Park at the end of the green, remain on the B4540. If visiting St Mary's Church at Studham, turn left at the roundabout and the church will be seen on the right of the village green.) As the route crosses Dunstable Downs, it passes through part of the Chilterns Area of Outstanding Natural Beauty. At the bottom of the hill, the route meets the B489, turns right and runs down West Street to the crossroads in the town centre. (To visit the Priory Church of St Peter, continue across onto the A505 towards Luton but immediately watch for the church carpark which is on the right.)

27

At Dunstable's central crossroads, the route turns onto the A5 and stays on this road until it is approaching Markyate. Having passed the park and private house, which stands on the site of the nunnery, turn sharp left and rejoin the main route.

As you drive up the hill, with the park still on your left, you are safely back on the main route.

NB: If wishing to visit any of these churches, remember to check if they are open, before leaving home.

The Cost of Hospitality

Not just Dunstable Priory but all religious houses were expected to provide (mainly free) accommodation and all forms of social service. Here, the canons were responsible for the Prior's House (for royal and other very important travellers), a hostel, an almonry and two leper hospitals. This was why they were desperate to acquire and to keep all manner of gifts. It was probably in the late 14th century that, to provide extra accommodation, the canons opened The Saracen's Head. Although in a mainly rebuilt building this inn can claim to be one of the oldest in England. Early in his reign, King John exchanged the royal palace, on the other side of the road, for quality hospitality at the prior's house. From then to the Dissolution, virtually all the kings of England stayed at the priory.

They did not pay for this accommodation but left expensive gifts. These were probably gratefully received but silken altar clothes or large quantities of wax could not replenish the prior's store cupboards. One precaution that was often taken before royal parties set out was to order casks of their favourite wine to be sent on in advance.

The Social Services

It was the care of the poor and sick travellers that caused the priory so much expense. On at least two occasions, the king wrote to the prior ordering him to move the poor people who were squatting around the town. From this we can imagine a shantytown of homeless people, camping on the waste land alongside the roads.

Manorial Problems in Dunstable

The notice that King Henry I sent out, inviting businessmen to settle in his new town of Dunstaple, promised them the same freedom as that enjoyed by the businessmen of London. When he gave his new town into the care of the priory about twenty-five years later, he promised the prior the same control over the people of the town 'that he himself enjoyed'.

28

The prior's interpretation of this was that, with certain exceptions, he could treat these independent, sometimes international, businessmen as though they were tied agricultural workers. This contradiction of statements caused the same problems as in St Albans and therefore an active role in the Peasants' Revolt.

Dunstable also had its own revolt in the period 1220-1224.[1]

On this occasion the position may have been aggravated because the prior, a famous scholar and diplomat, was constantly away from Dunstable, working for the king, the Pope and the Archbishop of Canterbury. The 1381 revolt was not as serious here as in St Albans and by the mid 15th century, the prior and the businessmen were working together to promote the town and develop the travel industry.

> ***ROUTE***
> **Carefully turn on to the B4540, which is heading towards Slip End and Caddington; climb the hill and, if visiting Caddington, watch for a left-hand turn.**

After the Dissolution

Because of this co-operation, the town continued to prosper after the Dissolution; all the scattered priory estates went to Henry VIII and one by one, officials sold individual inns and other buildings. However, uptil the 1860s the manor court and some of the buildings belonged to the Crown.

CADDINGTON

Edwin of Caddington made an exceptionally early (surviving) will c1053. He bequeathed his land at Watford to St Albans Abbey and the rest of his scattered estate to his son Leofwin. He asked to be buried at the abbey.

Leofwin* was a wealthy man but like the rest of the Saxon noblemen, lost his lands in 1066. He had already divided Caddington along the county boundary and given half to the canons of St Paul in London. The Bedfordshire (Luton) side, which was a community of about six cottages, went to St Paul's, while the larger, Hertfordshire side Leofwin kept for himself. This supported about twenty-eight families and looked down on the important crossroads which would become Dunstable. Following the Conquest, King William added this to the piece already owned by St Paul's.

1 Evans, V. Dunstable with the Priory 1100 to 1550
* He may be the Leofwin who, in 1086, had a small farm, Boarscroft, near Tring

St Paul's Cathedral

This was staffed by resident canons (clergymen) and with others who lived away from the cathedral. Many of the canons were given a specific estate for their support - these men were referred to as 'prebends' and their estates were 'prebendaries'. St Paul's divided Caddington into two small and one larger estate so that they could support two prebends and still keep the larger, Dunstable side to produce food for the cathedral.

The latter was probably represented by what became Zouches Farm. However, when that was rented out and was independent of the main manor, the manorial headquarters moved to Bury Farm. The former were known as Great Caddington (later Prebendal Farm) and Little Caddington. The stalls used by these two canons can still be seen in the cathedral today.[1]

An Inventory of the Household Manor

The Dunstable side of Caddington, together with Kensworth, was farmed by a tenant were; the rent was to produce sufficient food, drink, firing and necessary funds to totally support the residents and visitors at St Paul's for one week. The inventory of 1299, when one of the canons took over the tenancy, gives a good picture of the type of house that a cathedral thought suitable for one of its retired members.[2]

The farmhouse had a large hall open to the roof with a pantry and buttery at one end, with a room over them and at the other end, an upstairs room with an adjoining wardrobe (lavatory). From one side a passage led to the chapel, while the kitchen, bakehouse and brewhouse were under a separate roof. One part of the main roof was tiled but the older part was thatched. There was also a cellar, reached via a small outside porch.

Each building on the farm was listed, including the two great barns, the new barn, two sheep-sheds and a hut for the shepherd.

Documents from the Manor Court

Many papers have survived, some in Latin, some in English; they are now stored at the Guildhall, London. A typical entry for the 16th century gives a good picture of life in a late medieval village at a time when many monastic villages were changing to secular ownership, eg:

1. No cattle to be loose or tethered in the cornfield until everybody has cut and carried. Fine 10 shillings (50p).

1 Sutton, F. A History of Caddington and its People
2 BHRS Vol I

2. No cattle to be let into the common field until the grain has been carried three days. This was to allow time for gleaning. Fine 10 shillings (50p).
3. Hedges to be made and kept in good repair. Fine one shilling (5p).
4. The owner of hogs (pigs) caught doing harm to be fined tuppence (about 1p).
5. Bellewes (lead sheep) must wear a yoke (triangular collar). If they break a hedge, fine one shilling (5p).

The Church of All Saints

Edwin or Leofwin may have provided a church but it is more likely to have been built by St Paul's. Written records go back to 1181, when it is made dear that Caddington is in the lordship of 'the church at canons' ie St Paul's.

After the Dissolution

Changes took place at St Paul's after the Dissolution but it was not closed and they retained their ownership of both Caddington and Kensworth. In the 19th century both villages were taken over by the Ecclesiastic Commissioners.

LUTON

The boundary between Chaul End, Caddington and Luton includes an extremely old hedge. The land on the Luton side, across Dallow Road, represents what was the church land of Luton.

Bishopscote (Biscot)

King Offa gave this to St Albans Abbey but it was lost during the Danish raids.

ROUTE

The route continues on the B4540, over the county boundary into Bedfordshire (Woodside Animal Farm is immediately on the left). The road is now heading towards Slip End but, at a small crossroads, facing a public house, the route turns right, towards Pepperstock. It crosses the M1 motorway and continues until it meets the A1081. Carefully cross the traffic and head south towards St Albans. (If visiting Luton, turn north on the A1081).

The Dallow Manor

Before the Norman Conquest and until the 1150s, this estate was attached to St Mary's Church but it was then given to St Albans Abbey. About 600 acres (which supported fifteen to eighteen families) were recorded in the Domesday Book. It must have been very frustrating for these workers as they observed the workers on the secular manor of Luton gradually gaining their freedom from the tied feudal system. As late as 1455 two men were each fined twenty old pence (approx 8p) for fishing in the abbey's millpond.

31

ROUTE

Once on the A1081, be ready to take the first left-hand turning, signposted New Mill End. This road passes the back (private) gate to Luton Hoo, before meeting the B653.

The Farley Hospital

This was also near Caddington; it was probably a cross between an almshouse and a hospice. In the mid 14th century it was put into the care of St Paul's Cathedral.

NEW MILL END (LUTON)

The Abbey had a tithe barn on the Dallow farm and a watermill and small water meadow near St Mary's Church. As the years went by, they were given several pieces of land in and around Stopsley and at East Hyde. The tenants and workers at this end of the town considered the barn at Dallow too far to carry their tithes. So in 1461 the Abbey purchased a house and seventeen acres of land on which they built a 'new' watermill and a new tithe barn. This mill was taken down c1890 to improve the river and to make a trout stream.

ROUTE

This is the main Luton to Wheathampstead road, so turn right and follow it as it passes through East Hyde and then Batford. (If visiting Harpenden, watch for the right-hand turn when approaching Batford). The route stays on the B653, eventually meets a roundabout, remains on the B653, as it turns right into Wheathampstead village and out again on the other side. It is now heading for St Albans.

EAST HYDE

Although the people of this hamlet, like the rest of Luton residents, had to pay tithes to the Abbey, it was actually part of the manor of Luton. Of the six manorial and two Abbey watermills, the only one to survive is at East Hyde. It has been rebuilt and is an important part of Luton's history.[1]

BATFORD AND WHEATHAMPSTEAD

The name of the first village may have come from an early Saxon family who settled on a ford and the second one may have been the village where wheat was grown. Both were included in Edward the Confessor's gift to his new abbey at Westminster.

Westminster Abbey

The name 'Confessor' as given to King Edward, signified a holy person; sometime before the year 1060, he began to plan the foundation of a major Benedictine monastery. St Peter's Church was consecrated during 1065 and richly endowed, but work continued on the monastic buildings.

1 Austin, W. The History of Luton

32

King Edward was buried there the following year. This prestigious monastery received lavish gifts from later kings and from other influential people but King Henry III decided to rebuild it.

Centuries later, when Henry VIII was arranging to close the religious houses, he planned to divide some of the over-large diocese. It was decided that St Paul's should remain as the cathedral for London, but that Westminster should continue as a collegiate church ie a district church with several clergymen. It had been an extremely rich monastery and the change was made quite smoothly.

Wheathampstead

This rich agricultural area has evidence of human occupation over an amazingly long period, but it was the Saxon settlers who developed the rich and fertile land along the river. By the time of the Norman Conquest, there were thirty-six families ploughing the arable land, grazing their oxen in the water meadows, and their pigs in the woods. There were three other watermills in addition to the one at Batford. The clerks collecting the information for the Domesday tax records particularly noted the presence of a priest, although, not having any taxable land, the church was not mentioned.

Amazingly, the charter describing the estate which King Edward presented to the 'convent which is called Westminster' has survived and is in the Hertfordshire County Record Office. This boundary has been researched, identified, walked and published by Harpenden and St Albans branches of the Workers' Educational Association.[1]

The Church of St Helen, Wheathamstead

St Helen was the mother of the Emperor Constantine who, soon after 313AD, decreed the toleration of the faith throughout the Roman Empire. Very little of the Saxon church is left, except the remains of a round-headed doorway in the south wall. It is a lofty cruciform church with extremely fine carved stonework, an interesting feature of which is that the bells are rung from the central crossing. Much of the church is 14th century, but the stone corbels supporting the wall posts of the nave roof are Victorian.

Tenants of Westminster Abbey

Westminster Abbey officials lived at the manor house, probably Bury Farm; they kept half the land as a home farm and the rest was shared by the estate workers. In return for their share of the land, the thirty-six families had to work

1 *Wheathampstead and Harpenden. Vol 1 published 1973 by the two societies*

without pay in the abbey fields for four days a week, from Michaelmas to Christmas. They ploughed and harrowed sixteen acres of abbey land and sowed corn seed, which they themselves had provided. They also had to share the harvesting and each family had to deliver a bag of oats and half a bag of wheat to the Westminster kitchens. Nevertheless, the village prospered and groups of people cleared areas of woodland; soon there were many scattered settlements. Although most of the trees have long been cleared, the settlement names remain to this day; there are nineteen local names ending in 'End' and eighteen ending in 'Green'. Because of these settlements away from the river, in the late 12th century, Westminster Abbey had to develop another manor house and administrative buildings at the other end of their land. This was at Harpendenbury, near Redbourn. This led to more development and by 1217, a 'chapel of ease' had been built.

The Church of St Nicholas, Harpenden

St Nicholas, Bishop of Myra was the patron saint of travellers, so this gave the Harpenden people a chapel in their own community when it was too wet and muddy to walk to Wheathamstead and also a method of collecting alms from travellers. Harpenden became a separate rectory in 1865.

After the Dissolution

Throughout the area, including Harpenden, the people gradually got their freedom from work service and paid money rents instead. Also because of the smaller settlements in the clearings, there were compact, enclosed farms as well as the traditional open fields. Because Westminster Abbey survived the Dissolution, the estate prospered and between 1500 and 1642, the population nearly doubled and even more houses were built. Because of this the area is rich in medieval buildings. Much of the waste land was enclosed and some farmers gained control of groups of strips and put hedges round to enclose small areas of the common fields. Westminster kept control of all these changes, taking both licence fees and rents. As more and more trees were cut, the remaining woodland had increasing importance and again Westminster kept strict control. When they let woodland in 1587/8, the tenants could 'cut, fell and carry' but at the correct time of year to allow the woodland to 'renew, come and grow again', the tenant also had to agree to keep the wood well-fenced and drained.

ROUTE

Just as the route is approaching Nomansland Common, it passes the Wicked Lady public house. The B653 and the route continue through Sandridge and on into St Albans.

34

NOMANSLAND COMMON

This popular leisure area was once an important common for grazing livestock. It gets its name because of the frequent disputes between the two Benedictine abbeys of Westminster and St Albans. The Wicked Lady public house is so-named to commemorate the shooting of the 'Wicked Lady' of Markyate.

SANDRIDGE

Once over the border at Sandridge, the route is back on land which once belonged to St Albans Abbey. In fact this is thought to be one of the first gifts to have been given to King Offa's new abbey after its foundation. By 1086, it was well-populated and a very useful food-producing estate with arable land for growing cereals, meadows for hay, woodland for pigs and grazing for the oxen. There was also a watermill for grinding the corn. At first, much of the food produced at Sandridge was carted direct to the abbot's barns and only a small proportion went to the Abbey's kitchens, but at a later date, some of the produce, including cheese, was directed to the use of the Kitchener. Probably because the Sandridge land was so close to the Abbey and constantly observed by any travelling officials, there were even more disputes here than on some of the more distant manors.

Even though a religious house owned the village, there are no references in the Domesday Book to either a church or a priest. No doubt there was a chapel or designated room, attached to the house where the Abbey manager lived. One of the ordained monks would have visited to take services. The first reference to an independent, consecrated chapel appears in 1094. The Bishop of Norwich, who was probably staying at the Abbey, dedicated the chapel to St Leonard. This chapel continued as a dependency of the Abbey church until a vicarage was instated in the 14th century.

The abbey had a difficult time in the 13th century as they were in dispute with their own knights over hunting rights and with their tenants concerning work service. One man in particular called Mesun continually defied them and refused to carry out the customary work service. Negotiations became very bitter; the Abbey officials claimed that there was no cause for argument because Mesun had only recently bought his freedom. Anyway, Mesun refused to do (or pay his workers to do) the unpaid work. As a result, the Abbey officials repeatedly confiscated his oxen and horses and eventually broke the doors and windows of his house and impounded his furniture. When he protested, they put Mesun into the village lock-up! He was released on bail and sent a formal complaint to King Henry III. The king referred the case to his travelling judges. Mesun produced witnesses of his free status and claimed £40 for the loss of his animals and £100 for the damage to his house and furniture. He offered to pay a regular 'quitrent' in lieu of work service. The judges delayed giving a verdict and ordered that the court rolls should be searched to find evidence of the terms of Mesun's tenancy and also of other, similar Abbey tenancies. These could not be found; Mesun did not attend the judges when they sat at distant Canterbury and with glee, the abbot's representative claimed to have won the case. By this time (1273), Henry III had died and Mesun appealed to King Edward I. He sent for all the papers concerned with the case and ordered both parties to attend parliament. For some reason, Mesun failed to attend and so he lost the case.

This dispute lasted about four years and is included here because it illustrates some interesting points concerning tenancies. Whether or not Mesun had been born free, he had certainly reached a substantial position. At that time, horses were so valuable that they were only owned by merchants not farmers or dealers; yet amongst the livestock impounded by the Abbey were no less than eight horses. Also Mesun had powerful friends who could bail him from the local lock-up and help him to present his case to the king. Despite this, the Abbey was prepared to pursue the case for all those years. Had they once allowed a freeman to change the grading of tied land, they would have opened the floodgates for appeals.

Looking at the status of workers, rather than of land, it was nearly two hundred years before there are references to work-service tenants at Sandridge receiving their freedom. Needless to say, the Peasants' Revolt was particularly bitter in Sandridge.

Conclusion

This chapter set out to point to the importance of the religious houses and the control that they had over the lives of their workers and tenants. Less people in the early twenty-first century will appreciate their role as a channel of prayer but we must remember that for centuries they were the main providers of education, books, music, medicine, healthcare, agricultural improvement, town planning and business development. All this needed money, especially to provide care and accommodation for travellers. To keep the money coming in, they had to be completely ruthless with both their tenants and their workers.

CHAPTER 2 • *ROUTE 2*

The Royal Forest of Ashridge

Berkhamsted • Northchurch • (Aldbury)
Ashridge Monument • (Ivinghoe Beacon) • Ringshall
Little Gaddesden • Hudnall • Water End • Piccotts End
Hemel Hempstead (spur to Kings Langley)
Water End • Potten End • Berkhamsted

Introduction

This route is approximately 20 miles long and has an optional spur of about 3
miles to Kings Langley. It starts and ends in Berkhamsted and passes through old
Hemel Hempstead. Although part of it makes use of main roads, it passes in and
out of beautiful forest scenery and includes the attractive village of Little
Gaddesden. At various places along the route, there are historic churches,
public houses and other old buildings; there are also opportunities to walk and
picnic.

The remains of Berkhamsted Castle, Ashridge House, its grounds and
museum, the Monument and nearby National Trust Discovery Centre, shop and
tea kiosk are all, at times, open to the public. Dates and times can be obtained
from the Tourist Information Centres.

The Historical Background overlaps with other chapters of this book and is
based on the subject of pilgrims and pilgrimage. Many of the details are
uncovered in the Historical Highlights.

These start with a brief history of Berkhamsted Castle and the control that its
owners had over the people of the forest. They then move on to Ashridge
Monastery, its shrine and the life of the canons. Frequent, royal visits were
probably one of the reasons that the discipline broke down, during the years
leading to its closure in 1539.

Princess Elizabeth lived there for a short time but most of the latter half of

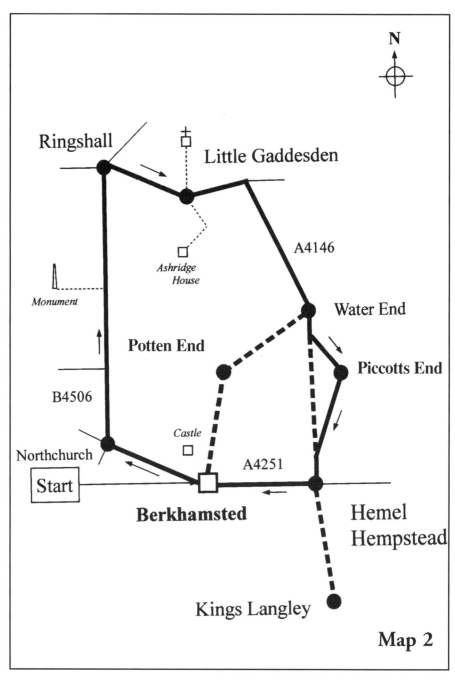

N

Ringshall

Little Gaddesden

A4146

Water End

Piccotts End

Monument

Potten End

B4506

Castle

Northchurch

A4251

Start

Berkhamsted

Hemel
Hempstead

Kings Langley

*Ashridge
House*

Map 2

General View Berkhamsted Castle (E.H.)

Back View Ashridge House

this section covers the life of one of Elizabeth's senior ministers, Sir Thomas Egerton, and his descendants. In the late 1920s, the family sold the estate and, before moving on to a description of Little Gaddesden Church and the family monuments, a brief adult education is included.

Although the important wall-paintings at Piccotts End are no longer open to the public, their known history is included, before the route heads into old Hemel Hempstead and, via St Mary's Church in Kings Langley, which is now linked to Hemel Hempstead by a main road but was once linked by a bridleway through the forest. This section of the book ends with the story of Kings Langley's royal palace, park and friary and the mystery of a king's tomb in All Saints Church.

In total, this chapter of the book opens up the interesting history of a beautiful and popular part of Hertfordshire's countryside.

Historical Background

The aim of this section is to uncover some supplementary background history to this important royal forest. As much of the theory has been covered in other chapters, only additional details have been included here under specific headings.

A little about the National Trust (the protectors and managers of the forest) will be found under 'The Preservation of our Heritage'. The history of the Order of Augustinian Canons is included in 'The Influence of the Religious Houses' and the chapter concerning the historical houses of Luton is based on the Luton Fraternity Register. This includes information about the attitude that medieval people held concerning purgatory and their desire to provide good 'quality' prayers, ie prayers which were welcomed by God on behalf of their loved ones who had recently died.

Pilgrimages and Shrines

Pilgrimages were extremely popular and families or individuals would save for years to visit one of the more important shrines. At first glance, a pilgrimage might appear to have been a glorified holiday, a chance to escape from a hard or boring routine. In many cases this must have been at least partly true, but many were undertaken because of ill health or a recent bereavement. Occasionally people went voluntarily, or on the order of a judge, to compensate for a crime. The majority (including the latter category of penitential pilgrim) 'registered' their intention in church or private chapel and had to guarantee that they had the permission of their husbands/wives, had settled any quarrels, had made peace with any enemies and settled any debts.

The roads were too dangerous to travel long distances unaccompanied and much of the pleasure, and health-giving properties of pilgrimages, was to be found in the company of fellow pilgrims; the change of air, scenery, food and water also helped. To cross the seas and visit Jerusalem, Rome or Compostella was not only extremely expensive, but was also dangerous and involved leaving one's workplace for several months. In England the shrines at the great Benedictine monasteries of St Albans and Bury St Edmunds were very popular and after 1172 many people tried to visit the tomb of Thomas à Beckett at Canterbury. However even these three English sites were too far for many poorer people to reach and in most counties there was a more humble local shrine.

The patrons who founded these later shrines were prepared to accept the expense of obtaining the 'relic' and of providing an honourable shrine because it illustrated their respect and devotion to the saint involved and, through that saint, their humble love of God. From the point of view of spiritual advantage, the patron and his family would benefit for years to come from the prayers of the residential community that they put in charge of the shrine. They also hoped that in centuries to come they and their families would be remembered in the prayers of pilgrims who visited the shrine. In a more worldly way, the provision of a shrine demonstrated the patron's ability to pay for such an impressive edifice.

The Honour of Berkhamsted Castle

A manor was an estate where the landlord had legal rights over his tenants and workers. It had nothing to do with size or value; Totternhoe was two separate manors whereas the whole of Houghton Regis, plus Sewell and what is now Dunstable, was one manor. Each manor had its own court. Occasionally one person owned a large number of scattered manors, held lordship over them and controlled the manor court in each of them. This would be called an Honour.

After the Battle of Hastings, in 1066, William I (the Conqueror) gave Berkhamsted and many acres of Ashridge Forest to his half-brother, Robert, Count of Mortain. There was already a small castle to the south of the village but Robert set men to work to start building a very large, residential castle. The remains we can see today were built in the 1150s and include Totternhoe stone mixed with flint and other building materials.

The original settlement and church, which became known as Northchurch, remained but a small town grew up around the castle. There were several more villages and hamlets in and around the forest eg Little Gaddesden and Aldbury which are still on the outskirts of the forest today and the present towns of Hemel Hempstead and Kings Langley which have grown out of the forest villages. All of these and many other scattered villages made up the Honour of Berkhamsted.

Ashridge House

As the centuries went by, several royal princes held the castle and honour, which included the valuable hunting rights in the forest. In 1225, King John gave the castle to his second son, Richard. He held it for the rest of his life and died there in 1272. His son, Edmund, divided the honour when, in 1283, he founded the monastery in the centre of the forest. He was living there, not at the castle, when he died in 1300. Much of the honour was still attached to the castle, but Edmund gave a piece of the forest and many of the villages to help to support the monastery. The castle continued for some years as a royal residence but required constant repairs and several royal visitors preferred to stay at Ashridge monastery rather than at the crumbling castle. In the reign of Queen Elizabeth, it was finally taken down and the stone used elsewhere.

Henry VIII regularly stayed at the monastery to enjoy the hunting but nevertheless, he closed it down in 1539 as part of the Dissolution of the Monasteries. Because of all the royal visits, part of the monastery was as comfortable as a royal palace. So, after Henry's death, it became a country residence for his daughter, Princess Elizabeth. The year following her death, the estate was sold to her friend, Lord Keeper of the Seal,* Sir Thomas Egerton, Baron Ellesmere. His descendants continued to own Ashridge into the 20th century.

* *Nearly equivalent to Lord Chancellor*

Historical Highlights/Route

BERKHAMSTED

For several centuries the owner of the castle also owned the town, the surrounding forest, the deer and other wild animals and in early days the people who lived in and around it. The livestock were strictly protected and any of the cottagers who dared to trap a rabbit were punished through the brutal game protection laws.

The Castle

When William I (The Conqueror) led his army in a wide circle around London in 1066, it was at some previous castle building on this site that the Saxon bishops and secular leaders met and invited him into the capital to be made king. William gave Berkhamsted to his half-brother, Robert, Count of Mortain, who quickly built (or re-built) an earth-walled, stockaded castle to watch over the surrounding countryside. By the time of the Domesday tax report in 1086, not only was there a thriving agricultural estate which included 2 water-mills and 2 fields of grape-vines, but also a busy town with 52 burgesses.

The son of the count rebelled against Henry I and the castle was razed to the ground. It was, however, soon rebuilt as a stone castle and was later given to Thomas à Beckett during his time as chancellor. Some of the stonework of this period (1155-1165) still exists.

The castle was damaged during the first civil war when, in 1216, the barons, backed by Prince Louis, the French Dauphin, surrounded the castle and held it to siege for two weeks. In the middle of the 13th century much money was spent to make it into a residential castle, suitable for royal visits, and there were chambers for the king and queen, plus a royal chapel and nursery. However, during the 14th century it was again in very poor repair, although some of the rooms were made habitable as a comfortable prison, when King John of France was captured in 1361.

The castle was often associated with the Earldom of Cornwall and in 1366 it was granted to Prince Edward, the 'Black Prince', son of Edward III, becoming

> *ROUTE*
> From Berkhamsted the route follows the A41 towards Northchurch, but if starting at the Castle, follow residential Bridgewater Road and at the T-junction turn left (with the gasometer on your left), go over the canal and you meet the A41, at another T-junction with traffic lights.

43

one of his favourite homes and where he spent his honeymoon. The last royal resident was Cecily, Duchess of York, mother of Edward IV. She died in 1495 and from then on the building was no longer repaired and was soon in ruins.

Queen Elizabeth I leased the ruined castle to Sir Edward Cary for a rent of one red rose. He ordered a new courtyard house, which became known as Berkhamsted Place and the remains of the castle was allowed to crumble and fall.

The Church of St Peter

This is a very large church dating from about 1200 when the castle was still a royal residence. It was probably built to replace an earlier building. The new sanctuary is particularly worth a visit to see its beautiful reredos screen, which was adapted from a 15th century room screen with twelve decorated statuettes of saints. There is a brass commemorating John Waterhouse, brother of Thomas Waterhouse, the last rector of Ashridge monastery, who died in 1558. Nearby is the arcaded tomb of a 14th century knight, thought to be Henry of Berkhamsted, porter and later constable of the castle. There are many more memorials, including the east window, dated 1872, to the memory of William Cowper, the poet and hymn-writer; he was born at Berkhamsted, where his father was the rector, in 1731. There is also a large black and white marble chest tomb of John Sayer who died in 1682. He was chief cook to Charles II and went into exile with him. In 1662 he came to live at Berkhamsted Place, which was demolished in 1967. He bequeathed £1000 for almshouses for the relief of the poor. The Sayer almshouses can be seen in the High Street. Do not miss the Elizabethan Court House which stands near the church.

ROUTE

Turn right towards Northchurch and, as you pass the school, turn right onto the B4506, sign-posted Ashridge.

NORTHCHURCH

This is thought to have been where the original church and settlement stood before the building of the castle. The Church of St Mary was originally the focal point of the parish of Berkhamsted St Mary. The parish of St Peter was first formed in the 13th century.

44

ASHRIDGE FOREST

Thousands of people visit the forest each year. They enjoy one very small area near the Monument but do not realise how wide an area it still covers or how great an influence its owners used to have on the local people. Ashridge Forest was protected for the king and the owners of first Berkhamsted Castle and then Ashridge House. They controlled the lives of the people who lived in or near the area which once stretched from Little Gaddesden across to Berkhamsted and far beyond.

ROUTE
The route (which passes through beautiful woodland scenery) is heading towards Ringshall and Little Gaddesden. Even though it is a main road, watch out for animals and picnicking children.

The Monastery of the 'Good Men'.

In the 13th century the brother of Henry III and his son Edmund were visiting Germany when they saw a box of gold, which, they were told, contained a phial of the True Blood of Christ; they bought it and returned with it to England. When his father died in 1272, Edmund inherited the title of Earl of Cornwall and the box with the relic. He gave a third of the blood to the Abbey of Hailes (which had been founded by his father) and in honour of the relic, he himself founded a new religious house at Ashridge and deposited the rest of the blood there. The house was given into the care of monks called the Bonhommes. These 'good men' were members of the Augustinian Order, whose responsibilities included the honouring and care of relics and the care of both sick and healthy pilgrims. There were some differences from the traditional Augustinian houses; they were very small houses, called colleges rather than priories and their leaders were rectors rather than priors. In addition they wore grey not black robes and had a strict regime of conduct and education. Edmund richly endowed the house in 1283 and during the next few years he and his friends added to the original endowment.

When Edmund died there was disagreement concerning his burial. Eventually his bones were buried at Hailes and his heart and flesh at Ashridge. This was not the end of royal interest. In December 1290 after the sad funeral procession of Queen Eleanor, wife of Edward I (which was commemorated by an 'Eleanor Cross' at every stop en route, including Dunstable), Edward retired to Ashridge for Christmas. He stayed for five weeks in the peace of the monastery and in January 1291 parliament was obliged to visit him there. The Annals of Dunstable Priory record the hardships suffered by the town in helping to supply food for the royal party.

45

ROUTE

(Along this road there are several optional diversions from the route.

1. After some distance there is an optional left turn down a very steep and winding hill to Aldbury. This is not on this route but in medieval times was a key village on the Berkhamsted/Ashridge estate.

2. If intending to visit the official picnic area, the Monument, the exhibition room or café, watch out for a sign pointing left up a short straight road.

3. On the edge of the forest at Ringshall, is an optional left-hand turn to Ivinghoe Beacon. This is not on the route but in earlier days Ivinghoe, Pitstone and several villages nearer to Dunstable were all connected with the estate.)

Over this period other kings visited and gave gifts. The Black Prince, son of Edward III, re-endowed the house in 1376 and in his will gave his 'Great Table of gold and silver furnished full of precious relics and in the middle of it a holy cross of wood of the True Cross; and the said table garnished with stones and pearls, that is to say 25 rubies, 34 sapphires, 15 great pearls......'[1]

All this wealth and royal interest brought many pilgrims to Ashridge and it continued to prosper but this popularity also carried disadvantages for the canons who were expecting peace and seclusion. Henry VIII was a personal friend of the last rector and made several visits, treating the place as a hunting lodge. On a visit in 1530 he paid 20 shillings (£1) for livery, 2 shillings (10p) for badges, 7s 6d (37$\frac{1}{2}$p) to the keeper and some money to 'Edmond the Footman' for 'the dogs to draw water'. The latter is a reference to the deep well, which can be seen at Ashridge today and to the dogs which must have been used to work the water-wheel. The former expenses probably meant 'livery' as in stabling for his horses.

The monks were eventually contaminated by all the worldliness about them and in 1515 the bishop's visitor found no grammar teacher employed and a general sense of grievance among the brothers, because insufficient practical workers were being employed to allow them time to study. There were even suggestions that brothers had been seen fishing and that one or more ladies had visited the house and stayed the night! Three years later matters were even worse. The evening silence was no longer kept and sometimes brothers remained in the hall after supper, drinking wine instead of returning to their rooms to study and pray. There were no teachers, lessons or leadership and by 1530, discipline had completely broken down. Drinking took place regardless of rules; the farmer's wife was encouraged to sleep at the college and the senior brothers caused much disgrace. The physician was in charge of the cellar and the brother in charge of the farm sold off the poultry for pocket

1 Coult, D. A Prospect of Ashridge

money and added to his income by poaching. A lady from St Albans frequently stayed overnight and other ladies visited occasionally. It was claimed that the seniors quarrelled openly in front of the other brothers, the medical students argued and fought amongst themselves and there was no love or charity within the house. The college was eventually surrendered to Henry VIII in 1539.

The rector, 14 brothers and a novice were awarded pensions and several of them went on to work in local parishes. The rector, Thomas Waterhouse, received £100 per annum plus 50 loads of firewood and for some years was rector at Quainton, Buckinghamshire. He died in 1554 and was buried at Hemel Hempstead church. It was a great pity that the house had such an unhappy end to what must have been a glorious and useful life.

Ashridge House Becomes a Royal Residence

After the monks left Ashridge, the house became a minor royal residence that all three royal children visited from time to time. Without understanding the causes, Henry had a great fear of plague and regularly sent the children out to the country. Some time after the death of her father, Princess Elizabeth came to live at Ashridge. She was frequently visited there by Lord Thomas Seymour, who courted her against the wishes of his brother, the Protector and one of Edward's Council of Guardians. There were even scandalous rumours that she gave birth while living there. After a detailed enquiry Thomas was executed and Elizabeth was moved to Hatfield House. This was in 1549 when she was only sixteen years old!

Elizabeth inherited Ashridge from her father; Edward transferred it to her on 17 March 1550, adding Hemel Hempstead and Berkhamsted to the estate in 1551. She returned to live at Ashridge until Queen Mary, fearful that her enemies would meet there, summoned Elizabeth back to court. She was too ill to ride but eventually agreed to travel in the queen's personal litter. She went to the royal apartments in the Tower of London as a

ROUTE
The route continues through Ringshall; watch for a right-hand turn towards Little Gaddesden. A small castellated building on the right of this turning was once a gatehouse to Ashridge House. The route is heading through Little Gaddesden to Hudnall and the A4146. Having turned right, there is an outdoor swimming pool called the Deer Leap, immediately on the right. After some distance, the Bridgewater Arms pub can be seen on the left.
(If wanting to visit Ashridge House or take a short-cut back to Berkhamsted, watch out for a sudden right turn (by a small monument), going through a white gateway and dropping down into the forest.

prisoner but was soon allowed her freedom on the understanding that she agreed to remain in the London area and did not return to Ashridge.

In 1556 she agreed to lease the house and estate to Richard Combe of Hemel Hempstead and from then on there were many different tenants. She never did return to Ashridge and the year after her death, October 1604, the house and estate were sold to Sir Thomas Egerton, Lord Keeper of the Seal. It remained with his family for almost 250 years and was then held by more distant relatives for another seventy-eight years.

The Egerton Family

Sir Thomas was the illegitimate son of Sir Richard Egerton of Ridley in Cheshire and Alice Sparke, a housemaid. Despite this apparent disadvantage he eventually became Lord Chancellor of England. He was a trustworthy man and a favourite of Queen Elizabeth. Although he bought land all over England, it was at Ashridge that he created the main home for his family. Despite there having been several tenants in the house, the bed once used by Princess Elizabeth, together with a pair of her gloves and stockings, remained at Ashridge until this century.

Sir Thomas spent much money on the estate but his heirs neglected it, due to their financial instability. His son, Sir John Egerton, paid about £20,000 to obtain the title of first Earl of Bridgewater. His grandson, another John, besides inheriting debts of more than £80,000 had financial losses due to the civil war, when several times food, horses and provisions were stolen from the house.

Royalty still had an interest in Ashridge Forest as illustrated by a Royal Warrant, dated September 1660, the year that Charles II came to the throne. He was concerned that his game at Ashridge was being destroyed by 'divers disorderly persons with greyhounds, mongrels, setting dogs, trammels, tunnels, nets and other devices'. The second earl had orders to protect all the game within ten miles of Ashridge[1] for royal use.

The 'Canal' Duke of Bridgewater.

In the 18th century Ashridge was once again improved; an inventory shows that at that time the house had 90 rooms. Scroop Egerton, named after his maternal grandfather, the Earl of Sunderland, married Elizabeth Churchill, daughter of

1 Coult, DC. A Prospect of Ashridge

John Churchill, Earl of Marlborough. Through the influence of his mother-in-law, he had several positions at Queen Anne's court and became the first Duke of Bridgewater. Scroop had two sons, both of whom were rather weak and sickly. When Scroop died and 11-year-old Francis became the second Duke of Bridgewater, he was still a pupil at a boarding school in Markyate. After a period at Eton he went with his tutor on the Grand Tour, where he studied both the theory and practice of canals. He returned home in 1755 and, when he was twenty-two, fell in love with a famous widow, the Duchess of Hamilton. The young Duke did not approve of her notorious sister who, although the wife of the Earl of Coventry, was having an affair with Lord Bolingbroke. The engagement ended and soon the duke was living on his Cheshire estates, planning a canal that would carry coal from the family mines at Worsley, right into the industrial, northern towns. He became one of the largest employers in the country, with an enormous wage bill to pay and with many engineering and political problems to solve. The capital outlay for this work was so high that there were no funds to spare for Ashridge. The house ceased to be maintained as a home and when he visited the estate, the duke stayed at the lodge.

When success came to the canal and the duke returned south, he decided it was too late to save his old home. An auction of the pictures, furniture and household items was held in 1800 and the building materials (including the bells and turret clock) were sold two years later. The Duke died in 1803 and his heir (and cousin), Lieutenant General John William Egerton, completed the demolition and was responsible for the present building. He wanted a house to represent the achievements of his famous cousin and the architect, James Wyatt, was chosen to design the new building, which was completed in 1810. The grounds were re-designed by Lancelot (Capability) Brown and the farms and cottages for miles around were renovated or rebuilt.

The dukedom had died out, but the 7th Earl bequeathed the earldom, together with £18,000 a year, to his brother, who lived in France. In his will, this 8th Earl left a design and £13,000 to erect an obelisk as a memorial to the last Duke. This monument, which is often open to the public, is 108 feet tall, with a viewing platform.

Later Members of the Bridgewater Family
When the 7th Earl of Bridgewater died in 1823, the title passed to his brother but he left the house to his wife for her lifetime. When she died in 1849, the heir was Viscount Alford, husband of Marian Alford, great-nephew of the 7th Earl

of Bridgewater and son of the 1st Earl Brownlow. He died two years later and his twelve-year-old son inherited the estate. It was this boy's brother who became the 3rd Earl Brownlow and married the youngest daughter of the Earl of Shrewsbury. (Look out for her memorial a few hundred yards along the route on your left). During their stay at Ashridge there were many famous visitors, including Benjamin Disraeli, Mr Gladstone and Queen Mary.

In his will the 3rd Earl directed that Ashridge should be sold and, as there were no children, the earldom came to an end. This was when the National Trust bought the park.

Ashridge House Becomes a College

In 1928 the house and immediate grounds were bought for the Conservative Party to use as a training college, which was known as the 'Bonar Law College', or the 'College of Citizenship'. It offered residential courses in political science, economics and current affairs.

During the war it became an emergency hospital but in 1947 it was able to re-open, this time on a wider basis and without political bias. Financially it became too difficult to support the important historic building and in 1957 there was complete re-organisation. In 1959 it re-opened as Ashridge Management College.[1]

Ashridge House Today

The architect, James Wyatt, died in 1813, before the new house was completely finished. His nephew, who was to become Sir Jeffry Wyattville, not only finished the original work started by his uncle, but also added an east wing and the present main entrance. The arms of the Bridgewater family can be seen above the porch and the heads of Edward VI and Queen Mary are on either side of the great doors.

The crypt and 'donkey well' are the only parts of the monastery building which survive today. The well has been cleaned and floodlit and a pair of oak doors, originally from the monastery and dating from about 1400, has been hung in a corridor behind the ante chapel.

Much of the 4,000 acres, landscaped by Capability Brown, are now owned by the National Trust, while the pleasure gardens surrounding the college, which were planned by Humphrey Repton, are periodically open to the public. There is now a museum which houses documents and interesting items illustrating the important history of Ashridge House.

1 Senar, Howard. Little Gaddesden and Ashridge.

LITTLE GADDESDEN

Over the centuries, this was developed as a typical estate village. The influence of the manor house can be seen in many parts of the village. As early as 1854, Lord Brownlow appointed a schoolmaster to teach the children during the week and adults on Sundays. Until 1858 (when the schoolroom was ready for use) the lessons were held in an upstairs room at the Bridgewater Arms.

This provision of education was typical of their advanced ideas. In 1858 Lady Marian Alford arranged for piped water to be connected to the estate cottages and several members of the family employed top architects of the day to design the village cottages. By walking round the village with Howard Senar's book it is possible to identify not only the age but also the architect of many of them.

The Bridgewater Arms

The porch, with its Doric columns and doorway with fan-shaped over-window, are both early 19th century. The first reference to the issuing of a licence to sell alcohol is 1815. Although Ashridge House has many rooms, it has been suggested that this property may have been built to provide extra accommodation during large house-parties. At different times there have been seven beer-houses in the village and scattered hamlets but only the Bridgewater Arms survives.

Memorials in the Village

On the road leading through Little Gaddesden there are two large memorials. The cross at the entrance gate was unveiled on Sunday 21st June 1891 in memory of Lady Marian Alford. Mother of the 2nd and 3rd Earls Brownlow, she provided almshouses and cottages in the village, built to her own design. For a few years after the erection of the cross Mrs Wheatley, who had helped with its design, arranged for local children to gather there once a year to receive bags of sweets in memory of Lady Alford.[1]

ROUTE
As the main route continues through the village, the memorial cross to Lady Marion Alford is near the side-road entrance to Ashridge House and nearly opposite is the attractive war memorial.

Another cross stands further along the green; this is in remembrance of Adelaide, wife of Adelbert, 3rd Earl of Brownlow, who died in 1917. This lady was also remembered with affection because of her interest in and care of the village people.

1 Senar, Howard. Little Gaddesden and Ashridge.

ROUTE

If wanting to visit the church in Little Gaddesden, look out for the signpost pointing left. The Church of St Peter and St Paul is 1/2 mile off the route with a car-park at the end of the road.

The Church of St Peter and St Paul

The original Saxon settlement and village were on the edge of the forest, near where the springs once gathered to form the River Gade. There are 10th century connections between the village and St Albans Abbey, but the first written reference to a church was in 1161. This was at a time when the village was still on its original site. By the 17th century the majority of villagers lived over half a mile away in the present village. However, the Bridgewater family chose to make this distant church the site for their mausoleum. It also contains their very impressive monuments and memorials.

The church booklet 'Little Gaddesden Church' describes each one and explains the family connections. All eight earls (as well as other members of the family) are buried in the vaults. The 'Canal Duke', the 3rd Earl of Bridgewater, has a monument on the south wall and the 7th earl (who rebuilt the house) is remembered by the beautiful 'Westmacott Memorial' over the altar in the south chapel. He used Jeffry Wyatt (nephew of James) to build this chapel and the profiles of the earl and his wife are carved on either side of the church porch. An eyewitness account of the 7th Earl's funeral gives some idea of the pageantry this old church has witnessed. The cortege consisted of: the park-keeper and 6 keepers on foot, 2 porters on horseback, the mounted valet with coronets on a cushion, 2 more mounted porters with staves, a cart carrying a plume of feathers, a hearse drawn by 6 horses and 5 mourning coaches, each followed by more servants on foot. This official party was followed by large crowds of people from the various villages that made up the estate. The 2 churchwardens had 70 assistants to help them to keep order.

One of the most striking memorials is that to Elizabeth Dutton, daughter of the eldest son of the Sir Thomas Egerton who originally bought Ashridge for the family. She married a Cheshire squire in 1611, while she was still sixteen years old. On her wedding day she was riding on horseback behind her husband when his horse stumbled and he was killed. She died of a broken heart within the year. This monument was originally in St Martin's in the Fields church but was moved to Little Gaddesden in 1730.

> 'Here rests in peace of whom 'tis truly said
> She lived true spouse and widow, dyed a maid.'

The Village Centre

As the Tudor family spent so much time at Ashridge, the outskirts of the forest became a popular residential area. Several handsome Tudor houses still survive alongside the green. The earliest is probably John of Gaddesden's house. There was a 'John of Gaddesden' who signed the deeds of endowment for the college in 1283 and the famous Dr John Gaddesden (who wrote one of England's first medical textbooks) was probably his son; Dr John was court physician to Edward II. Although he finished his training at Merton College, he probably started his education at Ashridge. His famous medical book was called 'Rosa Angelica' because he said the rose had five sepals and the book had five parts. Some of his ideas such as hygiene, good food and foot-care have stood the test of time and some of his herbal cures still sound sensible today. However, the use of pig excrement for haemorrhage or eating frogs for toothache are somewhat frightening!

The house that became known as The Manor House was originally built in 1576. After the Dissolution and the closing of Ashridge Monastery, the manorial rights were purchased by Henry, Earl of Essex. His heir sold them to Robert Dormer of Wing, High Sheriff of Buckinghamshire and Bedfordshire. It was his descendant, another Robert, who built the manor house.

ROUTE
The wide green runs along on the left of the road and there are several very interesting historic houses including the manor house and John of Gaddesden's house. Further along the green is the memorial to Adelaide, wife of Adelbert, third Earl Brownlow. Soon after the memorial the road divides. The route turns left towards Hudnall and then continues to the A4146.

PICCOTTS END

Two of the four attractive cottages, which lay back from the road, used to be open to the public; this was because they contain important wall-paintings. Unfortunately public opening added to the cost of insurance and preservation and they are no longer open.

Standing on the edge of the forest beside the busy Hemel Hempstead road, they were probably built as the monastic hostel. All religious houses were obliged to offer hospitality to travellers but the definite site of the Ashridge hostel is unknown. In 1953 Mr AC Lindley discovered, in one of these houses, hand-woven linen, under layers of wallpaper; these were carefully removed by experts, revealing medieval wall-paintings

ROUTE
It is heading into Old Hemel Hempstead, via Piccotts End.

Street Scene Old Hemel Hempsted (O.R.)

showing religious scenes and symbols. The building is about 600 years old, well back into the monastic period and the paintings are quite unique in this country.

The houses are made of flints, oak and wattle and daub. When, nine years later, the next cottage became vacant, Mr Lindley found an Elizabethan painted room, an early panelled room and a so-called 'priests' hide'. After the Dissolution of the Monasteries, the building was converted into a Tudor house and early in the 18th century it was divided into four cottages. In 1826 Sir Ashley Paston Cooper, surgeon to King George IV, used them to establish what is thought to be the first cottage hospital in England. Seven years later the hospital moved to larger premises and the building was converted back into four cottages.

OLD HEMEL HEMPSTEAD

At the time of the Domesday report of 1086, this was a prosperous agricultural community with the added advantage of having the River Gade running through. There were four mills and a thriving eel fishery.

The Earl of Cornwall gave the mills plus a fulling mill to the Ashridge monastery, which gradually gained control of most of the agricultural land. They were very strict landlords and at the 'Peasants' Revolt' of 1381, the farmers of Hemel Hempstead stormed the gates of Ashridge demanding a new charter; they failed but were not deterred. In 1409 justices were sent to enquire into a rumour that the tenants of the house of Ashridge had

> **ROUTE**
> The A4146 crossroads is on the Bedfordshire/ Hertfordshire border. Turn right and drive towards Water End and Hemel Hempstead.

leagued together to refuse to do their service (this was the work service that they owed to their monastic landlords). An agreement made between the college and its tenants in 1418, shows how strict they really were. Land that owed plough service could not be divided without permission and if a 'free' man took on land that owed service, he must work that service, as the land could not become free land. If a group of men took on a piece of land, they must all pay a licence fee before starting to work it and if a man built a second house, he and the new occupier must both pay a licence fee. Up to the Dissolution, the rector of Ashridge kept control over the people of Hemel Hempstead, restricted development and kept the community as a medieval village.

Looking at the busy town today it seems strange to think that in those days the plough fields came right down to the church and that in 1531 the farmers who lived along the High Street were agreeing not to put pigs or sheep on the nearby common.

In 1539 (the year that the college was dissolved) the town received a Charter of Incorporation, which included the right to elect a town bailiff, hold weekly markets on a Thursday and an annual fair. The plough land was pushed back and a hard surface made for Market Street (now High Street) and building began.

In the church is the Combe Memorial. Richard Combe leased Bury House, Burymill and the dairy from the Crown. Some time before 1595, he pulled down the old manor house and built a new mansion with a total of about fourteen rooms, including eight bedrooms. The ruins of one door can still be seen at the end of the walled garden, between the church and the river.

The Church of St Mary

This is a fine old church in which a large amount of the original Norman work still stands. Building started in 1140 and the chancel and sacristy are thought to date back to 1145, with the central tower a little later. The walls are of stone and flint, with some Roman bricks inserted; these may have come from the villa across the river. The amazing 130ft fluted leaden spire is thought to date from the early 14th century and, with the gilded weather-vane, reaches a total height of almost 200ft.

The Boxmoor Trust

In what is today a bustling modern town, evidence survives of the connection between Hemel Hempstead and its rural past. The long green field between the road and the canal is still common land, controlled by trustees; certain householders can apply to graze horses, cows, donkeys and geese during strictly observed summer dates. The Boxmoor Trustees, elected by the 'Inhabitant Householders of the parish of Hemel Hempstead and the hamlet of Bovingdon', administer the charitable trust on behalf of the community. Two full-time herdsmen are employed on the husbandry of the moors and commons and also for the supervision of the grazing. This is not a trust formed at the time of enclosure, but a gift, made around 1600, to the inhabitants of Hemel Hempstead and Bovingdon. During the 19th century, Trust land, or its income, was used for St John's Church, Boxmoor, a hall and a swimming pool. At different times, land has been made available for a wide variety of outdoor recreational facilities.

KINGS LANGLEY

This is not part of the direct route but is linked historically and is therefore an interesting, optional detour.

Berkhamsted Castle was not the only royal residence in this corner of Hertfordshire. Long before the Norman Conquest a profitable part of the manor of Langley had been given to St Albans Abbey and afterwards William's steward added the remaining land to the extensive estates attached to Berkhamsted Castle. For many years its history was similar to that of Berkhamsted but in August 1279 Queen Eleanor of Castile (first wife of King Edward I) leased it from her cousin by marriage, Edmund, Earl of Cornwall. Changes then began which led to the two manors named 'Kings' Langley and 'Abbots' Langley.

ROUTE
The route then continues through the old part of the town. (At this point it is possible to turn off the route to Kings Langley)

Although the queen accompanied her husband as he continually travelled both in England and France, she appears to have taken a personal interest in the work at Kings Langley, where a master builder was put in charge of enlarging and modernising the existing house. Eleanor was only twelve when, in 1254, she married fifteen-year-old Prince Edward (later King Edward I). Their first child to survive into adulthood was not born until 1270. Of their first four sons, only Edward (later King Edward II), born in 1284, lived beyond the age of ten.

A Country Estate for Queen Eleanor

Just over £400 was spent on stone, timber, plaster, ironwork and tiles to produce a suite of rooms for the sole use of the king, queen and young prince. However, once Queen Eleanor realised the suitability of the site for a family home, she commissioned more work. The hunting park was re-stocked, the moat deepened, cleaned and extended and a new well was dug out. Undoubtedly Eleanor saw this as a healthy country retreat to which she could escape from the noisy and unhealthy palaces in and around London. For her safety a new gate and gatehouse were erected and fine draperies were purchased for her comfort. Contemporary accounts suggest that she greatly missed the land of her childhood, so at Langley she ordered a vineyard to be laid out in the park and a cloister to be built, through which she could walk. She also imported apple trees from France to be planted in the extensive, newly designed gardens between the house and the church. To tend these gardens, which she hoped to develop in the style of her homeland, she brought Spanish gardeners to England and arranged for them to be housed at Langley.

57

Edward and Eleanor were crowned in Westminster Abbey on August 19th 1274, five years before she leased Langley. The couple continued to travel widely in England and Wales and spent from May 1286 to August 1289 abroad, travelling from one court to another. Even when they returned to England, they continued to travel from town to town and it was at Harby, Nottinghamshire, that Eleanor died on 28 November 1290. Before her death, she managed to make short visits to Langley and Edward continued to visit the house after her death. He was there with a house party on All Saints' Day 1299 and sent for the Abbott of St Albans to celebrate mass.

Edward may have visited Langley when, following Eleanor's sad funeral procession, he spent Christmas 1290 at the Ashridge monastery. During the next twelve months he ordered a new wine cellar and during 1292 paid Henry of Bovingdon to fit two louvres into the roof of the hall, which, at the time was being completely repainted and decorated. A local painter was paid 4d (1.7p) a day for 52 days and a London artist was paid £2.10s (£2.50p) to paint a mural frieze of 54 shields. A bailiff was employed to oversee the estate, together with a park-keeper and two gardeners. A resident chaplain was appointed and other household staff taken on. This modernised and well-appointed house became the country home of Eleanor's only surviving son, Prince Edward.

The Next Generations

Prince Edward was twenty-seven when, in 1307, his father died and he became King of England. The following year he married Isabelle of France and during their lives, that of their son (the future Edward III) and their grandson (the future Richard II), there were frequent royal visits. Much money was spent on the property, not only on repairs and modernisation to the existing buildings, but also on new buildings. There is reference to a paved bathhouse made from stone brought from 'Eglemont' quarry (see Totternhoe). There was a hot-water cistern with pipes to carry hot water to the bathhouse and drains to take the used water away. It is interesting to note the local craftsmen who worked at the palace; William and Henry Bovingdon were the main carpenters, John of Whipsnade the mason, John Smith fitted a fireplace in King Edward III's bedroom, which he had carved from Eglemont stone*. Edward III spent a great deal of money on his private suite at Langley and spent an increasing amount of time there during the latter years of his life. A young man who regularly stayed at Langley was his fourth son, Prince Edmund of Langley, later Duke of York. He had been born

* *The Totternhoe quarry*

there in 1341 and made it his main country house. He installed an organ, kept his own stables and even brought a camel to Langley and kept it in the park!

The royal interest in Langley did not end with the death of Edward III but from then on, most of the money was spent on repairs, rather than on new building work. Both Henry IV and his son, Henry V, visited Langley and after the death of Henry IV, his widow, Joan of Navarre, spent some years of her widowhood living there. She was probably the last person to live there for any length of time. There was a serious fire in 1431, after which it appears as if there was some delay in carrying out repairs. When she died in 1437, the roofs were reported as being in a grave condition and that, as a result, rain had poured in, damaging the walls and internal fittings. This time there was no major overhaul. From time to time, money was spent on essential work and the main reception rooms were still in good enough repair for the newly consecrated Abbot of St Albans to use them for the banquet that followed his inauguration in 1467, but from then on they were left to decay. By 1600 only the gatehouse and a few scattered walls were left standing.

The Park
Even after the palace was no longer fit for use, the park was still a valuable asset. In total there were nearly 700 acres but these varied in their use and value. Many years later, King Henry VII ordered the improvement of the grounds and in 1543 John, Lord Russell of nearby Chenies (later 1st Earl of Bedford), rented the rabbit warren. The following year he became 'Keeper' of the royal park. It was retained by the Stuart kings but long before the civil war it had passed to the Capell family of Hadham, who returned it to agricultural use. They were ardent royalists and Lord Capell was executed in 1649, but Charles II restored the estate to his son when he gave him the title Earl of Essex. It remained in the family until 1900.

The Dominican Friary
Eleanor of Castille was a great supporter of the Dominican friars so that when her son Alphonso died, she arranged for his heart to be buried in the Blackfriars Church, London. In 1312 Alphonso's brother, Edward II, invited a group of Dominican friars to settle in the park at King's Langley. He allowed them to use one of his lodges until their own house was built and encouraged them to build their own church. In 1368 Edward III paid for a clock to be installed in the belfry of this church. After the Dissolution, Lord John Russell took over the

friary and its land but in 1557 (approximately a year before she died) Queen Mary took back the house and some of the land and installed some Dominican nuns. Mary died in November 1558 and in less than a year her sister, Elizabeth, dissolved the nunnery and it became, once again, a secular estate. It repeatedly changed hands and most of what remained of the house was demolished c1700. A very small portion has been incorporated into a private school.

The Friars' Church

Because of its position within the royal park, this church was used for several interesting burials. Piers Gaveston, favourite of Edward II was often at Berkhamsted and when he was beheaded by the barons in 1312, his body was brought from Warwick to Langley. Edmund of Langley, Duke of York was also buried here with his wife Isabel. Richard II, who abdicated shortly before his death in 1400, was brought from Pontefract Castle and buried here on the orders of King Henry IV (see below). The church was dismantled after the Dissolution.

All Saints' Church, Kings Langley

Much of this church was rebuilt in the 15th century although there is evidence of the 13th century building.

King Richard's Tomb?

When the Friars' Church began to crumble, it was realised that the extremely elaborate chest tomb that contained the bodies of Edmund of Langley and his wife, Isabel, was at great risk. In 1575 it was rescued and placed against the north wall of the chancel in All Saints' Church. During repairs in 1877, an eastern extension was made to the north chancel, to house this important tomb. Although it was so extremely elaborate, no one had queried whether it was actually the tomb of the Duke of York, though it was known to contain the bones of both a man and a woman, and was approximately of the correct age. The last clue was that Edmund had stipulated in his will of November 1400 that he wished to be buried in the tomb at Langley ' ...by my well-beloved erstwhile partner Isabel...'

In the magazine 'History Today'* the Rt Hon J Enoch Powell MP published the results of a study he had undertaken after visiting the tomb. He realised that the shields were each carved and attached separately and that over the years their

* *Vol.15 No.10 1965.*

position could have been changed. Looking back through the records, he discovered that when King Richard II's first wife had died in 1394, he had ordered a double tomb which was to be placed in the Chapel of Edward the Confessor in Westminster Abbey. The final payments were made early in 1399 and in his will dated April 1399, Richard decreed that when he died, he should be buried beside his late wife. It was this King Richard who ordered that his aunt (by marriage), wife of the Duke of York, should be buried at Langley and the theme of the article is to explain, with use of the heraldic devices, that this tomb, with the bones of Edmund and Isobel, which had been moved here in Queen Elizabeth's reign, was in fact the original tomb which had been prepared for Richard. However, when Richard died in 1400 and Henry ordered his burial at Langley, there is no record of a tomb being commissioned or of the exact place in the church where he was buried. Fourteen years later, Henry V ordered that Richard should be moved from Langley and be buried beside his wife in the gilded tomb that he had prepared for them both.

ROUTE
The main route is heading back to Berkhamsted but as you cross the new town, the signposts indicate Aylesbury, rather than Berkhamsted.
The A41 links Hemel Hempstead with Berkhamsted but if the driver is unfamiliar with the area, it is probably easier to turn back up the A4146, as far as Water End, and approach Berkhamsted via Potten End.

Were Edmund and Isabel buried in the single royal tomb originally built for himself? Even now we are left with a further mystery. The tomb not only contained the bones of a husband and wife but also the body of another young lady!*

*I am grateful to Miss M Atton for pointing out this article to me.

61

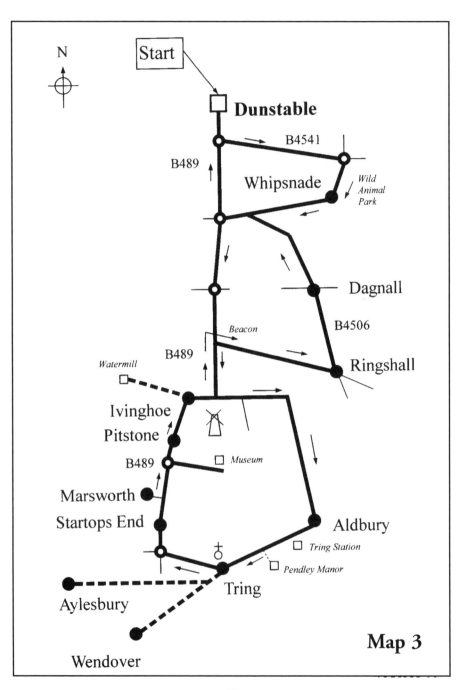

N

Start

Dunstable

B4541

B489

Whipsnade

Wild
Animal
Park

Dagnall

B4506

Beacon

Watermill

B489

Ringshall

Ivinghoe

Pitstone

B489

Museum

Marsworth

Startops End

Aldbury

Tring Station

Pendley Manor

Aylesbury

Tring

Wendover

Map 3

CHAPTER 3 • *ROUTE 3*

The Preservation of our Heritage

Dunstable • Dunstable Downs • Whipsnade
(Ivinghoe) • Aldbury • Pendley
Tring (spur to Wendover or Aylesbury) • (Marsworth)
Pitstone • Ivinghoe • Ivinghoe Beacon
Ringshall (spur to Little Gaddesden) • Dagnall • Dunstable

Introduction

This Route is about 31 miles long, and weaves in and out of South Bedfordshire and the neighbouring areas of Hertfordshire and Buckinghamshire. It crosses both Dunstable Downs and Ivinghoe Beacon, runs past the canal and reservoirs near Tring and crosses the edge of Ashridge Forest. It starts in Dunstable and visits several pretty villages, historic buildings and the market town of Tring. Extra spurs are offered to the historic towns of Wendover and Aylesbury. There is a Natural History Museum, a farm museum and several historic buildings, which at times are open to the public. There is also a hotel whose grounds are famous as the site of outdoor productions of Shakespeare plays.

The Historical Background to this route examines the difficulties surrounding the subject of conservation and the Historical Highlights points out, with gratitude, the efforts that are being made by official bodies, charities, commercial organizations, church congregations, local history and archaeological societies and many individual people to preserve our heritage.

Over the last few years, a surprising number of towns and villages have started their own local history and heritage societies and these can be traced via local libraries. They may not all campaign to actually preserve our heritage but, as a named body of interested people, they are often consulted by local planning officers. Also the research and recording carried out by local archaeological and historical groups provide valuable information about why certain sites and buildings should be protected. In the case of this route, particular credit should be given to the committees and supporters of the Ivinghoe watermill, the Pitstone windmill, the Pitstone Farm Museum and St Mary's Church, Pitstone. These overlapping groups have been together for a great many years and have contributed to both the preservation and the understanding of our heritage. The Manshead Archaeological Society of Dunstable should also be commended for over forty years of patient digging and above all, the recording of their many excavations.

Historical Background

English Heritage and the Listing Process

On an early edition of the then-popular BBC 2 television programme 'One Foot in the Past', English Heritage was criticised by representatives of one town for not having sufficient local consultation, and from those of another town for letting the process of consultation run on too long! In the first place a much-loved, local building regarded as part of the historical background to their lives had been pulled down because it had not been given the legal protection of 'listing'. In the other case a building which English Heritage did want to list was seriously damaged while they waited for public consultation.

One of the statutory duties of English Heritage is to advise the Secretary of State on heritage matters. Lists of buildings of architectural interest, compiled over the years by the Government, have been reviewed on a systematic basis by English Heritage inspectors and the list revised by the Secretary of State upon their recommendation. Since newer buildings become eligible for listing after they are 30 years old there is an ongoing backlog of new potential candidates for assessment. Changes in Government policy have also encouraged a systematic review of vacant or about-to-become-redundant buildings such as hospitals, mental hospitals, prisons and Ministry of Defence-owned buildings of all ages, so that a representative sample of these may be recommended for listing and therefore preserved from damaging changes. When English Heritage has decided upon its recommendations they are presented to the Secretary of State for consideration and agreement and his decision may take some time to emerge.

The Listing of Properties

In addition, requests for grants or planning permission may reveal buildings which, in the opinion of English Heritage, should also be listed. These are referred to the Secretary of State as they occur. In cases where there is a threat to the building, 'emergency' listing can take place but is sometimes not completed sufficiently quickly and the building is lost.

The process of listing is not intended to stifle all development. Buildings are listed in three grades. Grade I buildings are of national importance and include some public buildings such as cathedrals, churches and town halls, but can also be private houses which retain the majority of their original features. Grade II* buildings tend to be of major regional interest and Grade II tend to encompass the types of 'vernacular' buildings such as cottages, chapels and other 'local' types which give the distinctive 'local' flavour to an area. Groups of buildings can be listed as an 'entity' if they contribute to the vernacular flavour of the street scene. This is the case in part of Dunstable.

The process of listing is not based purely on age or excellence. A very late medieval church may be listed as Grade I because it has escaped unfortunate restoration or modernisation and remains an excellent example of its type. On the other hand a particularly early church may be down-graded because a Victorian land-owner or congregation restored it in such a way that its medieval character was lost.

The Problems of Listing

A new notification of listing is not always welcome. Notification may delight the local heritage-caring, members of the community but infuriate the owner, whose alterations from then on will be restricted and whose repair bills may rise if he has to use traditional but more expensive materials.

Visitors from around the world admire our historic buildings and sites which commemorate the past. In theory none of us would like to see them go but in practice it is often very difficult. Many councils, congregations and private individuals have agonised over these decisions. No-one wants to think that theirs is the generation which let some familiar feature which had survived for many centuries, disappear forever.

Churches

The most obvious example of the inability of owners/users to care for their historic buildings is the parish, whether town or country, where most of the congregation has moved away from the medieval church. These churches were usually built by the Lord of the Manor on his own land, regardless of how close it was to similar buildings.

In 1969 Parliament, in conjunction with the Church of England, set up a charity to preserve churches no longer needed for regular worship. In their last report of the millennium they pinpointed twenty of the exceptionally important churches in their care. One of these was the church of St Mary the Virgin, Edlesborough. Liz Forgan, chairwoman of what is now known as the Churches Conservation Trust, pointed out that 'More and more people from this country and all over the world are visiting our churches.' This is borne out by looking at the visitors' books in some of our most isolated churches.

Edlesborough is an example of a small village originally having a very scattered population, which may have been why the church became redundant. Pitstone St Mary is also in the care of the Trust and both churches will be described later in this chapter.

The Church as a Suitable Case for Tourism

Overseas visitors rate 'visiting churches' high on the list of attractions they enjoy when visiting this country. Churches which are particularly old, those with fine stained-glass windows, with interesting monuments or connected with a famous author or musician will help to sell themselves. However, most churches if advertised as part of a 'package' with other local attractions will soon prove to be of interest to visitors. They are nearly always the oldest buildings and will have watched over the community for many hundreds of years. Efforts to attract tourists can occasionally give offence to a few members of the congregation but those people who have become involved in the churches' 'ministry' of tourism have found that there are spiritual benefits in addition to financial ones.

Other Buildings Requiring Preservation

This is such a wide area of concern that instead of trying to list examples here, the route has been designed to cover as many different types as possible. In addition, the Mid-Bedfordshire Scenic Route points out numerous ways that enterprising people are preserving our historic houses.

DUNSTABLE

The Priory Church of St Peter

The 'Priory' church is not just a very active parish church and a focus of the town's Christian heritage but it is also a constant reminder of its exciting history. It links the present town, troubled by too many cars and heavy lorries, with the times when kings, queens, bishops and judges made constant visits, blocking the crossroads with their horses, coaches, baggage waggons, hunting dogs and servants. It reminds us that in those days the roads were not only thronged with travellers passing through but also with people walking and riding from all over the country to worship at the shrine of St Fremund or to consult the king's judges when the Crown Court was held at the Priory.

Affection for and interest in this important, historic building led, in 1995, to the founding of :-

The Friends of Dunstable Priory Church

Church-goers in the comparatively small town of Dunstable have the choice of attending services in at least fifteen different buildings. The congregation of the Priory Church of St Peter, one of three Anglican churches in the town, is responsible for the maintenance and constant repair of the Grade I* listed building. The 'Friends' is an active organisation, made up of people from several different denominations and some with no particular religious beliefs who are united in fund-raising to help preserve this important historic building.

The Marshe Family Charities

One of the greatest problems of preservation is the situation where the building at risk is owned by a charity which is itself in constant need of funds.

Around the walls of the Priory Church are several monuments commemorating the lives of this illustrious family. William Marshe died in 1651; he had a large family and although several of them became, or married, London businessmen, they retained their local interest in Dunstable. Evidence of their charities can be seen at all four corners of the town. Several of these buildings are now over 250 years old and important historic buildings in their own right.

The Ladies' Lodge

From the churchyard you can see a long white building set back from the road on the other side of Church Street. This is the 'Ladies' Lodge', which was started by Blandina Marshe in 1741, as an almshouse, originally for six poor maiden gentlewomen.

The Jane Cart Almshouses

In High Street South are Jane Cart's almshouses. Mrs Cart was another Marshe granddaughter. She died, aged 83, having out-lived nine of her ten children. She gave the Priory many gifts, including the pulpit cloth on show on the north wall of the Priory Church. The almshouses were for widowed or unmarried ladies who did not have the means to run their own homes. In her will she provided income to pay two shillings and sixpence (12.5p) each, for them to have a dinner each year, ten shillings (50p) each, for clothing and six shillings and eight pence (once known as 'half a mark' and now 33p) for fuel. In 1830 this meal was held at the Sugar Loaf. Their dinner and beer cost fourteen shillings (70p) and the meal included roast beef, boiled mutton and caper sauce, pies, puddings and pastries. It ended with bread, cheese and celery.

The Ashton Almshouses

In 1715 Jane Cart's sister, Frances Ashton, also provided a building to house six alms women; originally in West Street, it was found to be in a very poor state of repair and in 1969 was replaced by six new flats in Bull Pond Lane.

The Ashton St Peter VA Lower School was opened in 1865 with income

from land bequeathed by the same Frances Ashton.[1] It will shortly be moving to a completely new site on the Middle School playing field, West Parade.

The Ashton Grammar now Middle School

When the Midland Railway bought some of the land originally purchased by Frances Ashton for her almshouses, more capital became available. In 1888 income from this money was used to start the Ashton Grammar School in High Street North; it continued as a boys' grammar school until 1971 when Bedfordshire changed to the Comprehensive system. It then became the Ashton Voluntary Aided Middle School while the Manshead Voluntary Controlled Upper School, which replaced the Ashton Grammar School, moved to a new site on the London Road, leading out of Dunstable towards St Albans.

1 Evans, V. Proud Heritage

The Ladies Lodge Dunstable

Chew House Dunstable

The Chew Schools - now Chew House and the Little Theatre

If you walk across the Priory Gardens (beside the church) into High Street South and turn left, you will come to the most famous of the charitable buildings, Chew House. William Chew, a grandson of William Marshe, was at different times Sheriff of London and Middlesex and High Sheriff of Bedfordshire. When he died in 1712 he left instructions in his will that money should be set aside for the endowment of a charity school in the town where he was born. It was opened in 1715 for forty poor boys who were provided with uniforms which are portrayed by the two boys mounted over the door.* The boys had to be over seven years old, born in wedlock, able to read from the New Testament and regular attenders at the Church of England. They had to leave when they were fourteen but there was money available to help with apprenticeships.

When the Education Act was passed in 1870, the governors agreed to erect another building and start a grammar school. However, the new building, now the Little Theatre, was no longer needed when, in 1888, the other grammar school was opened and in 1905 the Chew School was closed and the money used for educational grants.

Chew House now houses the Parish Offices of the Priory Church and rooms are let out to groups and societies in the town.

The National School

The little building in Church Street now used as the Priory Church Hall, is not one of the Marshe charities but was built in 1839 as a 'National' Church of England School.

Other Town Centre Buildings

Because Dunstable did not really begin to grow until after the 1841 census, all the really old buildings will be found along the four main roads. In addition to the increasing problem of high rents and commercial rates, some old timber-framed buildings are not suitable to bring up to modern health and hygiene requirements for food processing and storage. They may, however, be an added attraction to bookshop or gift-shop browsers. Buildings which have been renovated or enlarged in the 19th century may, from the front, appear to be quite modern but from the back, or sometimes inside, their medieval character can still be seen. The same applies to some of the many hotels and public houses, although sometimes their 16th or 17th century origins have been completely lost.

* *These valuable statues were stolen in 1998 but were replaced in the year 2000. They were re-created, after extensive research, by Ian Rank-Broadley.*

Unfortunately, at the present time, the owners of some public houses think their younger customers will be put off by the traditional old names and despite protests from the local community, the medieval names are lost.

A selection of Dunstable's old commercial buildings must include Middle Row. This run of shops, facing the east side of High Street South and apparently forming the west side, were originally built in the 14th century by tenants of the Priory. They gradually replaced some of the market stalls which were erected in the middle of the road. Although the individual shops have been greatly altered, there are 14th century timbers in at least one of the roofs. and several of them still have their timber frames hidden under a more modern exterior. The booklet 'Middle Row', published in 1986 by Dunstable Museum Trust, grew out of an adult educational project run by the Dunstable branch of the Workers' Educational Association. Each building was researched back to at least 1800.[1]

Clues to Dunstable's proud history of hospitality are sometimes difficult to uncover. Some of Dunstable's oldest inns can only be recognised by surviving details or even by searching through the records.

The Saracen's Head is possibly the oldest public house in Bedfordshire, which is still open for business. It was provided as an inn by the Priory at a time when many of their visitors were crusaders or pilgrims setting out on their hazardous journeys to Jerusalem. The road (A5) which passes the door has been repaired so many times that like its near neighbour, Priory House (built in the 13th century), one now has to enter the front door by going down two steps.

Several of Dunstable's public houses, including the Bull and the Nag's Head, had opened for business by the early 17th century, but their buildings were greatly altered or even rebuilt at a later date. The Sugar Loaf did not open until after the Civil War. When Jane Cart bought it, c1715, to provide a rental income for her charity, she had it partly rebuilt. From then on it became one of the top inns on the London to Holyhead road. After the opening of the London to Birmingham railway in 1838, it experienced financial difficulties. For a few months it closed altogether but re-opened when its owners realised that there was still a good local trade in addition to the many high-class travellers who preferred horses to trains. Too small to be used as a modern hotel and too old to have a modern image, it has become a town-centre public house and restaurant. The stone archway in High Street North (west side) was once part of the White Horse Inn where Henry VIII stayed in 1537 and on all subsequent journeys

1 Also see Evans, V. Proud Heritage, which includes details of the other old shops in the town

through Dunstable. The Halifax Building Society paid to restore both the archway and the adjoining building that became their offices. During restoration they uncovered a fireplace decorated with Tudor roses and bearing the date 1646. It is now on show to the left of the front door.*

The Wall Painting inside number 20 High Street North was restored by the Nationwide Building Society. This was once Charlie Cole's cycle shop and it was known that upstairs there was an important wall painting. Painted around 1600, it portrays a forest and a hunting scene. Nationwide paid for the cleaning and restoration of the painting and had the main panels re-mounted on the ground floor, where everyone could see them. Some smaller panels are on display in the library. This building may have housed the 17th century Three Black Swans or some other undiscovered inn.

The Grey House (Number 59 High Street South) is an interesting old building and a good example of one owner after another finding a way of using it so that it can help to support itself. Its original use is unknown; it backed onto the small paddock owned by the Priory and the tenant may well have rented enough land to support it as a small farm. In the early 18th century it had its own malt kiln and with the expansion of the travel industry, it was opened as the Star Inn. When this industry failed it was adapted as a bonnet-sewing room. In living memory it has been a small hotel, offices, a fish restaurant, a private club and a wine bar. It is currently being used as a restaurant. The elongated windows at the back are one of the few remaining examples of windows designed to increase the light for bonnet-sewers.**

Grove House stands at the other end of the town, in High Street North. It was built as a high-class inn during the 18th century, when it was known as the Duke of Bedford's Arms. For many years it was a private house, but in 1989 it was completely restored by Dunstable Council and is now their headquarters. The impressive gardens at the rear are open for public use.

The Maypole, 16 - 18 West Street is a most important medieval building, which was in use at the time of the Priory. Typical of many listed commercial buildings, at one time the renovation appeared to be too costly for its commercial value. Thankfully it has now received a complete overhaul but still retains its medieval timber frame. In the 18th century, when the Chew Trustees

---

* *Sad as it is that so few retail stores can afford town-centre premises, we must be grateful to the financial services companies who are prepared to restore our important buildings*
** *A recent owner has changed the colour of the 'Grey' House*

occasionally used it for their annual dinner, it was a small inn known as The Maypole. At that time it had already been a small inn or beer-house for several centuries; it had previously been known as The Green Man and, back in 1635, The Leaden Porch. It had its own big yard at the back, which retained the name 'Maypole' long after the inn had been divided into two shops and a workroom. The building now houses two successful and attractive shops.

The Vine - once 'Ellis the Barber' - West Street, stood a few doors from Ashton Street. This 19th century beer house was identified via the 1851 census. At that time the publican was selling beer in an old medieval building of much the same age as the Maypole. Unfortunately this building was not saved. For hundreds of years it had stood looking out over the sheep-market, but in the 1960s developers insisted on its removal. Demolition workers were anxious to buy the old timbers but luckily staff from the Chiltern Open Air Museum offered to take the whole building to Chalfont St Peter. Every piece of timber was carefully labelled and is now awaiting reconstruction, to become an important part of their exhibition. When the site had been cleared, members of the Manshead Archaeological Society found that the chimney had been inserted into the previous simple house by making foundations of carved stone previously used at the Priory or the Dominican Friary.

A cautionary footnote to the above story is that the neighbouring house in West Street seemed so obviously an 18th/19th century house with a Victorian shop-front, that nothing was done to halt demolition. It was not until the bulldozers had partially destroyed the building that the medieval jettied frame was exposed.

The Old Palace Lodge and the Norman King in Church Street are not medieval but stand on an historic site. The palace where Henry I stayed in 1109 and which was used many times by medieval kings, was given by King John to the Augustinian Priory. In the deed of gift it is described as 'houses' and it appears likely that the Priory let it out to raise income. There is evidence that Sir William Cavendish, biographer of Cardinal Wolsey, owned what remained of it during the mid 16th century, but by the early 17th century it was the home of the Marshe family. By the 20th century it had long been a gentleman's house and farm. The Bagshawe family were living there around 1930 but in 1959 it was necessary to divide it into two. The eastern end was purchased by Creasey Hotels and converted into the Old Palace Lodge Hotel. At one time the farm buildings were let as a riding stable, but in 1961 Totternhoe stone of a suitable age was brought to Dunstable and the main barn was converted into the Norman King.

Although the Priory House in High Street South was never used as licensed premises, it was originally built, in the 13th century, as a hostel. All the other Priory hostels have long since gone, but this one remains with its original pillars. After the dissolution of the Priory it became a private house. In the late 17th/18th centuries it was owned by a member of the Crawley family of Someries (Luton) who used it as a cottage hospital, often for treating mental patients. In recent years it was bought and renovated as prestigious offices. The slender Norman pillars and vaulted ceiling are exposed and a Tudor fireplace, found in the back of the house, was moved into the front reception hall. This important building will shortly be opening as a restaurant. The beautiful Priory Gardens behind the house cover part of the area that was once the courtyard, farmyard and stables of the Priory and the adjoining Priory Meadow covers the rubble and foundations of the Priory buildings.

During the 1980s a group of 'Friends' saved the Il Millefiori Restaurant (Number 26 Church Street); it came on the market in such a dangerously unstable state that it was shored up to await demolition. Being such an important building, with jetties standing out over one of the little alleys leading through to the Priory, the Friends of Dunstable Museum fought to save it. They kept up continual pressure until it was eventually saved at a second public enquiry.* Like many of Dunstable's old buildings, it has been used for many different purposes. It may have started life as a house or workshop for one of the Priory's lay members of staff and may at one time have been a beer house. In the 19th century it was a small hat factory and during the 20th century became an antique shop. Since private restoration, it has been used first as a retail shop and now as a popular restaurant.

Opposite the Priory gates in South Street there once stood a Dominican Friary. The church and gatehouse faced into the road and the domestic buildings and gardens were at the rear.
None of the buildings survived but the Manshead Archaeological Society uncovered many of the domestic foundations and helped to uncover the foundations of the church, so that, although no actual buildings survive, plans and drawings plus a great deal of other information can be found in the Manshead magazines.**

Vaughan Basham (who died during the preparation of this book), was among those who organised the successful resistance to its demolition
**5 Winfield Street. A 19th century beer house, The Sportsman's Arms, later a private house, has been completely restored by the Manshead Archaeological Society and is now their headquarters*

DUNSTABLE DOWNS

The Five Knolls

The modern Icknield Way includes the A505 from Hitchin to Dunstable and the B489 from Dunstable to Aston Clinton. The original was not a road but a wide track along the hills with a ford near Marsh Farm. It ran from the north Norfolk coast across to Stonehenge.

Until about 6000 years ago, the people who lived in England had no knowledge of farming methods and for over 2000 years the Neolithic farmers did not have the skills of making metal; later farmers tend to be named by their knowledge and use of first bronze and then iron.Their sites are sometimes recognised by their differing pottery-making styles. Another way of separating different cultures of pre-historic people is by their customs concerning burial. Just as, at Toddington church, we can study the different styles of memorials used before and after the Reformation, on the high point of Dunstable Downs, one could once see different styles of 'barrows' or grave mounds.

ROUTE

Leave Dunstable on the B489 following the brown 'Elephant' signs up over the Downs, where there is a car park, picnic area, visitor centre and 130 acres of public access in the Chilterns Area of Outstanding Natural Beauty.

In pre-historic times any great mound of clean white chalk would have been visible for many miles along the Icknield Way. At different periods men and women were buried under bowl barrows, round barrows and long barrows. Worthington Smith, writing c1900, recorded seeing evidence of several other grave mounds, but now only the 'Five Knolls' remain. In their isolation they are very difficult to protect. During the late 1920s Sir Mortimer Wheeler excavated two of these mounds. A female skeleton which he uncovered can be seen in Luton Museum and a summary of his report can be found in the book 'Ancient Dunstable'.*

The Priory Rabbit Warren

During 1994 there was a flurry of publicity when English Heritage listed the site of the Priory's medieval rabbit warren, which had been identified on the further side of the hill.

Rabbits were once an important part of the available winter protein and the right to breed and catch rabbits involved buying a licence from the king.

* Written by CL Matthews, enlarged by JP Schneider and published by the Manshead Archaeological Society. 1989

75

Anyone found catching rabbits from the manorial warrens without permission was harshly punished. Rabbits have always run free but the warrener had to be prepared to provide the manor house kitchen with large numbers at fairly short notice. This was one of the reasons that they were semi-confined by a series of banks and ditches and provided with a network of artificial burrows.

Downland Management and Preservation

The building in the further car park includes the office of the Bedfordshire County Council ranger who has a special responsibility for the chalk downland. Every effort is made to prevent the growth of scrub and at times sheep are allowed to graze in controlled areas. Leaflets on sale at the kiosk describe the rare plants, birds and butterflies living on the chalk hills.

WHIPSNADE

Preserving Our Customs

So many of our ancient customs have been lost that those which survive are of particular importance.

Common Rights

When we complain that farmers who uproot hedges are destroying our heritage, it is a heritage based on the recent past. Until the various Enclosure Acts, the majority of farmhouses were situated along the village High Street. The farmers and farm workers walked out to work each day on the strips, which they or their employer held in the wheat or barley fields. Following enclosure, the strips were abandoned and the land 'allotted' in 'parcels'. The acreage of the allotments was decided in proportion to the number of strips, which the owner had previously held. After allotment the new owners or tenants planted hedges and sometimes built farmhouses on their land.

Before he began to allot the farming land, the surveyor had to lay out a network of roads. In each case

ROUTE

The route continues to Whipsnade crossroads and turns right through the roadside gates (don't forget these are occasionally closed) and across the common, passing the sign to the Tree Cathedral and then the gates of Whipsnade Wild Animal Park. Once past the gates watch out on the left for the penguins preening beside their pool and then for the bison and maybe wallabies and Chinese water deer in the big field. On the hill you have a close-up view of the chalk escarpment and a distant view of Edlesborough church and Ivinghoe Beacon.

there was one main road, which ran from the village centre to the nearest turn-pike road. These were usually long and straight, with wide grass verges to allow heavy wagons and coaches to share the road with drovers and farm carts. The other clue to an enclosure road is that the farmers of the newly laid out fields had a duty to protect the roads with a quick-growing hedge; this was often blackthorn or hawthorn. The Whipsnade road went straight through Kensworth and met the Holyhead Road (A5) at the Packhorse. Another of the surveyor's duties was to provide common grazing land for the occupants of those houses which had traditionally had grazing rights. This was arranged in different ways in different villages but quite often a piece of so-called 'common' land was set aside for what, in Whipsnade, were called stint-holders. These (or similar grazing rights) go back hundreds of years.

In many villages not only the list of stint-holders but the common itself has been lost. At Whipsnade the incumbent at the rectory, the village publican, now both private householders, Dell Farm, one or two other farms and six or eight cottages still have rights to graze two or three sheep 'at all times' and two or three 'cows common rights' from May 12th until November 12th. It is for this reason that there are gates at each end of the common and signs 'Gates may be closed'.

The Tree Cathedral

In 1926 Mr E K Blythe was so inspired when he saw the newly-built Liverpool Cathedral that he dreamed of creating a similar awesome building, using trees. Three of his friends had died during the First World War and he thought this would make a wonderful memorial to them. With the help of other friends, he managed to buy a piece of land at Whipsnade. It is an amazing design with an overall length the same as St Albans Abbey. The architectural features are all formed by different trees and shrubs; the font is represented by a dew pond. Since 1967 the cathedral has been cared for by the National Trust. Follow the marked path and you will find an amazingly peaceful and fascinating site where you can explore, study natural history or sit quietly and read or meditate. At least one service is held in the 'cathedral' each year.

The Zoo - 'A Pioneer of its Kind'

In 1927, Peter Chalmers Mitchell CBE, Secretary of the Zoological Society, fulfilled a dream and found a site where animals from the London Zoo could go for rest and convalescence. He also wanted to try to keep animals from other climatic regions in large paddocks in the English countryside. When he found

Hall Farm , Whipsnade, an outlier of the Woburn estate, he knew that it was just what he was looking for. He intended to open it to members of the Zoological Society but not to the public. Work started in 1928 and as there had been a great deal of local interest, members of the public were invited to come and look round. The response was overwhelming and gradually the zoo was open on a regular basis.

Whipsnade Wild Animal Park

Whipsnade has always set an example in the welfare of wild animals that are kept for showing to the public. As the years went by it took on a new role, helping to conserve rare breeds of birds and animals, which were at risk in their natural habitats. By the time of its Diamond Jubilee in 1991, over thirty million people had visited the zoo. However, because of the freedom enjoyed by the animals, there was little resemblance to a traditional zoo and it was decided to give it a modified name.

'Whipsnade - My Africa'

In 1990 Lucy Pendar (whose father, from the very beginning, was resident engineer) wrote a detailed history of the park and her own childhood when Whipsnade was her - Africa, Asia, Canada and Australia.* In his introduction to the book, the late Gerald Durrell (who, in his teens had been employed as a relief keeper) described Whipsnade as 'a pioneer of its kind in a zoo world full of bars and concrete, Whipsnade showed the way animals should be kept.'

Conservation at Whipsnade

Whipsnade continues to play a major role in the conservation of endangered species. The largest herd of rare white rhino in England run freely and Przewalski's horses, once extinct in the wild, roam on the chalk hills.

The White Lion

As soon as the lion's den was completed on the top of the chalk escarpment, the workmen were diverted to cut out more chalk further along and to 'sculpt' a white lion. This was based on the White Horses at Westbury, in Wiltshire.

Lucy Pendar's father drew up the plan for the proposed lion which was to be four hundred and eighty feet long with a tail thirteen feet wide and a total perimeter of three-eighths of a mile. It was not made by scraping away turf to

* Published by The Book Castle.1991.

The Endangered Species of White Rhino living safely at Whipsnade (W.W.A.P.)

The White Lion of Whipsnade (S.B.D.C.)

79

expose the chalk but by building up chalk to a height of six feet. Allowing for periods of bad weather, it took nearly eighteen months to complete and was finished for Easter 1933. Unfortunately it is not very easy to keep such a large area of chalk free from weeds and algae. Over the years groups of scouts and cubs, 18-plus and Young Farmers clubs and even students from the Royal Navy have all helped to keep it clean.

PITSTONE

ROUTE

The route continues down the hill where it meets the B489 and turns left towards Ivinghoe and Tring. At the T-junction on the outskirts of Ivinghoe, the route turns left for Aldbury; the Pitstone windmill is on the right. Just past the windmill the route leaves the main road and goes straight on, along a narrow winding road into Aldbury village. Watch out for a car park on the right-hand side that is an entrance to the long-distance Ridgeway and to various short local walks. The route passes right through Aldbury village but car parking is very limited.

The Windmill

This very rare post-mill is owned by the National Trust and bears the carved date 1627 although it was in use before this date. It is one of the oldest mills in England. Today it appears isolated from the village but in the days of the open fields, it had its own road to the village and another to Ivinghoe Watermill. In 1902 a freak storm struck the mill from behind, blowing the sails forward. They revolved the wrong way and crashed into the wall of the roundhouse causing damage so severe that it was not repaired and the mill never worked commercially again.

In 1937 the owner offered the mill to the National Trust who removed the broken pieces and strengthened the main body to keep it safe. They continued to do urgent repairs, but in no way restored it, so in 1963 the Pitstone Windmill Restoration Committee was formed. The National Trust gave timber and permission for an appeal to be launched for funds, so that voluntary labour could eventually return the mill to working order. To visit this mill is a truly remarkable experience because it represents the earliest form of windmill construction. The attractive leaflet describing the mill and its opening times is available at Tourist Information Centres.

For details of Pitstone Green Farm Museum and Church see page 97.

ALDBURY

As you are approaching Aldbury you pass Stocks House built in 1773. This is a medieval name and has nothing to do with the stocks on the green. On the left-hand-side of the road is the old dove house with the date 1753 worked in the bricks.

Aldbury is a village with a great deal of visible history. To get the most from the visit it is really worthwhile buying the 'Visitors' Guide'. On the green, by the duck pond, are the well-known, restored stocks and whipping post, while nearby stands an old house, built in the early 16th century. Many of the cottages were once farmhouses, which is typical of a pre-enclosed village when each man's land was scattered into strips, in two or more common fields and the farm houses were central. But why is there no manor house? As so often happens we have to look back through history for the answer to such village puzzles and are grateful to those who patiently uncover the answers. In this case it was historian Mrs Jean Davis.

In 1660, in his old age, Sir Thomas Hide married; his family had been Lords of the Manor of Aldbury since the middle of the 16th century. He had recently acquired the manor of North Mymms and it was there that the family lived and soon a daughter was born and christened Bridget. Shortly afterwards Sir Thomas died and his wife remarried; her new husband was the goldsmith Sir Robert Vyner, friend and banker to King Charles II.

Relatives of Bridget's mother were anxious to obtain control of her inheritance, so while she was only twelve years old a secret marriage was arranged between Bridget and her cousin John Emerton. The legal proceedings which ensued, as various interested parties tried to get the marriage annulled, lasted for nearly eight years. During this time Bridget left her husband and ran away with the heir to the future Duke of Leeds. She eventually became the Duchess of Leeds but her fortune and happiness were destroyed by her husband's extravagance.

Aldbury manor house, which Sir Thomas Hide abandoned after his marriage, had been allowed to fall into disrepair and was eventually pulled down on the instruction of the Duke of Leeds. The bricks and tiles were sold as building materials. That was in 1691, since when there has been no true manor house in Aldbury.

The full story of this melodramatic affair, which involved abduction, seduction and ambition is told in fascinating detail in Jean Davis' 'The Pretended Marriage' available in the village shop at Aldbury.

The Church of St John the Baptist

Although Aldbury has no manor house of its own, in the church is a fine chapel wherein lie the lords of the manor of nearby Pendley. There are effigies of Sir Robert Whittingham and his wife; Sir Robert wears a collar of esses, the emblem of Henry VI. The tomb is enclosed by a perpendicular stone screen and, together with the medieval floor tiles, was moved here after the Reformation, before Ashridge Monastery was acquired by Henry VIII. Also in the church is an attractive brass, dedicated to Sir Ralph Verney and his wife, dated 1547. Sir Ralph was also from nearby Pendley.

PENDLEY

Whereas Aldbury is a very successful village, but lacks a manor house, Pendley has a very interesting manor house, but lacks a village! There were seven cottages in 1086, when William I's sheriff gave the manor of Pendley to William's brother-in-law, the Count of Mortain. The village prospered and the population grew. Then in 1440 Henry VI granted Sir Robert and Lady Whittingham a licence to turn the arable land into a park, so depriving the villagers of their land. The Whittingham family lost Pendley for a few years during the Civil War because they stayed loyal to Henry VI but they retrieved it when their daughter married John Verney. Both families have memorials in Aldbury church.

ROUTE

The route leaves Aldbury passing the church on an unclassified road, to the right of the pond, heading towards Tring. After some distance it passes Tring station and the Royal Hotel. The entrance to Pendley Manor is a little further on, on the left-hand side.

In 1835 the old manor house was burnt to the ground and the estate became part of the Crown Estate at Tring. At the beginning of the 19th century a Dutch family rented Tring Park. They changed their name to Williams. Later they bought the Pendley estate and in 1870 the Rev James Williams started to build a new house. He wanted 'instant history' and asked the architect to design a house which would look like 'a Tudor manor that has been added to'. The Williams family came to live at Pendley in 1875.

During the Second World War part of it was used as a hostel for land girls. After the war the owner, Col VDS Williams, allowed his son, the late Dorian Williams, once famous for his connection with equestrian events, and in particular the Royal International Horse Show, to use it as a residential centre

82

Pendley Manor Hotel

Street Scene Wendover

for adult education. It opened in 1945 and after 40 years, 175,000 had attended 3,500 courses. Mr Williams was also founder of the Pendley Shakespeare Festival which continues to this day.

The manor house and grounds are now in the caring hands of Pendley Manor Hotel. By building on matching wings, of modern bedrooms and conference suites, they have managed to keep the original manor house and grounds in the style of a gentleman's house.

TRING

Until comparatively recently Tring was a small market town. It is believed that the market started around 1281 and stalls are still erected each Friday on one side of the large carpark.

ROUTE

Soon after this, the route joins the A4251 and is clearly sign-posted into Tring and from there to the optional Wendover and Aylesbury spurs. If, however, you are not intending to visit Tring, turn right onto the B488 towards Ivinghoe.

The market was particularly busy during the height of the straw-hat industry. People came from miles around to buy the prepared straw and to sell their finished plait to the local dealers or to representatives from the hat factories in Dunstable or Luton. The two-storey outbuilding, adjacent to New England antique shop, was once used as a bonnet sewing room. An interesting reference to Tring market is used to demonstrate the importance of the early straw-hat trade. To protect the general market, an order was issued before 1685 limiting plait sales to the morning. In 1899 the old market house, which once stood in front of the church, was pulled down and replaced by the present hall on the corner of Akerman Street and High Street.

The Rothschilds Came to Tring

Although there are legends connecting this house with Nell Gwynne, very little is known of its early history. After the Restoration, King Charles sold it to Henry Guy, Groom of the Bedchamber, who enclosed the 250 acres. Guy is thought to have consulted Sir Christopher Wren concerning a suitable design for his new country mansion.

King William III visited the house in both 1690 and in 1705 but decided to sell it to Sir William Gore, Lord Mayor of London. From then on it belonged to various wealthy merchants. In 1836 the banker, NM Rothschild, rented it as a summer residence for his family and in 1872 his son Lionel bought the house on behalf of his son, Nathaniel, who in 1880 became the first Lord Rothschild.

He and his wife Emma spent time at Tring and she was living there when she died in 1935, aged 91. He had died in 1915.

The Rothschild family greatly enlarged the house but Wren's design is still included within the outer structure. For some years the house was used by NM Rothschild's bank and although the family still own the house and park, it is currently used by the Arts Educational Schools.

Tring and the Rothschilds
The reason that Tring has a Victorian rather than a medieval appearance is due to the first Lord Rothschild who ordered the insanitary cottages and other buildings to be pulled down and replaced with the most modern cottages of his day. At the same time that he had the market-house moved, he also instructed the Red Lion to be rebuilt in an Elizabethan style.

The Natural History Museum
In 1898 Baron Rothschild gave his son, Lionel Walter Rothschild, a piece of land in Tring where he could build two cottages. One was to hold his collection of insects and books and the other for a caretaker. Lionel, later the second Baron Rothschild, then had a large building constructed to display his mounted specimens, which, in 1892, he allowed to be opened to the public. As the collection grew, the building was enlarged and in 1938 Lord Rothschild bequeathed it to the British Museum. At that time the collection contained 2000 complete mounted mammals and more than 2000 birds, in addition to 1000 reptiles and amphibians and 1000 fish.

The Church of St Peter and St Paul
The area of the church shows a striking example of old and new buildings carefully planned to complement each other. The church itself was much restored in 1880-82 but much of the 15th century flint and stone building still remains. Except for the nave, Ancaster stone has been used to replace the most seriously damaged Totternhoe stone. During the restoration of 1880 Portland stone was used in the nave. It is a beautiful church and there is much to see; there are elaborate memorials, stained glass of several different periods including modern windows by CE Kempe and others from his workshop (look for his mark of a wheat sheaf). There are also two 18th century panel paintings of Moses and Aaron. The pews were renewed in 1862 because the old box pews were damaged by the market-goers using them as a picnic place! Two

particularly interesting features are the stone corbels and the medieval tiles. At the springing of the nave arches are fourteen fabulous beasts. There is a dog or wolf fighting with a dragon, a collared bear, chained and muzzled and a fox carrying a goose. The tiles have now been moved to a safe place (some can be seen in the British Museum) but photographs of most of them are displayed in the church, including well-drawn groups of men and animals which tell stories about Jesus and probably date from the early 14th century.

The parish registers record that ancestors of George Washington were once connected with this parish. These registers are now in the County Record Office at Hertford.

Award-Winning New Buildings

To get to the parish offices you go through a brick and stone gateway beside the original vicarage, mostly built in 1828, to find some completely new buildings. These are the present vicarage, parish hall and the head office of the Sutton Housing Trust which combined as Sutton Court, received an RIBA architectural award in 1975.

It is, however, the Rothschild family who left their influence over the town and thanks to them we are lucky enough to have a branch of the British Museum (Natural History) in this area.

WENDOVER

Wendover is near Tring but is a spur from the route. It is well worth a visit to see its many well-preserved old buildings. 'Wendover' wrote Arthur Mee in the mid-1930s 'is clad in the beauty of the Chilterns.' This statement is still true and it is an excellent place from which to walk or drive out to explore the Chiltern Hills. There are also interesting walks around the village itself and it has much to offer the artist and photographer.

The Saxon village grew up on the crossing of the Upper Icknield Way (see Ivinghoe Beacon) and the route which became the main road from London to the shire town of Buckingham. By the time of the Norman Conquest its agricultural value had been recognised and it had become part of the scattered royal estate. There is still a pretty stream near the centre of the village today but in Norman times there was enough water to support the two water mills necessary to grind the grain from the very large area of arable land. There were meadows for making hay and enough woodland to support 2,000 pigs. Although no market was recorded until 1214, it is very likely that unlicensed trading took place long before that date. Agriculture remained a very important local industry but during the terrible rural unemployment of the early 19th century, the ladies could supplement the family income by making lace when the market was 'strong' and plaiting straw for Tring and other markets.

By the 16th century, a second form of employment had grown up to support the developing travel industry. The manor house was, and the church still is, 1/3rd of a mile south of the village centre and it is probable that the roadside village developed in response to the passing horse-drawn traffic. Nine inns and taverns were recorded in 1555; two hundred years later, the number had risen to twenty-seven. There are still several pubs in the village and many old attractive buildings. Some of these are on the outskirts and others in the town centre. Bosworth House, in the High Street, was a large 16th century house that has now been divided. Some of its important wall-paintings can be seen in Aylesbury Museum but the remains of a 16th century painting still survives, as do the Tudor chimneys. A stone piscina * was found in the building and is now included in the side entrance archway. Many very old inns were connected with the church and as seen in the chapter concerning St Albans, some of those were allowed to have their own chapels.

Still proudly standing in the middle of the High Street is the Red Lion Hotel. Although it was partly rebuilt around 1900, it has much of its early timbered frame, beams and inglenooks. It was a stopping-place for some of the London to Birmingham coaches that travelled via Buckingham. After the road was turnpiked in 1721, the road surface was greatly improved and speeds increased. The stagecoach from Holborn aimed to arrive in five hours and a local coach ran to and fro to London from the Red Lion.

AYLESBURY

When Alison Uttley published her book on Buckinghamshire in 1950, she expressed her delight in the country stalls that were erected in the Market Place on Wednesdays and Saturdays. Her particular favourites were the flower stalls 'heaped with every flower in season. Larkspur and Iceland poppies in summer, primroses and polyanthus in spring, chrysanthemums in autumn and holly at Christmas.' She explained that the ladies picked them from their own gardens and that they also made 'Victorian bouquets of charming variety, close-packed with colour [they contained] - bachelors' buttons, pansies, carnations and pinks, in a tight circle of colours.....' In 1950 these only cost a shilling. She goes on to

A small recess with basin and drain for washing holy vessels

discuss the fascinating variety of little shops that had held their own against the big stores, which were already beginning to arrive in the town. Little did she know that ten years later, plans would be discussed for a major redevelopment of the town centre.

Many of the little shops that she saw disappeared in this development, but the area of the Market Square is now far more pedestrian-friendly. The outdoor market is still held in the Square and, although most of the flower-sellers buy in their bouquets, they are still a colourful attraction. In addition, the monthly Farmers' Market offers all types of locally produced flowers, fruit, vegetables, meat and a whole range of other products.

Despite all the alterations, the area around Church Street, which leads to St Mary's Church, has many interesting and historic buildings, one of the most important being The King's Head. The first written reference to this inn is 1455, but it is thought that the original building dates back even earlier. The imposing iron gateway and sign stands on Market Square, but its yards, stables and outbuildings lead out into Temple Street and George Street. Together, the whole site gives a rare illustration of the ground plan of a coaching inn. In 1928, the widow and family of the Hon. Charles Rothschild presented it to the National Trust. It is still in their care today, but it is also a very busy town centre hotel. For the important stained glass, see the next page.

The Buckinghamshire County Museum

Preservation concerns more than just old buildings but in this case, the museum plays a double role. Standing amongst the other historic buildings, in Church Street is Ceely House, named after one of the founders of the Bucks. Archeological Society. This is part of the County Museum. Its handsome 18th century porch opens onto the street, but by entering from the yard, one walks back through history. The first room, before you come to Ceely House, is pleasantly modern and leads into the handsome 18th century rooms and the elegant staircase of c1720. Upstairs, carefully exposed for all to see, is not only a timber-framed medieval room and roof, but also a perfectly preserved wall-painting of the late 15th century.

Apart from the preservation of this historic building, the main work of the museum is to store and, where possible, display items concerning Buckinghamshire's archaeology, history, social and natural history. Because the county is large and the habitat diverse, they have a nationally important collection of geological finds, some rare aspects of the earliest periods of

The Buckinghamshire County Crest (Bucks CC)

The Dunstable Swan Jewel (O.R.)

89

archaeological finds and also some aspects of natural history. For those interested in Buckinghamshire, there is an exceedingly wide collection of articles connecting all these subjects. There are also collections concerning agriculture, lace and other rural industries. So diverse are the displays that, even though there are frequent, temporary exhibitions, many of the items are in store. These are catalogued on the internet and enquiries are welcome, so that individual items can be, by pre-arrangement, put out on display.

The County Town

Buckinghamshire is approximately 50 miles long and 10 miles wide and, as early as the reign of King Henry VIII, the position of County Town (administrative centre) was moved south to the more central Aylesbury.

The county badge is a red and black shield that bears the effigy of a swan, with a duke's coronet round its neck, to which is attached a heavy gold chain. When, in 1948, the County Council was granted a coat of arms, this 'Ducally crowned and gorged or' swan became the central symbol. To the right stands a swan (free from the restraint of the gold coronet and chain and, to the left, a buck, which is a punning allusion to the name of the county. Above the ducal swan is a white, Christian cross on a green background, representing White-leaf Cross, which can be seen on the Chiltern escarpment. The crest is a beech tree of the Chiltern Hills; the trunk is surrounded by a Saxon crown, to point out that the Saxons were the first settlers in the greater part of the county. The county's right to use the ducally-crowned swan came from the ancient family of de Bohun and the Gillards, who were Earls of Buckingham, and then from the Stallards, who were the first Dukes of Buckingham.[1]

The Swan Badge

This is incorporated into many of the official coats-of-arms and badges used in Buckinghamshire. It can also be seen in churches, paintings and carvings anywhere in England where the families entitled to the badge held land.

The White Swan pub in central Aylesbury has this as its inn-sign and an exceptionally early stained-glass window in The King's Head contains the de Bohun chained swan and the arms of King Henry VI and his wife, Margaret of Anjou.

---

1 Adapted from 'The Arms of the Buckinghamshire County Council', published by the County Council

The Dunstable Swan Jewel

In 1965, a solid gold swan brooch was uncovered in the centre of Dunstable by the Manshead Archaeological Society when excavating the site of the Dominican Friary. It is now titled the Dunstable Swan Jewel and has pride of place in the medieval jewellery collection at the British Museum.[1]

The romantic history and legend connected with the swan emblem have been the subject of much research. In 1959, Sir AR Wagner wrote a most readable essay 'The Swan Badge and the Swan Knight'.[2] This shows only too clearly how legend and history have, over the centuries, become intermingled.

The Legends of the Swan and Swan Knight

There are two separate legends that originally circulated in Western Europe. The best known is the legend of the 'Swan Children', which tells of a wicked stepmother with seven stepchildren, six of whom she turns into swans. The seventh has a task set that will give her the chance to turn them back into princes, but one remains a swan. The other legend tells of 'The Swan Knight', who appears in a small boat pulled by a swan and arrives in time to rescue a beautiful princess, whom he later marries.

Not only is the history of the Swan emblem confused with legend but the legend is confused with fiction!

The first legend, as told by AR Wagner, concerns a king who, while hunting in the forest, meets a nymph. They marry and have six sons and one daughter, born with gold chains around their necks. The nymph dies and it is the children's grandmother who causes them to be abandoned in the forest, where a hermit cares for them. Seven years later, the grandmother learns that they are still alive and has six of the gold chains cut off and brought to her, whereupon the six boys become swans. The girl, still with her chain intact and in human form, goes to the palace to tell the king, her father of the fate of his sons. As a result, five of the chains are returned and five of the swans become princes. The sixth chain had been melted down and re-used by the grandmother, so the sixth son remained a swan.

The second legend actually includes the names of real people. The knight, in his boat pulled by the swan, travels to the court of Bouillon (Boulogne). He

---

1 Evans, V. *The Dunstable Swan Jewel. This small booklet relates the finding of the jewel by Mrs Maxene Amey (née Miller), sets out the known history and speculates why it should have been hidden or lost in Dunstable.* 2 Wagner, AR. *The Swan Badge and the Swan Knight, Archaeologica (1850-51) See also: Maulder, R. and Mitcheson, J. The Wagner Companion.*

arrives in time to rescue the widowed Duchess of Bouillon and her daughter, Beatrice, from an attacker, whom he kills. He then marries Beatrice but makes her promise never to question him about his birth or background. They have a daughter called Ida and live happily for seven years, but then Beatrice breaks her promise. As a result, he puts Ida into the care of the emperor and returns to his boat to be towed away by the swan. When Ida is fourteen, she marries Eustace, Count of Boulogne.

The legend of the seven children is first recorded in France in 1190. There are other versions from Western Europe about the same time. During the 12th and 13th centuries, the chroniclers (paid by the different ruling houses) and the entertainers at the different courts were linking the two legends and making the Swan Knight an ancestor of several different families! Therefore, several different families claimed their descent from the Swan Knight and, because these families were so intermarried, the chroniclers found it easy to connect many other families with the legendary Swan Prince. The 'historic legend', which seems most likely to have connected English families to the swan, is that of Ida and Eustace II, Count of Boulogne. The first wife of Count Eustace II was the sister of Edward the Confessor. Eustace III came to England with William I, fought at the Battle of Hastings and was rewarded with land in England, including Tring and villages around Bedford. His daughter, Maud, married Stephen of Blois and became Queen of England.

History and the Swan Knight
Apart from Count Eustace of Boulogne, two other families have connections with the Swan Knight and with England; the Bohuns and the Tonys

Mr John Cherry of the British Museum, has traced the various families connected with the legend and much of this section comes from his fascinating article.[1]

If we look closely at the de Bohun family, for the period around 1400, we find that Humphrey de Bohun, the Earl of Hertford, Essex and Northamptonshire, died in 1371. He left two daughters, Eleanor and Mary. Eleanor married Thomas of Woodstock, the youngest son of Edward III; they both used the swan emblem. In 1388, Thomas gave St Albans Abbey a brooch; a swan with wings raised for flying, surrounded by a circlet set with jewels. Eleanor left her son a poem of the History of the Swan Knight and a psalter with clasps of gold enamelled with white swans. There is a very similar swan on her brass in Westminster Abbey.

1 Cherry, J. *The Dunstable Swan Jewel. Jnl. Brit. Arch. Assoc. 1969*

Thomas and Eleanor's daughter married Edmund, Earl of Stafford and their son, Humphrey, who died in 1460, became Duke of Buckingham. However, by that time, the badge had already been associated with Buckinghamshire through Thomas himself, who was created Earl of Buckingham at the coronation of Richard II in 1377.

Mary married Henry of Lancaster, later Henry IV. The right to the badge was then inherited by King Henry V who used it on his pennon at the Battle of Agincourt. It is carved on his tomb in Westminster Abbey.

The County Motto

As part of the design for a county coat-of-arms, it was necessary to select a motto. The one chosen was the family motto of John Hampden, the translation of which is 'no retreat' or 'we never go backward'.

John Hampden

Still recognised as one of England's great patriots, John was son of William Hampden of Great Hampden (Bucks). Despite his father's death when he was only three, John enjoyed the traditional childhood as son of a wealthy and influential family. He attended Thame Grammar School and Magdalene College, Oxford and before long was Member of Parliament for first Wendover and then Buckinghamshire. During his childhood, his family were on friendly terms with the royal family and both Queen Elizabeth and James I visited his home. In later years, he would make it quite clear that he was not fighting against his king but for his 'king and kingdom's right'.

Things Begin to go Wrong

King James I and even more so, King Charles I, ruled in an autocratic manner, giving offence to an ever-growing number of people. This led to a breakdown between the Crown and Parliament. Charles refused to discuss domestic affairs unless it was first agreed to set up a high tax to cover his expenses; Parliament insisted on the traditional period of discussion, followed by a vote. So Charles disbanded Parliament and set up a series of fund-raising methods, without the permission of Parliament.

The Ship Tax

The tax that gave offence right across the country was the Ship Tax. Depending on their population, each county had to supply sufficient money to build and fit-out a certain size ship. It was left to local officials to calculate how this tax should be divided into regions and then into households. Even during 1635-6, when the tax was imposed, it was difficult to collect; four years later, it was nearly impossible. More and more people refused to pay and were heavily fined. If they refused to pay their fines, goods to the value of the amount owing were confiscated. Eventually, King Charles was forced to summon Parliament; the tax was declared illegal and the complete breakdown in relationships which followed led to the Civil War.

John Hampden - the Patriot

As early as January 25th 1635, Hampden stood up in Great Kimble Church and protested against the twenty-five shillings tax that had been levied on his estate at nearby Stoke Mandeville. This became one of the first legal battles concerning the tax. He was defended by his cousin, Oliver St John of Bletsoe (Beds) and, although he lost the case and went to prison, the publicity brought him great sympathy. From then on, he was identified as one of the patriots who took the risk of fighting against the illegal tax.

The Last King to Enter the House of Commons

Hampden was not the only Member of Parliament to identify himself with resistance to the tax and, early in 1642, King Charles made a foolish attempt to arrest what he saw as the five ringleaders. On Monday January 3rd, he sent a sergeant into the House of Commons to demand their arrest and when that failed, the sergeant withdrew, but threatened to return the next day to take them by force. This gave the members time to call in supporters from the House of Lords and the Inns of Court. All five men attended the next morning, but to 'avoyd all tumult.... the five gentlemen went out of the house. A little after the kinge came, with all his guard, and all his pentioners, and two or three hundred soldiers and gentlemen'.

There are several accounts of these events that would lead to the outbreak of war; of those, the most detailed is probably the one included in Vol II of the Memoirs of the Verney Family During the Civil War. The above extract and also verses by Hugh Chesterman are included in 'Country Like This', published in 1972 by The Friends of the Vale of Aylesbury. The first verse starts:

> King Charles the First to Parliament came
> Five good Parliament men to claim

and each verse ends with the list of names, including '...Hampden, Gent of Buckinghamshire.'

The Civil War

In addition to Parliamentarian Oliver St John, Hampden was also a cousin of Oliver Cromwell and worked with him in the months leading up to the war. He rode to the opening Battle of Edgehill on 23rd October 1642, taking with him a troop of men from the villages around Aylesbury. After the disastrous battle, he and Cromwell met and discussed the confusion and the terrible loss of life. One of the examples quoted by Cromwell as the need for a new highly trained army, was the lack of skills shown by Hampden's 'old decayed servingmen and tapsters' who had fought beside him.[1]

Cromwell raised his New Model Army and went on to lead the Parliamentary army to a final victory. Hampden, on the other hand, did not live to witness the success of these trained and disciplined soldiers. He died eight months later, on 18th June 1643, when he met Prince Rupert's troops on a road near Oxford, in what became known as the skirmish of Chalgrove Field, Hampden was very badly wounded. Trying to get back to Great Hampden, he collapsed at Thame and died soon afterwards. He was buried in his own village church.

In 1863, Sir William Erle ordered a large stone cross to be erected in a field near the church. The inscription includes a reference to Hampden's stand against paying the Ship Tax and that, by 'resisting the claim of the King in legal strife he upheld the rights of the people under the law and became entitled to their grateful remembrance.' His statue in Market Square portrays him with his sword in his right hand and with his left hand pointing forward into the future.

THE GRAND UNION CANAL AND ITS RESERVOIRS

Having left Tring the main route will pass near to the reservoirs and canal. Originally called the Grand Junction Canal, it was one of the later canals to be dug. In 1792 there was a proposal to construct a new canal from Braunston on the Oxford canal to Brentford on the Thames. The Act of Parliament authorising the new canal received the royal assent in April 1793 and by December 1793, 3000 men were at work. The barges could carry up

ROUTE

From Tring, the route doubles back and turns sharp right, by crossing over onto an unclassified road towards Long Marston. It passes between the Tringford and Startopsend reservoirs, before turning right onto the B489 towards Marsworth. (The car park for the Startopsend reservoir is on the right immediately before the hump-backed bridge).

1 Fraser, A. *Cromwell - Our Chief of Men*

to 70 tons and the locks were constructed to accommodate a pair of narrow boats.

One of the difficult tasks for the engineers was crossing the high ground at the summit near Tring. A cutting was made through the Chiltern Hills, over one and a half miles long and at one point over 30ft deep. The storage of water was solved by digging reservoirs. The length which led from the summit, south of Berkhamsted, was opened in 1799 and the length north of Fenny Stratford in May 1800. By 1815 a six-mile branch to Aylesbury with sixteen locks was working. Wilstone Reservoir was constructed in 1802 and eventually reached its present size in 1839. Marsworth Reservoir was completed in 1806, Tring Ford in 1816 and Startopsend in 1817.

Startopsend Reservoir has a car park near the hump-backed bridge. From there it is possible to walk along the Grand Union Canal or round Startopsend, Marsworth and Tring Ford Reservoirs. The paths are clearly marked and most of them are reasonably dry once you get away from the car park. The wildlife of the reservoirs is managed by the Nature Conservancy Council.

It is sometimes puzzling why a particular reservoir may be full in dry weather and low in wet weather. Since 1837, pumping from all the reservoirs has been concentrated at Tring Ford. The reservoirs are there to keep a good supply of water for the canals, for as the boats go up and down using the locks, the water from this difficult part of the system is lost and the pumps switch water from different reservoirs into the canal. This is particularly necessary at Bank Holiday weekends, as, from 1968, the Transport Act no longer classified the Grand Union as a Commercial but as a Cruising Waterway.

MARSWORTH

All Saints Church

Standing above the canal, the church congregation help each year to provide a service for 'Boat Sunday' - an impressive ceremony stressing the connection between Marsworth and the canal. The Lady Aelfgifu owned Marsworth in the mid 10th century and may well have had a church here. (see Wing) The first known church building was in 1190 but none of that remains above ground. All Saints suffered two bad restorations in the 19th century, but in 1880 local men learned stoneworking skills and greatly improved it. Leading into the churchyard there is a flint and stone lych or body gate. It is a very exposed

ROUTE
The route passes the fringe of Marsworth village, which is just off the route on the left.

96

churchyard and as the bearers at a funeral had to wait at the gate for the clergy-man to lead them, they needed somewhere to shelter from the weather. In some villages there was a table on which to rest the body.

PITSTONE

As far as the route is concerned, Pitstone is divided into two sections. Having left Marsworth it will come back into Pitstone from the other direction. In the 19th century this was a village, which was entirely reliant on agriculture and straw plaiting. The population grew in response to the large cement works, but this has now declined and the majority of people work outside the village. However, the farm museum not only restores and preserves farm and craftmachinery and tools, but also presents a picture of village life.

> *ROUTE*
> **Continue to Pitstone roundabout and then straight into the village. (Pitstone Farm Museum and Church are on the road to the right of the roundabout).**

Pitstone Green Farm Museum

This and St Mary's Church are a short distance, off the route, to the right of Pitstone roundabout. The farm houses a fascinating collection of farm and craft tools, pictures, documents, farm and kitchen memorabilia. These are attractively displayed in the original farm buildings, which together give a record of country life a century or more ago.

St Mary's Church

This church is no longer in regular use but is kept in good repair by the Churches Conservation Trust (previously the Redundant Churches Fund). Like Ivinghoe Church it was built in the 13th century and dedicated to St Mary the Virgin. It is, at times, open to visitors and is well worth a visit because it has examples of different types of decoration and items to illustrate the life of the church. There is a Norman font, a Jacobean pulpit and some medieval floor tiles, which date back to the 13th century. In the north chapel is a piscina carved with foliage and faces, originally used for washing the Chalice (cup) and Paten (plate) after the Holy Communion Service, the water draining away into the churchyard. There is also an aumbry cupboard where the sacred vessels were once stored.

IVINGHOE

Several old buildings have survived in different parts of the village. The Youth Hostel was started in 1937 in a handsome building that was previously the private house of the local brewery owner. The latter stood in the space between what is now the YHA and the church. On the other side, the much-restored Town Hall was built in the 16th century as a parish hall and courthouse. Some less pleasant aspects of village life can be seen outside Ivinghoe Church. Screwed to the wall are a thatch-hook and a mantrap. It is impossible to say if and when the latter would have been used, but in the days of thatch, the former would have been kept in every church to pull the thatch away from cottage roofs to stop a fire from spreading.

ROUTE

The route automatically runs from Pitstone village into Ivinghoe village.

The Church of St Mary the Virgin

Many 13th century churches were dedicated to St Mary; this one was built about 1230 and despite having suffered very much at the hands of Victorian restorers, there is still a lot to see. The walls and arcades are original, the north and south doors and doorways are both 13th century but with later porches. The west porch is 15th century with Lord Brownlow's arms added about 1871. There are brasses, an effigy and stained glass windows and it is well worth visiting to see the carved woodwork. The posts of the 15th century roof rest upon the grotesque heads of the corbels, which are said to represent Old and New Testament characters. Above and between the wall-plates are angels with outstretched wings and shields bearing emblems. The bench-ends were also carved in the 15th century. Flowers and leaves might be expected in a country church, but why the mermaid (with the double comb and mirror!) so far from the sea? Actually this carving had nothing to do with the sea but represented the vanity of human flesh and thus the risk of hell.

ROUTE

If planning to visit Ivinghoe Watermill, watch for a left turn when approaching the King's Head.

The Ivinghoe Watermill

The mill is half a mile off the direct route down the B488, on the left-hand side at Ford End Farm. It is impossible to tell how old the watermill is, but there has been a watermill in Ivinghoe since the 14th century. In 1798 it was grinding an average of sixteen sacks of corn each week and the owner had five horses, a wagon and three carts. The mill was used until about 1953 but the very nature of the work meant that it needed constant repair and about that time it became uneconomic to run. At the end of 1964 an appeal was launched and together with financial help from the owner, Mr Arthur Jellis, the Pitstone Local History Society was able to complete sufficient repairs to get it working again. The Society now leases the mill and the money collected on Sundays goes into further restoration work. About half a mile from the mill, springs emerging from the chalk flow down to turn the wheel or are stored in the millpond.

In the last century the watermill was a vital part of farm life; not only was the corn ground for bread making, but other wheels crushed grain for cows and horses and cut hay into chaff. The water was also used for sheep-washing. To fetch a better price for the wool, the sheep were penned near the mill just before they were sold and then, one by one, dropped into about five feet of water. Dressed specially for his unpleasant task, a stockman held each one under the running water before they were allowed to swim into the shallows and climb out.

Though the springs provide less water today the mill is still capable of working, and locally-ground flour is on sale. The Society has also arranged a small collection of millers' and seed merchants' equipment to show the kind of work associated with milling.

IVINGHOE BEACON

Starting at Ivinghoe Beacon, the Ridgeway Walk has now been opened along the general course of the Icknield Way and the route is marked with the sign of an acorn. There is a car park near the Beacon and another near Aldbury. Today the Beacon is marked on the map as a viewpoint and sometimes one can watch enthusiasts flying model aeroplanes and gliders. It is 230 metres (789ft) above sea level.

In the Bronze Age, perhaps around 700BC, a community lived on the hill, defended by a very deep ditch and rampart. Excavations in 1963-65 uncovered domestic finds such as spindle whorls (for wool spun from their sheep) and bronze defensive weapons including a winged axe and pieces from swords.

ROUTE
Once past Ivinghoe Church, the route swings right and then turns left towards Dunstable. For a short distance it is retracing an earlier part of the route but near the top of the steep hill it turns right, up over Ivinghoe Beacon towards Ashridge and Ringshall.

ASHRIDGE FOREST

The history of this once royal forest has its own chapter but this route ends by following a most beautiful, scenic route across one corner of it. The reason that

ROUTE

Having passed along the edge of Ashridge Forest, the route meets a T-junction in Ringshall and turns left towards Dagnall. From there it is clearly sign-posted back into Dunstable.

we have access to so much of the forest is that when the last Earl Brownlow died in 1921 and the estate was being divided ready for sale, a local resident, Miss Bridget Talbot, together with others, wrote to the Times newspaper appealing to people to join them in their attempt to save the estate. This was supported by Stanley Baldwin and several other senior politicians; fund-raising began and quite quickly money became available to the National Trust to enable them to buy their first 1700 acres. By 1934 £70,000 had been spent to gradually buy half of the original estate.

The National Trust

This major charity that protects all types of buildings, areas of our countryside and coastline, villages and archaeological sites, was created in 1895 to preserve the history and beauty of the country. It was incorporated by an Act of Parliament, passed in 1907, and relies on subscriptions paid by its many members, entrance fees to its properties and charitable donations.

Ashridge House (Just off the route in Little Gaddesden)

The history of this important building is set out in the Ashridge Route. Even though it was rebuilt in the 18th century, the cost of preserving such a large rambling building is frightening. During this century several ways have been tried to enable it to support itself as an establishment for adult education. The present company has now been managing the property for over thirty years and are carrying out a regular programme of restoration. They now have a small museum of artefacts, pictures, letters and other documents.

CHAPTER 4 • ROUTE 4

Some Interesting Old Churches

Leighton Buzzard • Billington • Edlesborough
Eaton Bray • Totternhoe • Dunstable
Houghton Regis • Chalgrave • Toddington • Tebworth
Hockliffe • (Heath and Reach) • Great Brickhill • (Soulbury)
Stewkley • Wing • Mentmore • Leighton Buzzard

Introduction

This Route is approximately 48 miles long. It starts at Leighton Buzzard, crosses South Bedfordshire, heads north and returns close to Leighton Buzzard. However, having entered the attractive wooded countryside of the Greensand Ridge, it then follows a smaller circle out into Buckinghamshire.

The Historical Background covers the arrival and development of the parish church system, which today we take for granted. Historical Highlights starts with the cathedral-like church at Leighton Buzzard and includes the important church at Wing (which still has many original Saxon features), the church at Dunstable, built by the Augustinian Canons in the 12th century, and a whole range of smaller ones. Between them they offer a wealth of carvings, stained-glass windows, brasses, statues and other interesting architectural features.

Along this route are two market towns, numerous pretty villages and Leighton Buzzard Railway, where you can experience the vanished world of the English Light Railway. Near Billington you will see signs pointing towards Mead Open Farm. This working farm has a wide range of established farm animals, an indoor pets corner, other outdoor attractions and a wonderful, indoor playbarn.

On Slicketts Lane, just off the Edlesborough - Eaton Bray road is the shop known as Arts and Crafts. This sells a very wide range of crafts and gifts, in a surprisingly long shed which has been likened to a 'Tardis'.

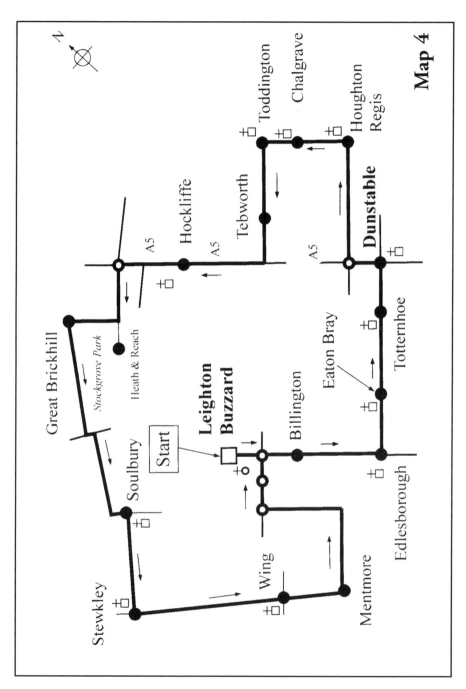

Map 4

102

Leighton Buzzard's Friendly Little Railway

Feeding time at Mead Open Farm (M.O.F.)

103

Historical Background

In the majority of towns and villages, the parish church is much the oldest standing building. Throughout the centuries, it has stood as the focal point of the community, witnessing the events that we learnt about in our history-books at school. Geographically it is not always in the centre because residential communities have sometimes moved. Before the Norman Conquest and in many places until the early 13th century, most priests were connected with monasteries or with 'minster' churches and travelled around from one community to another. Gradually the landowners built churches beside their own manor houses for the use of their families, servants and workers. It was 'their' church and these people were part of 'their' estate. It is probable that by the time of the Norman Conquest, most villages had a small wooden church somewhere near the manor house. There is written evidence of a wooden church at Studham but, not having land for its support, it does not appear in the Domesday Book.

Both Toddington and Chalgrave are thought to have had pre-Conquest churches, but today neither church stands beside a manor house and the latter stands a mile or more away from the community. At Toddington, the castle (which was possibly the first manor-house) stood beside the church, on what is now called Conger Hill. This was the first of three manor houses, the present house being nearly a mile to the northwest. At Chalgrave, the manor house, which once stood beside the church, gradually lost its importance when the last of the male members of the pre-Conquest family died in 1386. The majority of people were already living at Tebworth and Wingfield, so that when the manor house eventually crumbled away, the church was left isolated.

Chalgrave is also different from other churches on the route because the pre-Conquest owner, Albert of Lorraine, was chaplain to the Saxon king, Edward the Confessor, who was a relative of Duke William. Because of this, Albert was regarded as a friend, not an enemy and therefore was not dispossessed of his estates. Most manors and churches (if they existed) were taken from the Saxon families, who may have owned them for several generations, and given as rewards to the wealthy Norman families who had supported William in his successful fight for the English throne. In the 12th or 13th centuries, the descendants of these new Norman landowners often built or rebuilt churches on their estates.

The Minster Churches

These were a little like monasteries except that the men were all ordained clergymen. They were not enclosed and at first did not follow a strict rule. Some priests stayed at the motherhouse and travelled around the nearby churches, others lived on land provided for their support. It is assumed that many of the early Bedfordshire churches received visits from the clergy of St Paul's Church, Bedford, but there may also have been a second minster church at Luton.

The Augustinian Canons

At the very end of the 11th century, canons at St Botolph's Church, Colchester decided to follow a Rule worked out centuries before by St Augustine of Hippo. They then opened a second 'Augustinian' House at Holy Trinity, Aldgate. These canons who followed a Rule became known as 'Canons Regular'.

Dunstable Priory

Soon after he visited his new town of Dunstable in 1109, Henry I invited the Augustinian canons (each an ordained clergyman) from Holy Trinity, Aldgate, in London, to found a house opposite his Dunstable palace. By 1540 Dunstable Priory owned churches not only in Bedfordshire (including Studham) but also in seven other counties.

Newnham Priory

At Bedford c1166, the sheriff, Simon de Beauchamp, gave St Paul's Church land to the east of the town. They re-formed there as the Augustinian Priory of Newnham.

The Religious Houses as Owners of Churches

The secular owners of churches did not necessarily give them to the nearest religious house but to one with which their family had connections, perhaps as founders, or because a son or daughter was a member. They might, however, choose a house where they frequently stayed when travelling eg Dunstable Priory, a house that the family had started in Normandy, or where they recovered after crossing the Channel. Although all canons were priests, not all monks were. Quite often a poorly educated clerk was appointed to take the routine services, with one of their own ordained members being sent on special occasions.

The Appointment of Vicars

The above system was at best very inefficient and often left rural communities without a resident priest to care for their souls and supervise their welfare. The Lateran council of 1215 condemned the practice but Bishop Wells, of the Lincoln Diocese, had already insisted that resident vicars should be appointed. Many of our local vicarages were appointed at about this time. Although Dunstable Priory ordained a vicarage at Chalgrave in 1221, it was 1225 before two qualified priests were appointed to serve the parishioners of Dunstable and even then a wealthy merchant, Alexander Young, paid for one of them.[1] When the wooden Saxon church at Studham was given to Dunstable Priory, the vicar was a married man and after his death the Prior's officers had to make provision for his widow before the next vicar could move in.[2]

As the years went by, the position could become very involved and also open to abuse. Henry I divided the village of Houghton (Regis) between Dunstable Priory and a Norman baron called Hugh de Gurnay. After many bitter quarrels, the Prior built a manor house at Calcutt (near Chalgrave) and de Gurnay built another at Thornbury. Around 1153, Robert, Earl of Gloucester (illegitimate but much-loved son of Henry I) gave the parish church of Houghton, together with its sixty-acre farm, which some Saxon king had provided for its support, to St Albans Abbey. This meant that valuable church land now belonged to the abbey rather than to the village church and it was up to the abbey to appoint a vicar.

Tithes

Not only was the church land of Houghton lost to the village, but also the tithes. From 'time-out-of-mind' the people of every community had been obliged to donate one-tenth of everything they grew to help to support their church. The owner of the church collected these tithes and the corn was put in his tithe-barn. The money raised from the sale of the tithes was supposed to keep the church in a good state of repair. Although they had no choice but to obey, people bitterly resented paying tithes, particularly if they appeared to be lost to the village. At Houghton, where St Albans Abbey owned the church and church land and Dunstable Priory owned half of the manorial land, there were bitter quarrels concerning tithes and other church dues.[3]

The estate name 'Tithe Farm' comes from the tithe barn that the abbey built around 1400.

1 Evans, V. Dunstable with the Priory. 1100-1550
2 BHRS Vol X 3 Lovering, P. Royal Houghton

LEIGHTON BUZZARD

All Saints Church

When information was being collected in 1085-6 for the great tax report, which became known as the Domesday Book, few manors had their own stone churches and even fewer had churches with land provided for their own support. The afore-mentioned church at Studham (probably wooden) was the property of the landowner, in the same way as his barns and stables. However the church on the royal manor of Leighton had been given five hides (approx 600 acres) of land. This church and its land had been given to Bishop Wulfwy of Dorchester-on-Thames, who died the year following the Conquest. His successor, Bishop Remigius, remained in the post when the See was transferred to Lincoln.

Many of the canons attached to a cathedral worked as vicars at the parish churches that had been given into the care of the cathedral. Sometimes the church's land became their prebend (or source of income) and they were accordingly known as 'prebendaries'. The church land at Leighton was used by the Bishops of Lincoln as a prebend, the prebendary house being at the end of the High Street. In the 12th century the prebendary sent to Leighton was Theobald de Busar, while the cathedral had another prebendary, called Bromswold, who held Leighton in Huntingdonshire. In 1242 the cathedral clerk referred to them as Leighton 'Busard' and Leighton 'Bromswold'.

In 1220 the Bishop of Lincoln consecrated a site for the present All Saints Church, probably on the site of the Saxon church. A church as large and as beautifully decorated as All Saints took a long time to build and it was still unfinished when Canon Nicholas de Heigham died in 1288, leaving a generous bequest to complete the work.

Nicholas de Heigham was prebendary from 1269-88 and started to build the present cathedral-like church. His grand design was much appreciated by his parishioners and is now a 'treasure-house' of fine architectural detail. Much 13th century work remains and the font pre-dates the church. The broach spire, which is built of limestone and rises to 191ft, is 13th century (as is the oak eagle lectern, which may be the oldest in the country). The west door is modern but the decorative iron-work hinges, together with the hinges inside on the vestry door, were made by Thomas of Leighton, who, in 1294, made the iron grill for the tomb of Queen Eleanor in Westminster Abbey. When the Duke of Suffolk owned Grovebury (see below) in the 15th century, the Duchess made many changes to the church, including the 'East Anglian' style nave roof with carved angels. The choir seats were made for St Albans Abbey and brought here after the Reformation. Carefully lift the seats and you will see the beautifully carved misericords or ledges where tired choristers could rest during a long service.

There is a booklet for sale that describes the features of the church and many more treasures. Look out for the trademark of CE Kemp (a small yellow sheaf of corn) in the pattern of the stained glass. One window was made by his successor, who was called 'Tower' and has a tower with a wheat sheaf as a trademark. Note also the graffiti, the most famous of which is a low relief of 'Simon' and 'Nellie', the traditional story being that they are arguing about whether to boil or bake the simnel (Mothering Sunday) cake !

'We Shall Rebuild' was the heading of an emergency issue of the parish magazine, 'Saints Alive', hastily published in May 1985. This amazing headline did not mean that the parishioners of All Saints had become tired of their old church or, like medieval landowners, wanted something more modern and impressive. Their beautiful church had suffered a most terrible fire!

At about 10.30pm on Saturday 13 April a fire had broken out in the priests' vestry and quickly spread through the upper vestry into the chancel. Although the 13th century eagle lectern was removed to safety and the fire brigade managed to save many of the medieval treasures, the flames reached part of the angel-roof.

It took many years of fund-raising and exceptionally hard work, but All Saints was eventually re-dedicated.

Grovebury - The Manor-house of Leighton

It is not known where Leighton's first manor-house stood; maybe it was replaced by the Prebendary House ? An attempt is made below to explain why All Saints church appears to have been built a long way from the medieval manor house. Leighton has always been the market town for a wide agricultural area. In 1066 it belonged to the king and continued to do so until 1164 when Henry II gave the manor, but not the church, to the French Abbey of Fontevrault; they started the small priory known as Grovebury. This became the manor house of Leighton and, during the Hundred Years' War between France and England, the abbess tactfully granted Grovebury and Leighton to Mary of Woodstock, daughter of Edward I. During this period Edward I and II both visited the town and later Edward III granted it to the Duke of Lancaster's daughter, Maud. She

The Medieval Market Cross (S.B.D.C.)

Grove Church, now a Private House

stayed there when she visited the Dunstable tournament in 1342 and sent her brother, the future Duke of Lancaster, five quarters of wheat to help with his tournament expenses.*

A Succession of Royal Ladies of the Manor
After Maud of Lancaster, the next royal Lady of the Manor was Isabel, daughter of Edward III and a few years after her death it passed to Alice, née Chaucer (possibly the grand-daughter of Geoffrey) whose second husband was the Duke of Suffolk. Alice de la Pole, Duchess of Suffolk, held the manor from 1467-1475. During that time she paid for the exceptionally fine nave roof which has 'East Anglia'-style angels and saints, supported by carved stone corbels of angels, carrying shields. Her daughter-in-law was Elizabeth Plantagenet, sister of both Edward IV and Richard III, so that the tradition of royal ladies continued.

The Prebendal Mansion
By 1600, the town of Leighton had for many years been let to various London merchants. As the prebendaries of Lincoln were no longer using the house by the church and what had once been a very grand, comfortable house at Grovebury was now considered to be unfashionable and inconvenient, these businessmen (or their representatives) lived at the Prebendal House, which became the manor house for the town.

Some of the Church Charities

The Pulford School
It is probable that as early as the mid 17th century one of the businessmen provided money for the education of a few poor boys and by 1728 there was education provided for a handful of both boys and girls. The building in Church Square (now the Post Office) was built for these children in 1790. The vicar, Joshua Pulford, who died in 1710, had left property in trust for education and so the school was given his name. The new Pulford School, now a lower school, was opened in 1884.

The Wilkes Almshouses
Located in North Street, they were first built in 1630 and rebuilt in 1857. Edward Wilkes gave the almshouses and other gifts to the town and his son,

* *Details of her household expenses are included in BHRS Vol 3 and Evans, V Folk*

Matthew, left instructions in his will for an unusual ceremony to be carried out each year. On Rogation Monday civic and church representatives, accompanied by the choir and the verger carrying a nosegay, process from All Saints along the High Street to the Almshouses where there is a short service. The Clerk to the Trustees, wearing a wig, then reads the relevant part of Edward's will, while a choirboy or girl stands on his/her head! This ceremony was intended to include the beating of the bounds of the Wilkes' property and to call attention to the Wilkes' gift, so that it would never be forgotten.

A bill has survived for refreshments provided after the 'Wilkes Walk' of 1836. The boys received ale and bread rolls, which in total cost £3-4-6d (£3.221/2p)[1]

Leighton Buzzard Today

Having visited All Saints Church, allow time to explore the traditional shops, especially the small pedestrianised alleyways. It is a most attractive market town, still holding its market in the High Street every Tuesday and Saturday. The leaflet 'Historic Leighton Buzzard', which is available in the library, is very helpful in pointing out and describing the interesting buildings around the town.

The Market Cross

Erected originally about 1400, the figures, thought to represent Christ, Mary the mother of Christ, John the Baptist, a bishop and a king, were remodelled in 1852.

The Market House/ Town Hall/ Fire Station

This brick-built building, paid for in 1851 by the lord of the manor, stands near the cross. The original timber-framed building, built by the Lords of the Manor of Grovebury, was used as their tollhouse and the centre from which they ran the market. From 1919 to 1963 it was used as the town's fire station. Today its future is uncertain.

The Old Inns

As with most historic market towns, Leighton Buzzard has a wide range of old inns and beer houses.[2]

---

1 Brown, M. Old Pubs of Leighton Buzzard and Linslade
2 Brown, J. et al The Old Pubs of Leighton Buzzard and Linslade

ROUTE

When the route leaves Leighton Buzzard, it is heading for Dunstable via Billington and Edlesborough. Head out of Leighton Buzzard on the A4146 towards Hemel Hempstead (not Hockliffe). Continue on this road and just before passing the town boundary, you will see Leighton Buzzard Railway on your left. At the next roundabout continue on the A4146 towards Hemel Hempstead and Billington. Drive through Billington and remain on the A4146 into Edlesborough. With The Bell on your left and the church on your right, turn left through the village.

BILLINGTON

At the time of the Domesday Book, Billington was part of the manor and parish of Leighton Buzzard. It had a 'chapel of ease' (convenience) within the large parish and in 1650 won the right to appoint its own minister. At that time, the devout reformer, Oliver Cromwell, was in charge of the Commonwealth and when discussions arose concerning a wealthy village charity, the Commissioners of Charitable Uses decided that half the income from its estate was to be used to pay the stipend of a minister.

As the minister had full use of this divided charity estate, he became recognised as rector and, from 1722, the inhabitants of Billington were allowed to nominate their own minister. Although the nominees were likely to be put forward by the charity trustees or the churchwardens, the final election was open to discussion by the parishioners.[1] The present St Michael's Church, which stands on a low hill looking over the Ouzel Valley, was built in the 1860s but one or two details from the 13th century chapel were included.

EDLESBOROUGH

The Church of St Mary the Virgin is now closed and in the care of the Redundant Churches Fund. The vicar of Eaton Bray has the key, but the church is often open on summer Sunday afternoons when visitors are very welcome. It is a beautiful church with fine examples of 15th century carvings. The pulpit is described as 'wineglass' in shape and has a finely carved canopy of oak. There are some very interesting brasses and if you look carefully at the lectern you can see the inscription 'ereptum igne'- 'snatched from the burning'. We are lucky to be able to see any of the beautiful things in St Mary's for, during a violent storm on Friday 28th March 1828, the spire was struck by lightning. The wooden lining began to burn, the lead covering melted, dropped to the ground and the spire burst into flames.

1 Bell, P. *Belief in Bedfordshire*

The body of the church was saved by fire-engines from Ashridge, Dunstable and Ivinghoe, but the spire was lost; the present lectern was made from one of the charred beams.

EATON BRAY

This village has a church which demonstrates that size and decoration owe more to the interest and wealth of the landowner than the size of the population. There were approximately 450 people living in the village in 1671 and less than 600 in 1801.[1]

ROUTE
Continue by turning left along the High Street through Eaton Bray.

The Castle at Eaton (Bray)

At the time of the civil war between King John and the barons, the name was still 'Eaton' (the village surrounded by streams). William de Cantelupe, a senior civil servant of King John, had come to live in the manor house in 1205 but spent much of his time at court.

During the civil war the notorious mercenary officer, Falkes de Breauté, built a castle at Luton from where his soldiers terrorised the neighbourhood, including Eaton.[1] William de Cantelupe decided to build a new manor house which had such excellent defences that it became known as a castle. The moat, evidence of which is still there, is on private ground. It enclosed a site that was big enough for a large house, a private chapel and a granary. The moat had two drawbridges and there was an outer bailey with stables for sixty horses, cowsheds, piggeries and other buildings. Outside were two large gardens, a park and twenty-eight acres of woodland. William died in 1254 and the house gradually became neglected.

The male line died out in 1273 but continued through the female line via the family la Zouche. In 1483 John la Zouche was with King Richard III at the Battle of Bosworth, as a result of which he lost the manor of Eaton.

The Bray Family

During the same battle a Reginald Bray was fighting against King Richard III; he was an officer in Sir William Stanley's troop. It is said that Bray was with Stanley when they found Richard's crown and placed it on the head of Henry Tudor, thus proclaiming him King Henry VII. This may well be true as Bray was knighted shortly afterwards and in 1490 received the manor of Eaton.

1 Evans, V. Folk

By this time the old 'castle' was out of fashion and in a sad state of repair. Sir Reginald Bray KG, who was a respected architect, designed a Tudor-style house, which stood until the late 18th century. The male line of the Bray family held Eaton for only eighty-four years but their name is connected with the village to this day.

The Stanford Hall Connection
Among the collection of paintings, furniture and tapestries on show at this historic house in Leicestershire, owned by the present Lord and Lady Braye, is an interesting antique stone. Carved on it can be seen the royal arms of Henry VII, the crown of England, a gate of Windsor and the Bray badge of a hemp-breaker. A female descendent of Sir Reginald married into the Cave family at Stanford and in 1839, the Bray Peerage was taken out of abeyance.

The St George's Chapel Connection
Although this chapel was started by Edward IV, in 1475, the building process was very slow. It has been suggested that during his lifetime, Sir Reginald Bray KG influenced the design which may be why local Totternhoe stone was used for some of the internal carving. When he died, he left money and instructions to his executors, to have the chapel finished. He was buried in the chapel in the south transept, which bears his name. His badge, a weaver's hemp bray, appears 175 times in the parts of St George's Chapel which were finished with money from his bequest! It is thought that the stone at Stanford was originally in this chapel and travelled to Leicestershire via Eaton Bray.

The Church of St Mary the Virgin
This church was not given to Dunstable Priory but to another Augustinian Priory, Merton, in Surrey.

When William de Cantelupe came to Eaton he offended the prior by starting to build an elaborate new church. He had taken advice from Abbot John de Cella, of St Albans Abbey and no doubt the prior felt that Cantelupe would take advantage of the situation and claim ownership of the church and its vicarage. So Cantelupe changed his plans, obtained permission to include a chapel in his new castle and resigned all interest in the parish church. It was therefore left to the architect, Sir Reginald de Bray, to build on to the work started by Cantelupe.

The architecture is in two different styles. The north arcade and the south aisle are both thought to be the design of John de Cella. The font may be of the same period, but the wrought-iron work on the door leading to the south porch is attributed to Thomas of Leighton, later in the century. In the south porch, on the right-hand side of the door, are the remains of a 'mass dial'. When it was in use a hand would have pointed to the time of the mass.

When visiting the church, look out for the scratch-mark of Sir Edmund Bray's hemp-bray and the beautiful costumes on the brass memorial to the wife of Sir Reginald's nephew, Jane, Lady Bray and her children, dated 1539. The verse, apparently written by Jane's daughter, who died the same year, warned her friends -

'For as ye ar so was I and as I am so shall ye be'.

There is a particularly interesting and helpful guidebook.

TOTTERNHOE

The Village is Divided

To understand the history of villages it is often necessary to go back a long way to find why they are divided into a series of 'ends'. Totternhoe with its 'Church', 'Middle' and 'Lower' ends is a good example.

The Castle

Saxon settlers arrived in this area during the 6th and 7th centuries and usually chose sites near water but away from the main roads. By the arrival of William I (the Conqueror) most of our villages, with their Saxon names, were well established. William knew that at first he would face a period of unrest, if not rebellion, so he tried to prevent trouble. In Bedfordshire he gave the sites which would make natural defences to a family of Flemings. 'Totternhoe' comes from a Saxon word meaning 'Watchhill' and it was probably 'Walter the Fleming' who press-ganged the local people to dig out ditches, build up banks and make a simple motte and bailey castle on top of the hill. There is no evidence that it was a stone castle, although local stone was probably used to make the foundations. This was not a residential castle, as at Bedford or Berkhamsted and there is no evidence of it having ever been attacked. By the 12th century it was called Eglemont (the eagle's mount). Today, the castle mounds, which are known as Totternhoe Knolls, are classified as a scheduled Ancient Monument and the whole area is a Site of Special Scientific Interest.

ROUTE

The route continues into Totternhoe and at the T-junction, facing the Knolls, turns right towards Dunstable. Pass the Cross Keys and then, having passed the signpost pointing left to the Totternhoe Knolls carpark and having ignored Church Road, on your right, the route continues up Lancot Hill.

King William had a very good reason for defending Totternhoe; it had a valuable stone quarry which had been known to both the Romans and the Saxons. King William kept the quarry as his private property and the people who worked there formed a separate community. The quarry, which was under the chalk hill, was made from a series of tunnels and chambers. Men crawled along, cutting blocks of soft stone and hauling them out on the rollers. No wonder the church was dedicated to St Giles, the patron saint of cripples!

This stone was excellent for carving at buildings like Westminster Abbey and St George's Chapel, Windsor, where it was used for internal work. However for houses like Ashridge or Woburn and for local churches where it was used for the external structure, it has proved unsuitable for really long-term use. It does not wear well and eventually crumbles, letting in the rain. Because of this, many churches have been forced to organise appeals to help them replace the crumbling Totternhoe stone with something more durable. The last 'pit' at the quarry was owned by a local man, Jim Twidell; it was closed around 1914 and the entrances have been blocked for reasons of safety.

The Far End and Church End

In Saxon times Totternhoe had been under one lord of the manor but King William divided the village into two. Walter the Fleming, whose family had their main castle at Odell in North Bedfordshire, spent much of his time working for the King at Rockingham Castle but his steward, or a later owner, had a moated manor house built at 'Lower End'. One of William's civil servants, William, the King's Chamberlain, owned 'Church End', but he never lived there. Before long the Fleming family, who had become Barons of Wadenhull (Odell), owned most of Totternhoe and commissioned the building of the church, which they gave to Dunstable Priory.

The Church of St Giles

In the south aisle is an unusual stained-glass window, which includes some rare early English glass, taken from clerestory windows in the 20th century. Climbing up the window is the tree of life, one branch clearly showing oak leaves and an acorn. The theme of hope continues all over the church and the 17th century Bishops' chair is also decorated with the tree of life. There is a reredos over the altar in the south aisle with lilies, roses and vines and the sentence 'I am the vine, ye are the branches' commemorating the life of George Pratt, who died in 1888. In 1671 there was a Thomas Pratt in the village and the family name has continued there ever since. In 1971 William Pratt commissioned John Piper to design a new east window in memory of his wife and parents. Its brilliant colours dominate the chancel, as the phoenix bursts out of the ashes and butterflies alight on the branches of the tree of life.

Throughout the life of the church, people from Totternhoe have left their names and tributes. John Warwekyll 'sumtyme vicar of this church' died in 1524 and the people had a brass made to commemorate his life in the parish. In 1677 the churchwardens, Daniel Clithero and Reynold Wells, ordered a new parish chest with their initials carved on it. Thomas Michell was patron of the church in the early 17th century and put a brass in memory of his choirboy son, in the floor near to the altar.

DUNSTABLE

The Medieval Church

Long before the Norman Conquest the Saxon kings had owned all the land around the crossing, which was probably known as 'Dun-staple' - the boundary post, or the market place, by the downs. Most of the land was included in the royal manor of Houghton and soon after Henry I came to the throne in 1100, his officials planted a town on the crossroads*. Henry then commissioned the building of a palace for his family to use when they were travelling. The foundations of this palace are probably under or near the Old Palace Lodge Hotel and the Norman King public house.

ROUTE
When this road meets the B489, turn left into Dunstable and approach the main crossroads, (The Priory Church of St Peter is in Church Street).

In 1109 Henry came to stay at his palace of Kingsbury with a large party. It was during this visit that he signed the documents that allowed two Augustinian brothers to go from St Botolph's at Colchester to Aldgate in London. Later these same men brought a party of canons from London to start an Augustinian Priory in Dunstable.

By 1131 the Priory was sufficiently settled for King Henry to give the thriving town of Dunstable into its keeping. The church had two great towers; one on the northwest and one on the southwest corners. In 1222 there was a violent storm in which they were blown down. A new 'early English' door had to be built and this is why, on the west front, there is only one Norman door.

* Henry I planted a business centre on the crossroads but Dun-'staple' may refer to an unlicensed market held there in the previous century. See Evans, V. Proud Heritage

The gateway to the Priory courtyard still stands but the remains of the rest of the religious and domestic buildings lie under the nearby meadow. It is difficult to imagine the vast range of buildings which once towered over the medieval town. The church stretched back towards Priory Road. It was an enormous building with the roof ten feet higher than it is today. After the Dissolution the stone from the buildings was eventually sold or stolen but the remaining rubble makes Priory Meadow seven feet above the natural ground level. The site is legally protected and any form of digging is strictly forbidden.

After the last prior surrendered the house to Henry VIII, at the end of 1539, and the buildings were pulled down, the townspeople were allowed to keep the nave as their parish church. This is why there is a comparatively new wall behind the high altar. When the building was still part of the Priory, the lower part of this wall divided the parish nave from the canon's choir. The outline of the doors, which gave access to the choir, can be seen on either side of the altar. The carved wooden chancel screen has five open arches instead of one central one; this was to prevent it from interfering with the canons' Sunday processions. As a result, the congregation has an open view the full length of the church.

There is an excellent, inexpensive guide that unfolds to illustrate the different architectural features, such as the 'Marian Pillars' over the vestry door on the north side of the High Altar. These are ten wooden banisters each carved with motifs, including the royal badges of England and Spain; they date from the reign of Queen Mary. Catherine of Aragon (whose marriage to Henry VIII was annulled at the Priory) was Mary's mother and it is thought that a sympathiser of Queen Mary may have given them to the church. This may have been her friend, Sir Leonard Chamberlain, to whom she leased Priory House.

The two windows high on the west wall were made in 1972 by John Hayward. They show how modern artists can weave a story using pieces of glass. 'The Priors Window' includes a model of the Lady Chapel, crowned letters 'H' and 'C' and a broken lovers' knot. These tell the story of the annulment of the marriage of King Henry and Queen Catherine which took place in the Lady Chapel of the Priory.

On the walls of the south aisle are monuments to the town's 17th century benefactors, which are listed under the chapter 'The Preservation of our Heritage'.

HOUGHTON REGIS

The land on which Dunstable was planted was once part of this royal estate. By the time of the Norman Conquest there was a wealthy community of farmers and traders who enjoyed the privilege of having their own church.

All Saints Church

In 1086 this was the only village church in Bedfordshire that had an endowment of land for its own support. The sixty acres ran back behind the church,bounded on one side by the demesne land (home farm) of the king's representative and by Bidwell, previously 'Holywell' Hill, on the other.

ROUTE
Drive north along the A5, turn right towards Houghton Regis and drive through the village. Immediately before All Saints Church, turn left at the traffic lights towards Toddington.

We do not know what the Saxon church looked like because over the centuries it has been entirely rebuilt. Pat Lovering describes the various owners, and the features of different periods, in the book, 'Royal Houghton'.

There is a finely carved Norman font and nearby is a recessed tomb and statue, thought to be Sir John Sewell who died in 1438. He lies in what appears to be a private chapel where there is a 14th century piscina. However it is the Brandreth family, who arrived in the village in the mid-17th century, who are mainly commemorated in this church. There are hatchments, brasses and several other memorials and carvings. Their second manor house, built c1700, still stands on the further side of the Green.

Bidwell - An Important Christian Site

St Albans Abbey claims, quite rightly, to be England's oldest site of un-broken Christian worship. If we accept 'site' to cover an area of several hundred acres, then Houghton Regis can make a similar claim.

ROUTE
The route then continues down Bidwell Hill and up Lords Hill. Soon after this you will see Chalgrave Church lying back on the right, surrounded by horse chestnut trees.

'Well' in the Saxon language indicated a stream and there was a stream at the bottom of the hill. St Brigid was an Irish saint who died c542; this spring was dedicated to her. There is further evidence that the stream was considered holy because in the report of a court case at Westminster, on 12 November 1225, the hill is named as 'Holewellehulle'. It was listed as a boundary in a dispute between the Prior of Dunstable and the Norman landowner.[1]   *1 BHRS Vol 6 Part 2*

An Even Earlier Church

However, thanks to the efforts of the Manshead Archaeological Society, we now know that under a field on the rising land between Bidwell and Chalgrave there are the foundations of a Roman Christian church.

CHALGRAVE

Although there was once a large and impressive manor house next to the church, most of the people lived at Wingfield and Tebworth. Chalgrave is an example of a small medieval community that was deserted for reasons other than the plague. There is a well-recorded history and we can put together some of the facts which led to the eventual neglect of the manor house.

King Edward the Confessor brought a chaplain to England from Lorraine and as was then the custom, 'paid' him with grants of land; one of these was Chalgrave. He probably lived at court, seldom if ever visiting his rural land and manors. This original French owner is named in the Domesday Book as 'Albert of Lorraine'; he did not lose his land after the Norman Conquest and Chalgrave stayed with the family, whose name eventually became Loring. Albert's son or grandson built a manor house and by the 12th century there was a stone-built church. The Loring family were closely connected with Dunstable Priory; in 1177 they gave them the church and later, land from the manor of Chalgrave. This was then administered separately and referred to as their manor of Wingfield. At some stage a branch of the family appears to have partly separated Tebworth from the main manor.

Sir Nigel Loring - The White Knight

The descendants of Albert of Lorraine followed several typical steps in their climb up the ladder towards fame. They held several administrative positions, were in the army, at least one member married money, one was sent to France as a senior civil servant and another signed Magna Carta on the side of the barons. The most famous member of the family was Sir Nigel Loring who, from some date before 1335, fought for Edward III. He was a close friend of Prince Edward (the Black Prince) and when the prince started the order of 'Knights of the Garter', Sir Nigel was a founder member; his seat can be seen in St George's Chapel, Windsor 'Monsieur Neel Loring Primer Founder'.

When in 1340 the English army had a great victory, he was given a fast ship to bring the news back to England and the following year took part in a celebratory tournament in Dunstable. He then continued to earn honours throughout the French wars. The author Conan Doyle based his fictitious hero

Sir Nigel of the 'White Company' on Sir Nigel Loring of Chalgrave.

Sir Nigel had married Margaret, the daughter of Sir Ralf Beaupel of Knowstone in Devon, and they had two daughters. When he died in 1386 the Chalgrave estate went to his daughter Margaret, who had married Thomas Pever from the adjoining manor of Toddington and for many years the farmland of Chalgrave was managed with the land of Toddington. Wingfield stayed with the Dunstable Priory until the Dissolution and then continued to follow a different history from the land of Chalgrave.

Sir Nigel not only equally divided his land in seven counties between his two daughters but also scrupulously divided the Chalgrave manor house and home farm. They shared the reception rooms, the kitchens, the bedrooms, the gardens and even the farm buildings. He also left them 2,367 'great marguerite pearls'. At this date the Chalgrave branch of the Loring family died out but other lines continued and American descendants have recently visited the church.

The house had probably begun to deteriorate when, following the death of the two sisters, the church and manor were sold to Robert Braybroke of Colmworth, in the north of the county. In 1406 the Braybroke family started a chantry chapel in the church of Chalgrave and endowed it with the 'mansion' house, a garden, an orchard and a piece of meadow which, in the 16th century, were together let for only £1 per year. From then on little is heard of the mansion house.

All Saints Church

This is one of the great success stories of the diocese. It is very beautiful and has many features of great architectural importance but thirty years ago there was no electricity, there were holes in the roof and a wall was in danger of collapse! The vision and exceptionally hard work of a comparatively small group of people has resulted in a church with electric lights and organ and an amazingly successful restoration.

Inside Chalgrave Church there are two tomb chests, each with a sculptured knight. Pevsner suggests that the knight in the south aisle (with his feet on a lion) was erected in 1360-70 and the one in the north aisle in 1380-90. Sir Nigel died in 1386.

Also in the church there are several early 14th century wall paintings. Unfortunately they have been partly spoiled by a coat of whitewash but luckily much has survived. Over the north door is a large St Christopher, painted about 1400; the Loring shield is among those represented around the walls, while over the south door in the south aisle is a small picture of St Martin of Tours. He is seen on a horse and is using his sword to divide his cloak so that he could share it with a beggar.[1]

There are medieval graffiti on the pillars and a fine piscina in the chancel. It is a welcoming church, has an active congregation and a beautifully maintained churchyard that includes the grave of Enoch, father of author Arnold Bennett.

TODDINGTON

The Church of St George of England

There are many interesting features to be discovered in this beautiful church. There are medieval wall paintings, graffiti and wooden carvings as well as two outstandingly beautiful modern windows by Christopher Webb, which were dedicated in the mid 1940s. The very helpful church guide points out the different features and includes drawings of some of the carved angels from the nave roof.

Each church mentioned on this route has some feature of particular interest.

In Toddington's case it is monuments.* The seven monuments mentioned cover a period of more than two hundred years, on both sides of the Reformation. They are a valuable source of information for students studying the fashion in memorials, the fashion in clothes and changes in the design of armour.

The connection between the lords of the manor and the churches has been mentioned above. Standing looking towards the altar, the early landowners had their own chapel to the right of the nave and the land-owners of the 17th and later centuries, to the left. The so-called 'Cheney' chapel on the right is one of the oldest parts of the church. It was built as a mortuary chapel and dedicated to St James - perhaps one of the family had been on a pilgrimage to the shrine of St James at Compostella?

ROUTE

The main road through Toddington village leads to Bedford, but the route leaves this road by turning left immediately after the pelican crossing near the church. The Red Lion is on your left and the route bears left, heading for the A5 via Tebworth*.

The junction with the A5 can be dangerous and drivers may prefer to take the second left-hand turning after the pelican crossing, immediately opposite the church and join the A5 via Milton Bryan and then Hockliffe crossroads.

1 *Bedfordshire County Council. Discovering Our Past. No 3 April 1986*
Bedfordshire Parish Surveys No 6 - Chalgrave, is a pack containing maps and a most detailed account of the historic landscape and architecture.
* *Much of this section comes from the research of Joseph Hight Blundell*

Toddington Church and Green

Monument, Toddington Church of St George of England

The tomb on the west wall of the chapel is that of Nicholas Pever who died on 17 July 1361 as a result of a severe outbreak of plague. Set in the west wall of the chapel are his son, Thomas and daughter-in-law Margaret (nee Loring). In his will Thomas requested that a priest should 'synge' for him, his wife, parents and all Christian people in the 'Chapel of Seinte Jame in the chirche of Todyngton'. There is a very rare 'parvise' or chaplain's room and chapel on the northern side of the chancel. This may have been the home of the Pever family's private chaplain.

Thomas and Margaret were succeeded by a daughter, whose second husband was John Broughton of Chalgrave. Five generations later, in 1528, an Anne Broughton married Sir Thomas Cheney of Sheppey, in Kent. He was already well placed in the household of Henry VIII and lived on, enjoying royal favour at the courts of Edward VI and Queen Mary. He died in 1559 and is buried in his church on the Isle of Sheppey.

Due to the purchases that Sir Thomas had made, following the dissolution of the monasteries, his son, Henry, inherited large but scattered estates. He decided to make Toddington the centre and had a new 'mansion' built on the Tebworth road, which is opposite the church. Queen Elizabeth visited him there in 1563 and while she was there bestowed a knighthood on him. She returned in 1576.

Having had his mansion house built at Toddington, he chose to be buried in St George's Church. His tomb and damaged statue is the central one on the east wall. To his right is that of his mother Anne (nee Broughton) and on his left his wife, Jane (née Wentworth). It was she who introduced an even more important family to Toddington. She lived on for some years after the death of her husband but having no direct heir of her own invited her great-nephew, Sir Thomas Wentworth and his wife, of Suffolk, to come to live at Toddington. When she died in 1614 he inherited her estates. He went on to hold several posts in local and national government. In 1625 he was Lord Lieutenant of Bedfordshire and the following year he was created Earl of Cleveland. It was this first Thomas Wentworth who ordered the building of the other private chapel in the north transept. It was started in the early 1630s. (It is kept locked but can be visited by appointment.) He and his son (another Thomas) and several of their descendants are buried in the vault underneath this chapel.

The Earl of Cleveland had six children, of which only two survived to have families of their own. Thomas, Lord Wentworth, his son and heir, died before his father so did not inherit the earldom. His surviving daughter Anne married

John, Lord Lovelace. Another daughter, Maria, died aged 18 in 1632. She was the first of the family to be interred in the vault. Despite some damage, her life-sized memorial has survived in the chapel above. It portrays an attractive young lady, seated with a basket of needlework on one side and a needle, in its cushion, on the other. Six verses around the base tell of her goodness and include:

> 'Good to ye poore, to kindred deare
> To servants kind To friendshipp cleare
> To nothing but herselfe severe'

However, the pile of sewing has led to a village folk rhyme:

> The Lady Mary
> Sewed on Sunday
> Pricked her finger
> Died on Monday.

There is a finger missing from her right hand, which rests on the chair. Another legend suggests that the undamaged hand had a protruding finger, from which dripped a (stone?) drop of blood.

On the far side of the chapel is a much-damaged memorial to the above Maria's niece, Henrietta Maria who died in 1686 (see next page). Blundell describes other memorials in the church and brasses, which were once in the church but have passed into private ownership.[1]

Toddington Manor House

Less than $1/2$ mile off the route is the present Toddington Manor built on to one wing of the house built by Thomas Cheney. The house is not open to the public but the beautiful gardens, park, lake and woodland walk are sometimes open during spring and summer.

A survey made in 1719 shows that the house in which the Cheney family entertained Queen Elizabeth and in which the Wentworths entertained King James I was a very great mansion. When assessed for the 17th century Hearth Tax it had forty-five hearths, from which figure we can tell that it was one of the biggest houses in the county. It had three storeys, was built around a courtyard and had two more service wings in addition to a second back courtyard. The rooms, linked by four galleries and tower rooms were described in detail when they were sequestered by parliament in 1644.[2]

1 Blundell, JH. Toddington, its Annals and People
2 BHRS Vol 16 Toddington

The Great Toddington Love Story

The memorial mentioned in the previous page, to Henrietta Maria, Baroness Wentworth records that she died unmarried 'April ye 23rd 1686' but does not mention her great romance.

The Earl of Cleveland and his son, Lord Thomas Wentworth were extremely loyal supporters of King Charles I and went into exile with the future King Charles II. In 1660 they took an active part in the celebrations to welcome him back to England. Then in 1665 Lord Wentworth died, followed two years later by the elderly Earl of Cleveland. Charles II was in no position to financially compensate his supporters but when both his Toddington friends died within a few years of the Restoration, he allowed Lord Wentworth's seven-year-old daughter to take the title Henrietta Maria, Baroness Wentworth. This was the young lady who, when she was about fifteen years old, met and soon afterwards fell in love with the twenty-five-year-old Duke of Monmouth. He was the illegitimate son of King Charles who, at the age of fourteen, had had an arranged marriage with Anne, the eleven-year-old Duchess of Buccleuch. His growing affection for Henrietta was very embarrassing for the girl's mother who hastily took her back from court to Toddington. Lady Wentworth has sometimes been criticised for the events which followed, but what could the poor woman do when, a week or two later, the Duke arrived on her doorstep!

From then on he was a constant visitor to Toddington, but England was going through an unsettled period and trouble was brewing. The heir to the throne, Charles' brother James, was very unpopular because he was a Roman Catholic, while in some quarters Charles himself was also unpopular. Dissatisfied people suggested that the popular Protestant Duke of Monmouth was really legitimate and therefore heir to the throne. Willingly or un-willingly, he was drawn into politics and had a strong following of those who wanted his father to name him heir to the throne. When Charles refused to do this, in 1683 a plan was hatched to kill both the King and his brother, the Duke of York as they travelled near Rye House on their return from Newmarket. Circumstances changed and the attack never took place, but the story leaked out and many of the conspirators were arrested. Suspicion also fell on many other people including William, Lord Russell (of Woburn) who was eventually executed at Lincoln's Inn Fields, although it was accepted in later years that he was not guilty. In 1689 Parliament pronounced that he had been 'wrongly condemned'. The Duke of Monmouth was also implicated and although he was innocent, he was ordered to go into exile. However, he slipped away, and lived quietly at Toddington where both the villagers and the local landowners kept knowledge of his presence from the authorities.

Eventually both the Duke and Lady Henrietta went into exile in Holland, where they were the guests of William of Orange and had a very festive stay. When Charles died and his brother James came to the throne, the fugitives who had escaped from the Rye House plot and other hotheads persuaded the Duke to claim the throne. Whether or not he and Lady Henrietta were truly ambitious or whether the Duke was simply influenced by his friends, he set sail for England and landed at Lyme Regis in June 1685. There he proclaimed himself his father's heir and James a usurper and set out on a long march, gathering supporters as he went, but King James sent troops to scatter the Duke's followers and he soon became a prisoner. He was thirty-six years old when he was executed, Lady Henrietta was not quite twenty-five and when the sad news of his execution reached her, she sailed for England. Already ill by the time she arrived in London, she returned with her mother to live in Toddington. The Duke had been executed on 16th July 1685 and Henrietta died nine months later on 23rd April 1686 - it is said of a broken heart. In some circles her plight received little sympathy as it was thought that she had brought great disgrace to her family. Moves were made to forbid the tolling of the funeral bell, but the village bell-ringers outwitted them.

Henrietta's mother, Lady Philadelphia Wentworth, lived on for a further ten years. Wishing to wipe out any shame still attached to her daughter's memory, she included the following bequest in her will:

'....and to erect a Tomb for my said Daughter in the Room which is over the vault wherein she is interred and to spend in the said Tomb not less than two thousand pounds......'

This was a great deal of money to spend in 1696. Although slightly damaged, this memorial can still be seen today. *

The estate passed from Henrietta to her aunt, Anne Lovelace and gradually to more distant members of the family. In the early 1700s it passed to a different branch of the Wentworth family who had recently revived a much earlier family title, Earls of Strafford. The first Earl was buried at Toddington in 1739. His son William inherited a much-neglected house and estate and, in 1745, instructed that most of the manor house was to be demolished and the remainder to be converted into a house for his estate manager. During the 1760s and 1770s the great Elizabethan house was reduced to the kitchen wing and tower.

* *Pamela Hill has used the historical facts to create a very enjoyable story 'Knock at a Star'.*

Blundell mentions the sale of several of the antiquities, including pieces of wooden carving. Some of these can be seen decorating a wall on the Old White Horse at Hockliffe, one piece being dated 1561.

HOCKLIFFE

ROUTE
When the road meets the junction with the A5, turn carefully to the right, as the route is heading north through Hockliffe, before it eventually turns left for Heath and Reach.

Very little remains of the medieval village that lay to the northwest of the crossroads and has long since been deserted. The Church of St Nicholas still stands on its 'cliff' or small hill but the remains of the manor-house and cottages are deep under a nearby field.

Hockliffe House

Back in the 13th century when the lord of the manor had to provide accommodation for travelling lepers and other sick people, he chose a site on the main road by the southern village boundary. The 'Master' of the Hospital of St John the Baptist was under the jurisdiction of the Bishop of Lincoln. Later the work was placed in the care of Dunstable Priory.

Some years after the Dissolution it became an inn called the Red Lion, but when, in 1815, it was adapted to a private house, the beer-house opposite (then known as 'The Blackbirds') took over the name. Today the building is known as Hockliffe House. This house has a Georgian front but one of the original doorways and walls has survived at the back. After all these centuries, this building has once again become a place of healing, known as Wellsprings.[1]

The Inns

At some date unknown (but probably before 1600) inns were built along the main road and Hockliffe was a recognised resting-place for coaches, private travellers and drovers. The coming of the railways brought an abrupt end to the coaching trade and a more gradual end to the wagons and droving. However several of the important buildings have been saved.

On entering the village from the south, watch out for the pelican crossing and soon after on your right look for the redbrick house with very large, central, black-painted wooden doors. This was once the White Horse Inn and is still decorated with some of the wooden carving from Toddington Manor (see above). The Star, at the crossroads, is now a range of cottages. The central

1 Bowes, P. Wellsprings at Hockliffe House

bedroom window that is out of line with the rest marks the position of the (once) great gateway into the yard. The George and Dragon that was once a very old inn, gable onto the road, has also become cottages. The Red Lion, which has been partially rebuilt, and the completely rebuilt White Hart are still in business.

The Church of St Nicholas
This church, part of which dates back to at least the 14th century, still stands on its small hill or 'cliff'. The earthworks which are all that are left of the manor house, can be seen over the graveyard wall and one can imagine a typical manorial church, built as part of the Lord of the Manor's estate.

St Nicholas is one of the patron saints of travellers and it may well be that the thousands of pilgrims who travelled to and from St Albans and Canterbury, stopped here to pray before continuing on their journeys. The piscina and Easter sepulchre would have already been in use at that time.

Standing as it does, on the borders of South and Mid Bedfordshire, its walls are constructed of both chalk 'clunch', quarried at Totternhoe and ironstone from the Greensand Ridge.

SOULBURY

The Church of All Saints
This church, which is just off the route, is well worth a visit. It has many monuments to the Lovett family of Liscombe Park, including a marble group by Gibbons, dated 1690.

STEWKLEY

St Michael's Church
Just off the route, to the right of the war memorial is what John Betjeman in his 'Guide to English Parish Churches'

ROUTE
Take the second Heath and Reach turn, at the roundabout, this is before the A5 reaches Little Brickhill. The route is now heading for Great Brickhill. (Watch for the signs on the right to Stockgrove Country Park and drive down Brickhill Road. Once past the park gates, the road swings left, becomes very narrow and winding.) The route passes through beautiful countryside, but the roads should be used with care. At the 30mph sign, prepare to turn left for Soulbury, and do this as soon as you see the Old Red Lion in front of you.. After some distance, the Three Locks Golf Club and then the public house are on your right.

The route continues over a busy, staggered crossroads, heading towards Soulbury, Stewkley and Wing and then, on the brow of the hill, just before reaching Soulbury church, turns right towards Stewkley (keep going if visiting Soulbury church). Having turned right, continue to the T-junction in the middle of Stewkley village (the church is to the right). The route then swings to the left of the war memorial and follows the signposts towards Wing. At the T-junction with the A418, the route turns right towards Aylesbury and goes into the village. (The traffic through the village is very fast-moving, so if visiting All Saints' Church, be prepared to turn right down Church Road, which is nearly opposite The Cock public house.)

describes as 'A very fine Norman Church'.* It is one of the few places in the county where one can see a Norman church without too many later alterations. During the Norman period the village was divided between four landowners and no subsequent landlord has spoilt the original architecture. It was built about 1150 of local iron limestone mixed with limestone rubble and the great chancel arch has a span of 14 feet. It has an unusual frieze with thirty-seven small carvings and in the sanctuary the original ribs can be seen with lozenge (type of diamond) decoration. The architect, GE Street, restored the church in 1862 without spoiling the original decoration.

WING

Although it is easy to see that this village has one of the most architecturally important churches in this part of England, it is not so easy to explain why it should be here.

The Castle

There is a so-called 'castle mound' in the village but no evidence of a residential castle. However, before the Norman Conquest, Wing was held by a tenant of King Harold. King William's officials added it to the vast estates of the Count of Mortain, of Berkhamsted Castle; the Count held thirty-eight pieces of land in Buckinghamshire, most of which was let to tenants, but Wing was kept for his own use. It had an exceptionally high population; seventy-one families on approximately six hundred acres compared with thirty-six, thirty-two and forty-five families on estates on the king's much larger holdings at Aylesbury, Wendover and Risborough. Markets do not seem to have been recorded in Buckinghamshire but there had been no drop in value, despite fifteen missing plough teams and no mention of

* Simon Jenkins selected it as one of his rare 3 star churches and described it as 'Norman spectacular'

Hockliffe Church with Earthworks

Wing Church

other forms of employment. It therefore seems likely that, as at Houghton Regis, unlicensed trading was taking place.

All Saints Church

No church is mentioned in the Domesday Book as presumably it owned no taxable land, nor is there any reference to a Norman priest.* In 1066 'a man of God' held a small piece of land at nearby Soulbury but in 1086, the nearest priest was some distance away at Wingrave.[1]

However, there is both documentary and visual evidence to prove that there was a stone-built church here long before the coming of the Normans. It still has its early Saxon apse and crypt but it is not known when they were built. These seven-sided 'polygonal' apses are thought to have first been used when the Romans became Christian. They used the familiar design of the basilica, but placed the altar in the central position, which, in a law-court, would have been occupied by the special chair for the judge.

Miranda Hyslop, summing up finds from the two Saxon cemeteries excavated at nearby Leighton Buzzard, suggested that the Saxon features were possibly built, before 661, by Agilbert, Bishop of the West Saxons or between 666 and 669, by Bishop Wilfred who was a great supporter of the Roman style of worship.[2] John Morris, writing about Saxon churches of the mid 7th century, describes Brixworth Church, near Northampton, which was a principal royal centre, as one which: 'an Italian architect imposed upon the midland countryside a large basilica of the type most familiar at Ravenna....'
He points out that although Brixworth is unique, a similar church was probably built at Wing.[3]

A Royal Centre

Whether Wing was a royal centre in the 7th century is not known but it probably was by the 10th century, when the church was enlarged or rebuilt. A royal lady called Aelfgifu, who made her will in 975, bequeathed Wing to her brother-in-law, King Edgar. She refers to her shrine and to the relics, which she kept at Wing - presumably in the church. This village may have been the headquarters of her scattered estates and the place where she chose to spend her retirement.

* At Studham where the known church did not show up (not having any taxable land), a priest was living on the neighbouring manor. 1 Morris, J. Domesday Book - Buckinghamshire. 2 Hyslop, M. 1963 Archaeological Journal CXX. In doing this she refers to EDC Jackson and EGM Fletcher, the archaeologists who excavated at Wing - see Journal of British Archaeology 1962. 3 Morris, J. The Age of Arthur

It has been difficult to accurately identify this Elgiva because King Edgar had 3 close relatives of the same name. However on St Elgiva's Day (18th May) 1999, Arnold H.J. Baines published a detailed piece of research Lady Elgiva, Her Life and Times, which was produced for the Chess Valley Archaeological and Historical Society. This clearly identifies Elgiva of Wing as King Edgar's sister-in-law.* Her bequest also included land at Linslade, Marsworth and other places in Buckinghamshire. In 966, King Edgar (who reigned as king of all England from 959 to 975) gave Lhincgelade [Linslade], '..... in return for her most devoted obedience', to a 'certain noble matron' who was related to him by 'affinity'. She was called by 'the graceful name Aelfgifu' and was permitted to bequeath it to whomsoever she chose.

ROUTE

The route continues right through Wing but does not bear right along the main road; it goes straight on into the quieter, Park Gate Road, passing through open fields and then following a tree-lined road into Mentmore. Leave the impressive Mentmore House on your right and be prepared to turn left at the village green, as from this point. the route is heading back towards Leighton Buzzard by turning left and following the signs via Linslade.

This was a troubled period in English history, King Edgar and his elder brother King Edwy were the sons of King Edmund who, in 946, was murdered when he was only twenty-four years old. Edwy was king after Edmund's brother Edred. There are several versions of the story below but with or without permission from her mother, Edwy had married a girl to whom he was closely related. The coronation took place, but Edwy then offended the Archbishop by leaving the ceremony with his young bride, 'Aelfgilue' without asking his permission to withdraw.

Pressure was brought to bear on the young couple to separate and eventually their marriage was dissolved. King Edwy continued to offend both the church and secular leaders and within a year his brother Edgar had been asked to take over some of Edwy's royal duties. The lady who had been given Linslade because she had displayed 'devoted obedience' to King Edgar could be the same Elgiva whose prestigious marriage to Edgar's brother had been dissolved, and who had impressed Edgar with her 'devoted obedience'. Edwy died in 959 and when she thought her own end was near, Elgiva may have divided her property between the church and her royal brother-in-law.

Regardless of its history, this is a particularly attractive and interesting church to visit.

* I am grateful to June Masters for pointing out this important booklet.

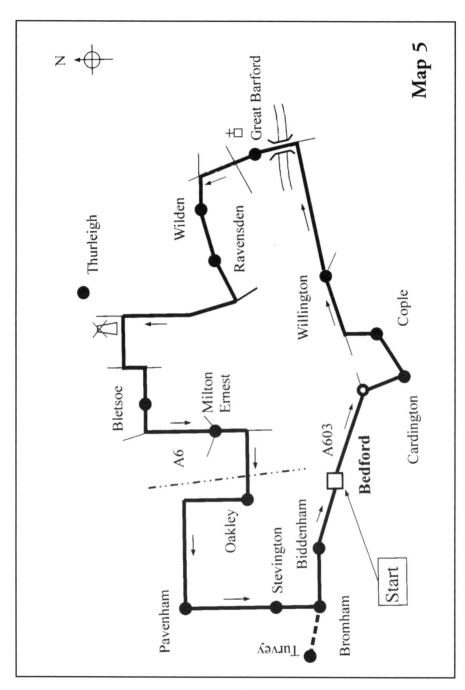

Map 5

134

CHAPTER 5 • *ROUTE 5*

North Bedfordshire Villages

**Bedford • Cardington • Cople • Willington
Great Barford • Wilden • Ravensden
(Thurleigh) • Bletsoe • Milton Ernest • Oakley
Stevington (spur to Turvey) • Bromham • Biddenham • Bedford**

Introduction

This Route is approximately 40 miles long; it uses good, well-surfaced roads and can be separated into two parts. It leaves Bedford and heads east, south of the River Ouse and then crosses Great Barford Bridge. From there it heads west until it is nearly back to Bedford. Having by-passed the town and still north of the river, it heads west and crosses again at Bromham. The last few miles are once again south of the river. In addition to the second loop, there is an optional spur to Turvey.

The Historical Background is based on the history of Bedford Castle and its sheriffs and includes the exciting siege that led to its destruction.

The early sheriffs carried a great deal of responsibility for the administration and defence of their counties. They therefore needed an income to support their castle and they also had to support a large number of knights.

The Historical Highlights picks out villages that the sheriff kept to produce food for the castle or which he let out to his knights. These villages have been selected because they are particularly attractive. They mainly have some feature that is open to the public eg the dovecote at Willington (by appointment through the National Trust) and Bromham Mill or, which can be seen from the road eg Cardington Cross and airship hangers.

Another feature of this section is that it is packed with stories: the story behind the brasses in Cople Church, the building of the new road from Barford Bridge to the Great North Road, the memorials to the 306 Bombardment Group on Keysoe Road and to the Mordaunt family in Turvey Church, the Civil War adventures of the Luke family of Cople and the Dyve family of Bromham - and many more.

Historical Background

At the start of the last millennium, far from being part of a United Kingdom, England itself was made up of a group of petty kingdoms. In the 8th century, King Offa came some way towards becoming king of all England but the raids, later invasion, by the Danes brought this to an end. When King Canute died in 1035, there was an uneasy peace and an attempt was being made to turn England into an economically successful country. For administrative reasons, it was divided into shires (counties), each one in the care of a shire-reeve (sheriff). However, these men were not just administrators; they represented law and order, civil defence and the nucleus of the country's army. Each one, with his family and a retinue of knights, lived in a castle; usually in a strategic position on a river.

The first reference to the name 'Bedford' occurs in the Anglo-Saxon chronicles for the year 918; this was before the Saxons and Danes had united to live and work together. At that time, the Danes were using Bedford as a regional headquarters and were being expelled by the Saxons. There was reference to two castles but little more is heard about the one on the south bank. Following more raids in 1011, a list was made of shires which had been overrun by the Danes and this included Bedfordshire.

By 1066, Bedfordshire had become surprisingly prosperous; the sheriff was assisted by a team of civil administrators, based on the districts called 'hundreds'. The bishop for the region had his see at Dorchester on Thames and his representative, the archdeacon, then, or soon afterwards, had his headquarters at Bedford.

The Saxon sheriff, Godric, was killed at the Battle of Hastings and Bishop Wulfwy died c1080. The Saxon landowners who survived the battle were dispossessed and it has been suggested that the 96% (approximate) Saxon population were organized by 4% resident Normans.[1]

The great tax assessment ordered by William I, in 1085, and presented to him in 1086, can be used in many ways to draw a picture of life in Bedfordshire. From an administrative point of view, we can identify that the sheriff held land in all parts of Bedfordshire. Some of this he kept in his own hands to provide food for the castle or to be sold and provide income; other pieces he let to support his family, senior officers and other dependents. Minor officials were also supported with land.

1 Godber, J. The History of Bedfordshire

The first Norman sheriff, Ralph Tallboys, had died before 1086 but his widow, Azelina, held Hockliffe and eleven other farms, mainly in Mid Bedfordshire. His nephew, Ranulph, brother of Ilger, held 600 acres in Pavenham but Ralph's position as sheriff, his castle and his vast, scattered estates went to his daughter's husband, Hugh de Beauchamp. The senior officers, Norman and Flemish, plus those people who had given William ships, money and/or soldiers to help him fight for his claim to the English throne, all had to be rewarded.

However, it was the policy of King William that no one man, not even his own half-brothers, should build up an estate big enough to challenge him for the throne. Each of the larger beneficiaries chose one estate on which they would establish their headquarters but would also have land in several other counties. Robert of Tosny, who held land in Oakley, Turvey and Studham, plus twelve other counties, had his main castle at Belvoir (Leicestershire). Judith, William's niece, held a great deal of land in Bedfordshire and also had land in nine other counties; her castle was at Fotheringhay (Hunts). Apart from the sheriff, two landowners built their castles in Bedfordshire. A family of Flemings held land in Bedfordshire and in three other nearby counties. Walter built his castle on the high land at Odell. Nigel of Aubigny had land in four counties, including a very large estate in Mid Bedfordshire. He built a castle at Cainhoe, near Clophill.

The Domesday Record

During 1085-6, clerks went all over England collecting material to make up the great report. Spot checks were made to ensure that it was accurate and then the whole collection was edited and arranged, county by county, under the names of the landowners. Amazingly, it was commissioned at Christmas 1085, and was nearly complete by the following summer.

Out of the thousands of entries, one of the few to be lost was Bedford itself. However, we know that the sheriff owned forty scattered manors; from Linslade across to Stotfold and from Risely down to Streatley. The route on which this chapter is based, links many of these villages, around Bedford. It could be called 'Beautiful Bedfordshire Villages', because each has been chosen because it is attractive and has historical features for us to see today.

Bedford Castle and The Beauchamp Family

Although the Beauchamp estates did not always pass directly from father to son, it was Miles de Beauchamp, grandson of Hugh, who first needed retainers to defend his right to the castle.

With the permission of the king, the large estates owned by Hugh de Beauchamp automatically passed to his heir but the position of sheriff and the charge of Bedford Castle was the gift of the king. The Beauchamp family considered that the charge of the castle should also pass with their barony. It appears that after Hugh's death, sometime early in the 12th century, his elder son, Simon, inherited his estates and was confirmed as constable of the castle and that when Simon died, sometime before 1136, the estates and the castle passed to Miles, son of Simon's younger brother. However, the following year Stephen was in great need of loyal and powerful friends and broke with tradition. Wishing both to help and to obligate the powerful Earl of Leicester, he arranged a marriage and income for the earl's younger and landless brother, known as Hugh le Poer (or Poor), with the even younger daughter of the dead Simon de Beauchamp, cousin of Simon's heir, Miles. King Stephen then notified Miles that he had created Hugh le Poer Earl of Bedford and that he wished Miles to surrender the castle to his cousin by marriage. Miles was greatly concerned fearing that his inheritance might be at risk and refused to hand it over.

The Castle is Besieged

Opinions differ as to where Stephen spent the great court festival of Christmas 1137. Worthington Smith, the Dunstable antiquarian, suggests that he was at Kingsbury, his royal residence in that town. Some time over the Christmas period, Stephen sent a final message to Miles and then marched his soldiers to Bedford where he set up a siege. The contemporary writer, Henry of Huntingdon, complains that Stephen set the siege on Christmas Eve and completely ignored the holy season. Miles and his brother, Payne, resisted the siege, having stocked all the available store sheds with food and produce, stolen from the townspeople of Bedford. Although Stephen had to take some soldiers away to settle another uprising, the main part of his army stayed in place, completely isolating the castle, for five weeks. Battering rams and armaments failed to take the castle but eventually, the stores ran out. Stephen's brother, Henry, Bishop of Winchester, arrived in Bedford and persuaded them to surrender and Hugh le Poer then became constable of the castle.

The Beauchamp family did eventually get it back but trouble started again when Stephen and his cousin, Matilda, were in dispute for the throne. Fighting took place in different places around the country; William de Beauchamp was captured and Stephen gave the castle to his mercenary officer, Falkes de Breauté. The subsequent events have led modern historians to refer to him as 'The Robber Baron'.

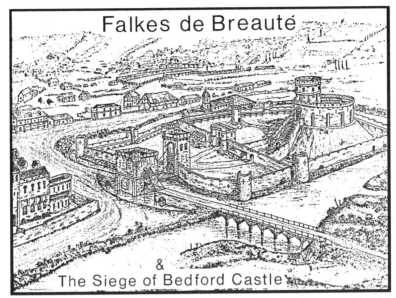

Model of Bedford Castle, made by Margaret Greenshields for Bedford Museum (B.T.C.)

The River Ouse Bedford

The fighting went on for several years but even when Matilda was victorious, she was so unpopular that she was forced to leave the country and Stephen remained king.[1]

The Future King Henry II

However, on or about 6 January 1153, Duke Henry, Matilda's son, landed in England to fight for the throne on his own behalf. He and his army marched from one of Stephen's strongholds to another, consistently winning people to his side. He did not stop to besiege Stephen's supporters, who were sheltering in Bedford Castle but set fire to the town and continued on his way to Wallingford in Berkshire. Both Henry and Stephen were anxious to undertake a decisive battle but their senior advisors persuaded them that no good could come of a battle where 'Kinsman was pitted against Kinsman' and whoever won, England would be left in great distress and bitterness, so a truce was arranged. The two armies continued to move about the country until November 1153, when at long last first a verbal, then a written agreement was worked out. During his lifetime, Stephen should remain King of England, Duke Henry would be his heir. Stephen died less than twelve months later and King Henry II was crowned in Westminster Abbey on 19 December 1154. Bedford Castle was once more restored to Payne de Beauchamp and responsibility for the castle stayed with the Beauchamp family until, some years later, when Payne's grandson once again had to fight for his inheritance.

King John and the Magna Carta

In the early 13th century, King John came to the throne, following the neglect of the country by his brother, Richard. During the first few years of his reign, he alienated members of the church, the law and the landowners. Eventually the barons (great landowners) asked John to sign a long list of points relating to the running of the country, but he refused. Arbitration proved useless and eventually, the barons raised an army to enforce their wishes.

The Beauchamp Family and the Magna Carta

From c1206 William Beauchamp was in control of Bedford Castle and his support for Magna Carta was very important; if he gave a lead, most of the other Bedfordshire landowners would follow.

1 Evans, V. Folk

During the years leading up to the signing of the Magna Carta there were numerous meetings, dispatches and appointments made and broken until, in desperation, the northern barons met at Stamford (Lincs), where they were joined by William Beauchamp. Together they marched to Northampton, where King John had promised to meet them. When he failed to appear, they marched on to Bedford Castle and as there was still no message from the king, marched towards Windsor, where he was staying. They camped at Brackley (Berks), where they were met by the archbishop and William, Marshall of England, and who took their charter to the king but John refused to accept it. So the barons raised a small army and laid siege to Northampton Castle. John's reply to this was to call for a truce and to suggest a court of arbitration, under a chairman, appointed by the pope. The barons were tired of pointless discussion and broken promises, so they marched on and successfully took London. Eventually in June 1215, they met in a field by the River Thames, called 'Runnymede' and after yet more discussion, King John signed a list of 63 articles.

For a few months, all went well but a letter from the pope, in September, described the charter as 'unlawful' and 'unjust' and declared it 'null and void' because, he wrote, the seal had been obtained by force. The barons realised that the charter no longer held and armed themselves against the king. Soon, groups of soldiers were moving about the country and by the end of November, mercenary John's officer, Falkes de Breauté, brought an army to Bedford and stormed the castle. William de Beauchamp escaped but on 2 December, the castle fell and Falkes was told to repair and strengthen it. His first local outrage was to take down walls of St Paul's and St Cuthbert's Churches and use the stone for the castle. Then he rode to St Albans and, on 18 December met King John at the abbey to discuss strategy; he then went on to defend London whilst John and his soldiers marched north to rally support.

Falkes de Breauté in the Reign of King John

King John employed numerous mercenary soldiers but Falkes was a professional soldier, who had settled in England and had become one of John's most trusted senior officers. In December 1215, he had taken Bedford Castle, in the name of the king and shortly afterwards, he was put in charge of it and held it for the next nine years. He continued to support King John throughout the war.

The struggle continued throughout 1216 until, during an October visit to Newark, at the age of forty-nine, John died quite suddenly from dysentery. Contemporary writers blamed his illness on a surfeit of peaches and new cider.

Henry III is Crowned

His son, Henry, was only nine years old and the barons knew that England would be administered by the respected William Marshall, so the fighting ended but Falkes de Breauté was still in possession of William de Beauchamp's castle and estates.

Falkes de Breauté in the Reign of King Henry III

Although most of the people were free to recover from the troubled years, the people of Bedfordshire were having an even more difficult time due to the activities of Falkes, his brother William and their officers.

While Falkes was in charge of William de Beauchamp's estates, he did great damage and sold off many of the livestock. When he needed to repair Bedford Castle, he not only took stone from the churches but also helped himself to timber from the woodland owned by Warden Abbey. In the struggle that followed a monk was killed and thirty other men, who tried to prevent the theft, were dragged through the mud and imprisoned in Bedford Castle.

Falkes de Breauté Causes Trouble in Luton

William Marshall junior had inherited the manor of Luton during the troubled period leading up to the struggle for Magna Carta. He actively supported the barons and so, when his young wife died in 1216, King John gave his estates to Falkes de Breauté. Falkes had a castle built between St Mary's Church and the River Lea. The river was diverted to make the moat, water mills were damaged and many people either lost their homes or had their ground floors flooded. His soldiers robbed the market stalls and terrified people for miles around.

Falkes de Breauté is Charged in Court

For many years Falkes had been a loyal and brave soldier and despite all the complaints, Henry was slow to interfere. The people of Luton had several times taken him to court but each time he failed to appear. When, in July 1224, they took their grievances to the king's judges, meeting at Dunstable Priory, Falkes knew they would have to find him guilty and so he again failed to attend.[1] The three judges arrived and thirty-two people from Luton made their claims, mainly of stolen land eg Roger de Ho accused Falkes of taking thirty acres from his father. Falkes was found guilty on all charges, heavily fined and it was recommended that he should be outlawed.

1 BHRS Vol 9

Kidnap at Dunstable

Falkes was away when his brother, William, and a group of soldiers, rode out from Bedford Castle to kidnap the judges! News reached Dunstable in time for them to escape in different directions; two of them got away but Henry de Brayboc rode straight into a trap and was carried off to Bedford Castle. His wife, Christiana, and her escort rode to Northampton to beg the king for help and this time Falkes had gone too far; when summoned to attend the king he escaped to the estates of his friend, the Earl of Chester, on the Welsh border. Henry sent for Falkes and when he realised that he had slipped away, he issued orders that Bedford Castle should be surrounded and began to plan for a major siege. Without waiting to finalise his plans, he set off southwards with his church leaders, chief justice and the barons who were with him. No doubt William de Beauchamp was consulted about strategic points concerning the castle's defence, although his presence at Northampton is not recorded. Henry was only sixteen years old but he had grown up with soldiers and sieges were a familiar form of warfare to him. He and his advisors made plans as they rode along and by the time that they stopped for the night at Newport Pagnall, Henry was ready to send off messages in all directions. These 'messages' were royal commands and were to be obeyed 'in haste' or 'without delay'.

The Siege of Bedford Castle

A siege was a slow operation and Henry prepared for a long wait; a royal tent was to be sent from London and thirty casks of wine. The cooks might be able to use locally produced food, supplemented with almonds, spice and ginger from the royal stillroom, but the wine that was to be provided from Northampton might not be good enough for use in the royal tent! Although he had sent for his sporting dogs, this was not going to be a country picnic where the attackers sat feasting until those in the castle starved; Brayboc and the other prisoners must be quickly released. The whole siege plan was prepared as they rode; many of the weapons were too big to transport, so their construction was allowed for on site. From Newport, messages were sent out ordering the local sheriffs to provide hides for making slings and cords and cables to work the engines; the Sheriff of London was to send wax to grease the cords, the monks at Newnham (near Bedford) were to provide 'rawstone' to be made into shot. The Sheriff of Bedfordshire was to send for quarrymen and masons (from Totternhoe?) to come with their tools to work the stone into shot. Smaller weapons could be transported, so at the Tower of London, smiths were to work day and night making crossbows for immediate use and others were to be transported from distant Corfe Castle. The waxed cords and hides were used to make slings and to 'throw' large blocks of stone by using a winch. The account of the battle, in the Dunstable Priory annals, describes the use of mangonells. These had to be set up some distance from the castle and to the horror of the local people, the church leaders stood by and allowed the engineers take down the towers of St Paul's and St Cuthbert's churches.

The letters went out from Newport on Thursday 20 June; at Bedford, on three successive days, a group of military and church leaders, including the Prior of Newnham, had demanded, in the king's name, the surrender of the castle. William de Breauté had defied them, saying that it was his brother's castle and that the king could not demand entry; when messengers told Henry this, he swore to hang them all! The Archbishop of Canterbury arrived and on 20 June, read the solemn service of ex-communication on all that held the castle against the king. On 21 June, the king himself arrived and the siege had officially begun. When, many weeks later, it was decided to make a major attack, 'the men of Dunstable', who had suffered attacks from Falkes and his soldiers and suffered the indignity of the kidnap, were allowed (a doubtful honour) to lead the attack. Their account is so clear that I now include a new translation by Mrs Elizabeth North.

'Meanwhile, when the destruction of the castle was imminent and the Bishop of Chester, the king's messenger, mediated, the earl returned to the king's court and Falkes to Northampton. While he was there, with the king's safe conduct and Martin of Pateshull and the Archdeacon of Bedford were conducting peace negotiations between him and the king, the castle was captured in this way. On the east there was one petrary and two mangonells that attacked the tower every day. On the west side, there were two mangonells that battered the old tower. And there was one mangonell on the south and one on the north, which made two entrances in the walls nearest them. Besides these, there were two wooden towers made by a carpenter, raised above the top of the tower and castle for the use of the crossbowmen and spies. In addition to these, there were several engines in which both crossbowmen and slingers hid in ambush. In addition, there was a siege-engine, called 'The Cat', beneath which underground diggers, called 'miners', could go in and out while they undermined the walls of the tower and castle. However, the castle was taken in four assaults. In the first, the barbican was captured, where four or five outsiders were killed. In the second, the outer bailey was captured, where several were killed and our men acquired horses with harness, breastplates, crossbows, oxen, bacon and live pigs and countless other plunder.

However, they burnt the outhouses with the corn and hay that were inside. In the third assault, a wall near the old keep fell because of the action of miners and our men entered there and seized the inner bailey, in face of great danger. In this occupation many of our men perished. Ten of our men, too, wishing to enter the keep, were shut in and held by the enemy. But at the fourth assault, on the Eve of Assumption, about the time of vespers, miners set fire to the keep so that smoke poured into the room in the keep where the enemy were; the keep cracked with the result that fissures appeared in its side. Then since the enemy despaired of their safety, Falkes' wife and all the women with her, and Henry, the king's Justiciar, with the other knights who had previously been imprisoned, were allowed to leave safe and sound and the enemy subjected themselves to the king's commands, hoisting his standard at the top of the keep, thus they remained under royal guard in the keep that night. But the following morning they were brought before the king's tribunal and absolved from ex-communication by the bishops; more than eighty were hanged on the instructions of the king and Justiciar.

After these events, Falkes was taken to Bedford with a small escort. His men were absolved but he remained under pain of punishment until he should restore to the king the castle of Plympton, the castle of Stokes-Curci, gold and silver vessels and the money that he had, thus he was brought to London. Afterwards, Falkes was absolved in London and because he had taken the cross, he was allowed to leave for Rome.'

Meanwhile the sheriff was ordered to destroy the keep and outer bailey, but to leave the inner bailey for William de Beauchamp to live in. The stone was granted to the canons of Newnham and Cauldwell and to the churches damaged.

After the Siege

William Beauchamp was allowed to build a house on the site but not a castle; he lived on for over thirty-five years. In 1234 he was appointed Baron of the Exchequer and was Sheriff of Bedfordshire and Buckinghamshire in 1235 and 1236. He did not die until 1260 but in 1257, when he was at least seventy years old, he passed the Barony of Bedford to his second son, another William.

The Last Beauchamps of Bedford

This second William died within five years of receiving the title, leaving a brother, John, who was too young to inherit and it was not until May 1265 that he legally received his inheritance. Three months later, he was killed in the Battle of Evesham, fighting with Simon de Montfort, who was also killed. John was still a young man and this was his first battle. 'Who' said the chronicler at St Albans Abbey 'could keep from tears at the death of John de Beauchamp'. The victory had been won by the skill of the young Prince Edward (later Edward I) and he was given the Beauchamp lands.

When John Beauchamp died, there was still a niece of his living - Simon's daughter, Joan. When her father died in 1256, Henry III had placed her under the guardianship of William de Clare. The poor young lady was passed from one wealthy and influential person to another. Marriages were arranged for her and cancelled and she died unmarried c1266.

Eventually, the Beauchamp land was divided between her female relatives. The site of the castle, still apparently in a derelict condition, passed to a distant relation and the distinguished name of Beauchamp was no longer connected with Bedford. The earthworks connected with the castle can be seen between the Embankment and the Bedford Museum, which stands in Castle Lane. A conjectural model of the castle can be seen in the museum.

The Role of Sheriff in Later Centuries

The destruction of the castle did not end the shrievalty but it soon became an annual, not hereditary, position. Different landowners carried out the administrative and legal duties from their own houses, supported by a team of magistrates who lived in different parts of the county. Because of this, it was no longer necessary for the sheriff to own such a scattered estate. Although for several centuries they were still responsible for providing and training soldiers for the king, the officers were other local landowners living on their own estates.

A sheriff (who may be either a country landowner or a businessman) is still appointed each year. Once the County Council was formed in 1881, the duties became more traditional than administrative or legislative and the sheriff is no longer expected to produce a private army!

CARDINGTON

The clerk who wrote out the Domesday entries spelt this name - Chernetone, which has been interpreted as 'Caerda's Farm; 'Caerda' being an early Saxon settler. By 1066, this was a very valuable estate of around 1200 acres. The sheriff, Hugh de Beauchamp, kept $^2/_3$ of it for himself. There was enough deciduous woodland to feed well over a hundred pigs and the cereals and hay produced on the farm could be sent back to the castle, via the river. In addition there was a watermill, an eel fishery and an enclosed hunting park for the use of the sheriff and his friends.

The remaining 400 acres had been allotted to 'Countess Judith'. She was a niece of King William and widow of the Earl of Huntingdon. Her main castle was at Fotheringhay, but she had land in many counties; her Cardington land was leased to a man known as Hugh.

There is very little woodland left in Cardington today and the last watermill was dismantled in 1926, but there are still several arable farms. Manor Farm, at the south of the parish, may represent the smaller, medieval manor. However, most of what can be seen in Cardington today is the result of changes made in the 18th century. The initials 'SW' (Samuel Whitbread) and 'JH' (John Howard) can be seen on several of the buildings. From the mid 18th century the Whitbread family bought an increasing amount of property and land in Cardington and contributed generously to the church, school and the rebuilding of cottages.

Another famous resident and landowner was the prison reformer John Howard. He and his family also took a great deal of interest in the wellbeing of the village and villagers. The workhouse and almshouses that they supported still stand today but are now used as cottages. A Parish cottage and hall built by the daughters of Samuel Whitbread, c1861, as

ROUTE
The route leaves Bedford by going south along the High Street and over the bridge; it passes both St Mary's and St John's churches before approaching the first of a series of roundabouts. Turn left onto the A603 towards Sandy and continue on this road until you see the bridge which carries the Southern Bedford bypass over the road. As you approach it, you will just see, on the further side, the Cardington Cross, which stands on the right-hand side. As you drive under the bridge, remain on the round-about and be prepared to turn onto the road leading to Cardington.

ROUTE
(The route will pass
through the village
and turn left at the
public house.)
Drive into the village
and, at the T-junction,
with the Kings Arms
on your left, turn left
towards Cople.

an industrial school where village girls could be taught the skills needed for domestic service. These also stand, but have been adapted into a private house and parish hall.

An enquiry into the availability of education in 1818, recorded that at Cardington there was a school for twenty-four children 'maintained by the principal inhabitant'. Other enquiries recorded six plait or lace schools and several Sunday schools. The Nonconformist chapels supported most of the latter. In 1884, the inspector appointed by the Church of England found that the master at the day school was 'sadly deficient in temper and skill'[1]. Soon after this Mr William Whitbread took a firm hand and in 1848, a permanent 'Parish' school was put up. This was opened in 1848 and was affiliated to the British Society. This meant that it was one of Bedfordshire's few village schools where the religious education was accepted by Nonconformist parents. Designed by Joseph Lancaster, if well run, this system provided excellent general education and the religious studies were bible-based, not prayer-book.

A Walk Around the Village

The book by John Wood, 'Cardington and Eastcotts' is light enough to carry as one walks around the village.[2] This not only contains a detailed history of the village, but also includes a brief description and history of each building. There is information about the Church of St Mary the Virgin, the barns at Fenlake, the distant airship hangars (which were built or enlarged in 1926-28) and Cardington's famous crosses.

Church Lane (which is not suitable for cars), contains Howard's House and other attractive buildings, such as cottages which were once the Howard Almshouses. These, and other buildings, mark the interest of both the Howard and the Whitbread families. One plaque notes that they were built by 'JH' in 1762 and the other that they were restored by 'SHW' in 1928; note the clay tile roof. The almshouses provided by the Whitbread family are on the Green.

The Church of St Mary was rebuilt, except for the chancel, at the end of the 19th century. The chancel is thought to date from around 1500 and Samuel Whitbread instructed Diocesan Architect, George Highton, to rebuild the

1 Bushby, D. The Bedfordshire Schoolchild BHRS Vol 67.
2 In the series 'Bedfordshire Parish Surveys'. Published by Beds County Council

148

rest in the style of a 15th century church. Next to the church is The King's Arms. There has been an alehouse on this site for several centuries, but the present building was mainly constructed in 1783.

At this stage you are facing a T-junction. If you walk along to the right, you can see several other interesting buildings, such as the original day and industrial schools (see above).

If you turn left towards Cople, the buildings at the Cardington end have 'JH', 'SW' or both, but as you move into Cople, the cottages have a crown and a 'B' (standing for the Duke of Bedford), as this was once a village connected with the Woburn estate.

The Airship Hangars

These can be seen to the southeast of the village. They are over 800 feet long, nearly 180 feet high and over 270 feet in overall width. The main doors which weigh 940 tons, are mounted on rails and are operated by electric motors.[1]

By the end of the 1920s, when the hangars housed the R100 and the R101, which had been built at Cardington, the centre appeared to have an important future. However, in 1930, the R101 crashed in France and all but six of the fifty-four passengers and crew were killed. Since then, the hangars have been used for various purposes.

The R101 Memorial

Standing prominently in the churchyard opposite the church, is a cross mounted on the memorial to the disastrous event of October 3rd 1930. It was designed by local architect, Sir Albert Richardson.

Cardington Crosses

The original cross, which stood near the main Sandy Road, was probably used as a shrine, where travellers could pause and pray; after the Reformation, it became a landmark. In 1778, a new village road was constructed and eight years later, Samuel Whitbread paid to have a cross built at the new road junction. It was only forty-one years later that William Henry Whitbread paid sculptor Sir Frances Chantey to design a completely new cross. This remains unchanged but when recent major road works took place, the cross was removed for safety and re-sited in a more suitable position.

1 Cox, A. Odd and Unusual Bedfordshire

ROUTE

The route then continues to the end of the road where All Saints Church is on the left. At the T-junction, the route turns left up Willington Road to rejoin the A603; at this junction, turn carefully to the right.

COPLE

Hugh Beauchamp's predecessor, Ralph Tallboys, was originally allotted a very valuable manor at Ware in Hertfordshire. It may be because, as part of his responsibility as sheriff, he had to provide for a number of knights, that he exchanged Ware for: just over 1000 acres at Cople, just under 1000 acres at Salph (Renhold) and about 750 acres at Goldington. In this way he managed to spread his interest in North Bedfordshire. He kept Salph for himself and with the other two was able to provide ten small tenancies. Six of these were in Cople; one of about 60 acres went to Roger, the priest, which suggests that there was an early church in the area. He also supplied land to support a priest at Great Barford; they may have been chaplains at the castle.

The Countess Judith also had a very small parcel of land in Cople, farmed by her tenant, Hugh and over the centuries, several well-known families were connected with this village, the most famous being the Lukes of Wood End.

The Luke Family of Wood End

Nicholas, son of Walter and Anne Luke, was a Commissioner for the Peace during the reign of Queen Elizabeth and became High Sheriff of Bedfordshire. His grandson, Nicholas (2) married Margaret St John, from the senior Bedfordshire family. Nicholas and Margaret had died long before the Civil War but both their son and grandson worked with their St John relatives to support parliament.

Sir Oliver Luke

Sir Oliver was one of a large number of respected Bedfordshire landowners, who wanted to raise the standards of the Established Church. He regularly represented either Bedfordshire or Bedford Borough in parliament. In the years leading up to the Civil War, he was a militant leader amongst the group who were working for the freedom of parliament. It was Sir Oliver Luke who, on 17 June 1642, was ordered to arrest Sir Lewis Dyve (see Bromham). In 1643, the family raised a regiment of dragoons, but Sir Oliver was wounded and took no further part in the fighting, giving his support to parliament by helping to raise money, food and supplies.

Sir Samuel Luke

At the so-called 'Long Parliament', which started in 1640, Sir Oliver Luke represented Bedfordshire and his son, Sir Samuel, represented Bedford. At the opening Battle of Edgehill, in October 1642, he commanded a troop of horse, which was dreadfully cut about by the Royalist attack. It was in the following year, with his own regiment of dragoons, that he took an active part in the Battle of Newbury; once again he was the centre of the fighting. A month later, the Royalist soldiers were driven out of the garrison at Newport Pagnall and by the end of the year, as Colonel Sir Samuel Luke, he became Governor. He remained there for the next eighteen months and when he left Newport Pagnall, after the successful Battle of Naseby, he returned to Cople and the quiet and peaceful pastimes of gardening and estate management.

Some Important Brasses in All Saints Church

Neither Sir Oliver nor Sir Samuel Luke had a good relationship with the vicar of All Saints Church. The Rev John Gwin,who was not appointed by the Luke family, was a supporter of Archbishop Laud and the strict branch of the Church of England. They made an excuse, involving the difficult road between themselves and the village to get permission to attend Cardington Church. However, there is a tomb chest in All Saints Church with a back panel, which includes kneeling brass figures of some earlier members of the family - Sir Walter Luke, a judge of the King's Bench, and his wife. He was buried there in 1544 and his wife, Anne Launcelyn, in 1538. She had been one of the nurses who helped to look after the young Henry VIII. It was Anne who brought part of Cople to the Luke family, having inherited it from her father, Thomas Launcelyn. An earlier couple, John Launcelyn and his wife, Margaret, possibly Anne's grandparents, also have brasses in the church, as do Luke and Anne's son Nicholas and his wife.

John and Margaret's brass of 1435 is a very old survival, but there are at least two that are even older. One commemorates the life of Nicholas Rolond, a barrister who died c1400 and the other, the life of Walter Rolond, also 1400, who is portrayed in full armour. This is probably the oldest military brass in Bedfordshire.

Brasses such as these in All Saints, are not just of interest to church, local and family historians but also to adults and children with an interest in costume and military uniforms.

WILLINGTON

ROUTE

(If wanting to visit St Lawrence's Church, Willington or the dovecote and stables, watch for the Willington sign and then turn left, down the clearly-marked 'Village Loop', which is on the left. This short rectangular diversion will rejoin the route at the junction.)

During the 11th century, the sheriff kept the entire 1200 acres for the use of himself and those lodged at the castle. This was another valuable riverside village with a mill and eel fishery. There was plenty of rich arable land and although it was short of woodland to support pigs, there were lush water meadows for making hay.

From the absentee Beauchamp family, Willington passed to another absentee family, the Mowbrays. During the 15th century, the Bishop's Visitor described the church as 'dark and ruinous' and the manor house at that time was also said to be tumbling down.

The local family who regularly held the position of bailiff was the Gostwicks. In 1529, a John Gostwick managed to buy the estate from the Mowbrays. At this date, King Henry VIII was on the throne and John and many other young men, had made their fortune by obtaining administrative jobs at court and in the shires (counties).

Sir John Gostwick

The young John Gostwick had gained an excellent position within the household of Cardinal Wolsey and rose to become a confidante and administrator. From this high role, he made friends at Court and was able to sense when Wolsey was falling from popularity. He then separated himself from Wolsey, so that his own career did not suffer and joined the followers of Thomas Cromwell.

After the Reformation, King Henry received the various taxes previously paid to the pope. One of Gostwick's better-paid jobs was 'Treasurer of Tenths and First Fruits'; in other words, he organised and enforced the collection and deposit of church taxes. His efforts were very successful and, in 1540, Henry rewarded him with a knighthood. He also managed to get the position of 'Particular Receiver' for part of Bedfordshire; rent collectors on what had been Warden Abbey lands brought their rents to his office, where he received them on behalf of the king.[1]

These positions not only brought in money but also influence, power and opportunities for other financial gain. Men who were involved in the

1 Finberg HPR. *The Gostwicks of Willington. BHRS Vol 36*

Cardington Cross

Willington Dovecote

administration of the ex-monastic estates were in an excellent position to get favourable purchases or leases. John Gostwick became farmer (tenant) of Caldwell Priory and its home farm, south of Bedford. Other members of his family also benefited. Edmund Gostwick had been the auditor for the Abbot of Warden Abbey and Robert Gostwick, who took over from him on behalf of the King, later bought the estate.

The Manor House

Previous Gostwick houses must have been quite modest but Sir John needed a really impressive mansion and estate where he could entertain his new friends and colleagues; so he began to build. All his work was carried out with good quality stone, some of which may have been brought down the river from Newnham Priory. The new manor house was particularly fine; in September 1539 he was able to entertain Thomas Cromwell and his followers and in October 1541, Henry VIII broke his journey at Willington and held a meeting of the Privy Council.

Sir John's descendants married well and for many years stayed in and around Willington but by 1713 they were seriously in debt and the estate was put up for sale. Some years later, there was a serious fire and the house was dismantled.

In 1779 it was bought by the Duke of Bedford, who used some of the old bricks to build a substantial farmhouse and a range of farm buildings. When, in this century, some of these were converted into houses, the foundations were found to be of carved stone.

The Godber family owned the farm in the 20th century and this is where the late Joyce Godber grew up. For many years she was the much-respected Head Archivist at the County Record Office and in 1969 the County Council published her major book about the county. She wrote several articles for the Bedfordshire Magazine, one of the most interesting being a brief but detailed picture of life over the centuries in Willington.[1] She also researched and wrote essays and complete volumes for the Bedfordshire Historical Record Society.

The Church of St Lawrence

As has been noted, the church was once in a poor state of repair but Gostwick needed a handsome, well-cared-for building on his doorstep. In 1539 he had received all the lands and property once held by Newnham Priory including the right to appoint the vicar at Willington.

1 Godber, J. Willington. Beds Mag Vol 13 No 103

He partly rebuilt, partly enlarged, St Lawrence's and his big, plain, tomb-chest still stands near the chapel that he built. He died in 1545 but had the tomb prepared in advance. Other more elaborate family tombs were built in the 17th century. Of particular interest are two helmets and an ancient tabard. The latter is reputed to have been worn by Sir John Gostwick when he accompanied King Henry VIII to his meeting with the French king at the 'Field of the Cloth of Gold'. Sir John's jousting helmet is in the Tower of London but one of those at Willington is a replica. The other belonged to a later member of the family.

By 1731, the Gostwick family was in financial difficulties and over the years, the church became neglected. The Duke of Bedford ordered repairs and in 1877 there was a major restoration.

The Dovecote and Stables

The (private) house, church, and other old buildings still form an attractive backwater just off the two main roads. The two secular 16th century buildings are owned by the National Trust. The best-known is the two-bayed dovecote. Inside, the building houses around 1500 nesting places for pigeons; outside, the stepped gables give it an exceptionally unusual appearance. It is thought to have been built at about the same time that the church was being rebuilt.

The farming of rabbits has been described in the Mid Bedfordshire chapter; the keeping of pigeons was also strictly controlled. Although they were allowed to feed freely on the land of both tenants and workers neither was allowed to catch them.Standing nearby is the stable block. This handsome stone building provided accommodation for horses on the ground floor and for stablemen above. It ws probably built in time to house King Henry's horses in 1541.

GREAT BARFORD

There are various suggestions as to how this village got its name but the early settlers probably named it for the birch trees that grew around the ford. Not surprisingly, the sheriff kept control of this village because, even before the Conquest, it was already an important ford.

In total, there were over 1400 acres of land, which was divided by the sheriff's agent between four tenants. One of these had the main watermill and eel fishery, the second a valuable arable farm and the third a much smaller farm. The fourth tenant was a priest, called

ROUTE
**The route follows the A603 until it meets the junction of five roads and then takes the second left towards Great Barford Bridge. After some distance, it crosses the dismantled Bedford to Sandy railway line.
And continues with the River Ouse on the left.**

155

ROUTE

There are traffic lights at the next T-junction to control traffic crossing the bridge. (The route turns left and is heading for the A421, which it will cross, on its way to Wilden.) Having crossed the bridge, the route continues through Great Barford, with The Anchor and All Saints Church on the right. As it continues up towards the A421, it passes more modern houses, as it approaches the crossroads. Very carefully cross the main road and head towards Colmworth and Wilden, following the signs towards Wilden. (At various points along this road, you will see the brown signs pointing to Bedford Butterfly Park. The route will pass through Wilden and Ravensden, as it heads for Bletsoe and the A6.)

Ansketel. With over 100 acres of arable, a meadow for making hay and a small watermill for grinding his corn (plus that of the ten families who worked for him), he was one of the best-provided priests in the county.

Barford Bridge

It is not known when the ford was backed up with the first wooden, or even stone, bridge. When Sir Gerald Braybroke, of nearby Colmworth, died in 1429, he left money to build a stone bridge. Over the centuries, this has been enlarged and partly rebuilt, but it is sometimes possible to see from the Barford side, a change in stone and pattern on the piers which separate arches seven and eight. These changes can also be seen on arches fifteen and sixteen. Together these few remaining stones mark the size of the original bridge.

The sheriff had overall responsibility to see that the local landowners and their workers kept bridges in good repair. In addition, bridge repairs were one of a group of 'charities' that people listed when making their wills - especially if they had had cause to use them. In 1501, John Canon of Barford, a farmer and dealer, with other property across the river at Biggleswade, left 6s=8d plus a bad debt of 26s=8d. Five years later, merchant Richard Manley of Blunham, who had a shop in Bedford and land in several other local parishes, left 6s=8d, while farmer, John Whitchurch of Ravensden (who, in 1521, was able to pass a cart and three horses on to his son) left 3s=4d to help to repair Barford Bridge.

However, just as with road repairs, the emphasis on local responsibility was not really successful and once the Civil War was over, Barford was one of a group of important bridges supported by rates gathered across the county.

Another problem along the Bedfordshire length of the River Ouse was that the fords prevented straightforward navigation. During dry weather, it was quite normal for boat-owners to have to pay the local millers to release water to assist their boats across the ford. Efforts were made before the Civil War to introduce a series of sluices from St Neots to Bedford, but they only reached as far as Great Barford. It was not until the 1670s that work was started on the other side of the bridge. Because of this, Great Barford developed as a busy, riverside community and had wharves for coal, salt and iron.

Great Barford and its Roads

Going southeast from the bridge, the Bedford road joined the Great North Road, via Blunham. Travelling north from the bridge, it joined the same road higher up, near Roxton. However, both of these roads were in a very bad condition, which did not encourage travellers to use them. People travelling from Bedford to London usually went through Shefford and Hitchin.

Because this bridge was so near Cardington, both the Whitbread and Howard families took a serious interest and during the 18th century, planned major alterations. In 1754, the parish register records that John King was killed by a fall from a horse and that James Green and Robert Dent were killed by the overturning of an empty cart. These were local men whose deaths may not have been caused by potholes. In August 1776, John Pedley admitted that his fall from a horse was because he had had too much to drink, but over the centuries, many travellers and horses must have suffered heavy falls.

On November 27 1773, the vicar recorded that men were measuring 'the new road'. This was planned from the bridge to Roxton Hill and would link the bridge to the Great North Road. However, it was eighteen years before he mentioned it again. In 1791 he wrote 'New Road made'* The delay was partly due to a problem met with today - disputes between landowners as to which line the road should follow.

John Pedley's diary (published as BHRS Vol 40) emphasised the role played by the two Cardington families. On October 27 1773 he was at Mr John Howard's 'about the Road', on November 2nd, he was with Mr Whitbread 'measuring the Road', and on September 17 he met the 'Commissioners of the Road and had a great dispute with Mr Whitbread'.

The traveller, Arthur Young, recorded his own tribute to John Howard. When he rode through Bedfordshire, in 1771, he described the roads as 'a cursed string of hills and holes'. However, when he reached some by-roads where 'John Howard Esq. of Cardington' had influence, they were level and free from ruts.

I am grateful to Janet Must for showing me the booklet 'History of Great Barford' by J Harold Brown JP, CA.

ROUTE

From the A421, it is approximately 2¹/₂ miles, along a country road with a series of bends, followed by some comparatively straight lengths of road, into Wilden village. The countryside is open and there are some good views across Bedfordshire on the left and Cambridgeshire on the right. When you meet the staggered crossroads, the route will turn left into Wilden village. The route passes right through the village, with a small stream running along on the left-hand-side; the school, pub and St Nicholas Church are also on the left. Beyond the village, also on the left, is Crowhill Farm and pond.

WILDEN

Coming into this village from Great Barford, the school, The Victoria Arms public house and the Church of St Nicholas are all on the left-hand side of the road. In places, one can also see the remains of what was once a fast-flowing stream.

The Village School

The school, which was built in 1851, is now a Voluntary Aided Lower School. Sometime in the early 1620s, a man called Thomas Peate became concerned about the boys of Wilden and planned to provide them with a schoolmaster. At that time, Wilden was a prosperous corn-growing area and Peate may have been one of the men who was enclosing land and improving profitability. On 18th December 1624, he nominated a house and land at Church End, Wilden to support the schoolmaster. The following year, he bought an extra piece of land at Thurleigh and set up a Trust. He obviously assumed that most of the parents would be prepared to pay a few pence for their sons' education, because he stipulated that only one village boy should attend free of charge.

Peate made a curious statement in the Trust deed; the trustees were to dismiss the master if he were to 'live disorderly or be contentious'. There were very few people in Bedfordshire in the 1620s who openly 'dissented' from the Church of England. At Wilden, the rector did not admit to having any Non-Conformists until the 1670s. Therefore, Peate did not add in injunction, as most later founders did, that the children must be taken to the parish church. However, the reference to contention may have been a warning to future dissenters. Certainly, the 18th century trustees assumed that it was a Church of England charity.

In 1717 and again in 1720, the Bishop of Lincoln ordered an enquiry concerning the availability of education in his diocese.[1] At this early date, there were well over fifty

---

1 This and most of the other references in the section come from: Bushby, D. BHRS Vol 67

158

Bedfordshire parishes where there was no provision at all, but Wilden still had its endowed school, attended by four or five children. They were taught the catechism and regularly taken into church. A hundred years later (1818), the value of the endowment had increased and twelve children were attending the school. At the end of this enquiry, the rector wrote 'the poor have sufficient means of education'.

The Charity Commissioners' Report

In 1821, there was a national enquiry into educational charities. At Wilden, the value of the endowment had risen and they found that the trustees had increased the number of free places, so that any poor parent could request places for their children. Despite this, there were only six free scholars (all boys) but there had been as many as ten, including one or two girls. In addition, there were eighteen paying scholars.

Three interesting pieces of information were included in the report:

I   They were taught reading, writing and arithmetic and were given instruction on the Bible but not on the church catechism, 'unless their parents desire it, which none at present do.'
II   That the master for the last fourteen years had been a dissenter (Nonconformist).
III That the master had qualifications 'from one of the universities.' However, it is also reported that he had been in the job for thirty-four years, having taken over from his father. Later enquiries would show that he was only about fifteen when he took on the job.

Thomas Peate had not made any reference to the denomination of his school-masters and when, in 1786, the appointment had been approved by the vicar and trustees, the master had still been a practising member of the Church of England. Maybe, when, around 1807, he began to worship with the Baptists, he was allowed to remain in the job because several of the trustees worshipped with him. This was certainly true later in the century and he did not leave the school until 1851. By that time, he was approaching eighty!*

The charity inspectors had also reported that, due to the poverty of the parents, children were often kept off school to work. At this time, there must have been

There are similarities here with the Whitehead School at Houghton Regis, where again there was confusion re the denomination and intentions of the founder and the difficulty of removing a very elderly master.

many employed men at Wilden who were only earning six or seven shillings a week. Because of this, a scheme was started whereby nine boys were employed at 2s=0d (10p) per week and one smaller boy 1s=6d (7¹/₂). This cannot have encouraged school attendance. In 1823, government inspectors recorded that 24 children attended the Daily School but noted that 8 males and 15 females attended the Sunday School belonging to the Established Church and 28 males and 29 females to one belonging to the Dissenters.

Eleven years later (1844), a government inspector wrote 'Poor schoolroom. Master appointed at the age of 15; has held the post 55 years'.

These government inspectors failed to comment on the denomination, which controlled the school, although the earlier Charity Commissioners report inferred that it was controlled by a Nonconformist master and trustees. The next published report was that set up by the Church of England during the year 1846-47. In suitable cases, they were prepared to arrange grants to build new, modern, church schools. Their detailed report uncovered the true position at Wilden. When recording numbers, they disregarded the Peate School because it was in the hands of the Dissenters. Their enquiries, probably from the vicar, uncovered the fact that 'it ought to be a church school.' However, as they were not allowed to see the deeds, they were unable to recommend a building loan. The next recorded enquiry was not until preparation for the Board School Act of 1870. A law that made education compulsory could only be successful if there were enough classrooms and desks to seat every child; in many cases, this was still not possible. At Wilden, the inspector recorded that:

1 there was no efficient schoolmaster
2 accommodation was required for 102 children
3 the Endowed School was large enough and could be made suitable
4 it was essential that a certificated teacher should be appointed

It was a hard struggle and in 1880, Wilden was one of only seven Bedfordshire schools which were not yet satisfactory. The problem must have concerned the teachers, rather than the building because, despite the negative report in1846/7, Wilden did get a new school building. This was so good that it is still in use today. In his fascinating book Wilden, a History of the Parish, Michael Rider has uncovered the local events of the mid-19th century. A Mrs Pritchard, who was a relative of the vicar, left a legacy of £100 towards a new school building. As this capital sum would open the doors for government and Church of England grants, this great educational opportunity must have encouraged the

160

Non Conformists to surrender the deeds. The new school, which included a house for the master, was opened in 1851 and the trustees advertised in the Bedford Times (Jan 11, 1851) for a 'Trained Schoolmaster and Mistress (Husband and Wife or Brother and Sister) ...Salary £50 per annum with House and Garden.' Even though this had to cover the two salaries, it was generous for a village the size of Wilden. The words 'Church of England' were not mentioned, but applicants had to have a knowledge of music '... sufficient to enable them to lead the singing in church.' The master appointed was Litchfield Norman, who pleased the trustees so much that they raised his salary. However, he cannot have had the necessary training certificate for he was still in the job when Wilden was criticised in 1870. The next teacher, who stayed for nearly ten years, was the one criticised for lack of training in the General Report of 1880, but, after 1882, when Jethro Boyse was appointed, Wilden settled down with a caring and responsible master.

On his first morning, 22 May 1882, he started to keep the school logbook and kept it going until his final day 17 April 1919.* This detailed book is of value to anyone interested in the history of Wilden or in the history of rural education. Year by year, he recounts his problems, trying to create sufficient interest and stimulation to keep the children in school long enough to receive a reasonable amount of learning. Even when he is able to hold their interest, he is hampered by their constant ill-health, their parents' need to keep them at home, child-minding or earning money and even by the heavy rain which caused the stream to flood into the schoolroom.

The 21st Century

This popular school, which has just celebrated its 150th anniversary, now successfully provides education for the 4-9 year-old age range of children from Wilden and from the villages round about.

RAVENSDEN (GOLDINGTON and PUTNOE)

The name Ravensden does not appear in the Domesday Book but the 600 acres entered as Chainhalle probably represents the same piece of land. These acres merge and overlap land from the other two villages. The sheriff kept

ROUTE
The route then enters Ravensden, via Church End, passing through the village, with the church and pub on the right and, as it leaves the village via a steep hill, the thatched houses to be seen on the right were once part of a pub called 'The Case Altered'.

* *This can be seen in the Bedfordshire and Luton Archive and Records Office*

161

ROUTE

This is because it was previously used as the village lock-up. Having left the village, the route crosses a stream and then meets a T-junction, where it turns right, heading towards Thurleigh. (At this point it is possible to turn left and head back to Bedford.)

Ravensden and added 500 acres from Putnoe and nearly 400 acres from Goldington - Highfields to provide food for the castle. Another 700 acres at Goldington, gained from the Ware exchange, were used to support three tenants.

Ravensden was yet another valuable estate with a watermill and eel fishery and along the river at Goldington - Highfields there was another. Today much of Putnoe and Goldington has been absorbed into Bedford but Goldington Green has been preserved.

RAVENSDEN

This is another village with a number of 'Ends', but both before and immediately after the Norman Conquest, it was in the hands of one important owner. Although today, the majority of the inhabitants live at Church End, on the high ground to the south-east of the parish, earlier this century the population was spread out among the different hamlets.

Whether the name comes from the Saxon words identifying a valley settlement where there were a lot of ravens, or a valley where a man called Rafn* settled, the main settlement was obviously in the valley.

By 1066, what is now Wood End and the area around Traysfield Farm, Manor Farm, Ravensden House, Brook Farm, Great and Little Wood were probably the centre of the manor. The clerk in 1086 recorded a valuable watermill with an eel fishery and meadowland, which later evidence places near today's Tilwick Farm.

There was enough woodland to feed 100 pigs. No land had been provided to support a church, but the sheriff was supporting priests at nearby Great Barford and Risely. The leaflet 'A Ramble Round Ravensden' describes the walk as covering 'some of the most attractive countryside in North Bedfordshire, including streams, woods and hills with wide views over the surrounding area.'[1] The village today stands up on the higher ground and looks down across the two streams and woodland.

* Or some similar spelling

1 One of the Parish Paths series of maps, produced by Ravensden Parish Paths Partnership with support from Bedfordshire County Council

Wilden Church

Ravensden Church with the Cross of Lights on the Tower (P.W.)

Newnham Priory

There was already a house of canons (ordained priests) based at St Paul's Church, Bedford, at the time of the Conquest. A hundred years later, the young Simon de Beauchamp, who had recently come of age, encouraged them to follow the Rule of St Augustin.* To support his new priory, he began to put together a parcel of scattered property ;this included twelve churches, including the one at Ravensden.

As their original church and other buildings were enclosed by the town of Bedford, he looked for a new, larger site, big enough for a range of buildings, gardens, orchards and a home farm. By 1178, they were moving out to Goldington. Once they were settled, the Beauchamp family and many other people began to add to their estates. From around 1200 they received several gifts of land in Ravensden and before long obtained a licence to set up a separate manor. This was based around Wood End.

The Manor is Divided

Once this first division was made to the Manor of Ravensden, several more followed. The Beauchamp family also gave a small amount of land, around Tilwick, to Warden Abbey, who used it as a grange (outlying farm). Some centuries later, there would be a big house called 'The Grange'. Over the years, the remaining land was divided between various tenants.

The tenant of the main manor, Ralph Morin, gave his name to the Manor of Morinsbury. His house was beside the Iron Age hillfort and the site is now known as Morinsbury Hill. Although some of these divisions were united in the 16th and 17th centuries, the various owners were absent; the village and the church suffered from the lack of an interested, resident Lord of the Manor.

All Saints Church of England

It has been suggested that the stone church was newly-built when it was given to Newnham Priory; at that time there was just a nave and a chancel. As a result of 20th century renovations, archaeologists have been able to investigate the structure of the building and to identify eight main stages in its development. These took place over two or three centuries

In 1218, Bishop Hugh of Wells installed a vicarage, but it was only a humble dwelling and the incumbent's salary was fixed at under £4 per year; lower than in most other villages.

See Dunstable Priory and Ashridge

After the Dissolution

The Prior of Newnham surrendered his house and its estates in 1537 and All Saints Church passed to the king. Sir John Gostwick of Willington, who was one of the king's rent receivers, was able to pick out estates for himself and his family. He bought the land that went with All Saints Church and the advowson (the right to appoint its vicar). The church stayed with his descendants for two hundred years. Later generations neglected their responsibility for maintaining the building and a 17th century enquiry revealed that the vicarage was a small half-timbered building with a thatched roof and only one hearth. In addition to neglect by the patron, the parishioners found it difficult to maintain their part of the church and churchyard. There were complaints in the 16th and 17th centuries, particularly about the churchyard.

The main problem was the low and scattered population. In 1671, there were less than 150 people in the whole parish and although the figure rose and by 1800 had passed 200, there was, by then, a growing group of Nonconformists who would have resisted paying more than their legal obligation.

A New Rector

The Duke of Bedford bought the living in 1774, but straight away sold the church land and advowson to an ordained clergyman. The Rev Robert Hart Butcher and the rectors who followed him declined to live in the dilapidated vicarage and installed curates or a resident vicar.

During the next hundred years, there were several absentee rectors, but towards the end of the century, the church and its advowson passed to the Bishop of Ely, who, in 1893, appointed the Rev. R Wood Samuel as vicar. The Diocesan Fund provided money for the complete overhaul of the vicarage and urgent repairs were carried out on the church roof. Two years later, a major restoration began; a new font and organ were purchased and work began on the bell tower. By the time that Samuel left, in 1899, the church was, once more, in a good state of repair.

The Role of the Churchwardens

The modern definition of churchwardens explains that they are lay representatives of the parish, elected to assist the incumbent in the organisation of the church and its affairs. By the 13th century, there was legal recognition of their role and by the 15th century, two wardens were elected each year at a meeting of all the adult parishioners. In those days, and for several later centuries, they were both guardians of the parochial morals and trustees of the church goods.

The former included the denouncement of people thought to be 'living in sin' or pursuing suspected fathers of illegitimate babies. This heading also included reporting those individuals who did not attend their parish church, or worse still, were suspected of being dissenters. Under the latter heading they were responsible for the entire church and its contents, apart from the chancel. Historically, the patron was supposed to use part of the profit from the church land to repair the chancel.

The Civil Role Imposed on the Churchwardens

During the reign of King Henry VIII, the closing of the religious houses and the gradual lessening of manorial control left gaps in local administration. As town and county councils did not appear until the mid to late 19th century, a new level of administration was needed. During 1532-3, an Act of Parliament was passed, making the parish responsible for the destruction of rooks and crows. To make this possible, many churchwardens bought nets. As the years went by, regular payments were made to individuals who presented nets of dead sparrows or the tails of dead foxes and badgers.

More Voluntary Officers were Needed

Medieval wills frequently included bequests to the parish to help with the repair of the local road or to care for the local sick and poor. Straightforward cash gifts were used by the wardens, as requested by the donor, or as they thought best. However, gifts of land involved the wardens both in finding tenants and in rent collection.

The Road Surveyors

Roadside parishes occasionally received alms from travellers, but on the other hand, they became increasingly involved with the support of sick travellers and the wandering unemployed, known as vagrants. By the time that Queen Mary came to the throne, the maintenance of local roads made too much work for the churchwardens; in some places roads were becoming impassable. A new Act of Parliament, in 1555, put the full responsibility onto the parish and before long, new voluntary officers were being elected at the main Easter Vestry that was the main parish meeting. These officers were called surveyors or sometimes stonewardens.

Guardians of the Poor

Throughout the Tudor period, poverty became an increasingly serious problem. In 1536, a formal 'collection of alms' was ordered, after the Sunday morning service. This was not particularly successful and so, at regular intervals, the clergy were expected to preach on the subject. This also failed and, in 1563, a levy was demanded, which gradually became an organized method of collection. By the end of the century, parishioners' property was valued and contributions, known as rates, were collected accordingly. New officers were now being appointed at the Easter Vestry - Overseers of the Poor. Both these and the Road Surveyors were answerable to the local magistrates. However, the work of the rent officers overlapped that of the churchwardens, who, after 1558, were also partly responsible for archery practice and maintaining the parish butts!

To pay for these varied duties, they relied on church rates, which they had been empowered to collect from the mid 14th century. In addition, there were bequests, gifts and money raised by festivities, such as May Day and patronal festivals.

Churchwardens Today

These men (and women) are still elected to help the clergy and to be responsible for the church building and its contents. They are also responsible for 'Maintenance of Order' and are empowered to remove persons who disturb the performance of services - this does not happen very often. They are still responsible for the collection of alms and for the normal collections.

The Churchwardens' Accounts

There are two of Ravensden's books in the Bedfordshire and Luton Archive and Records Office. They start in 1716 and uncover an interesting picture of village life.

Charges that we would expect to find are:

3s=0d (15p) for the account book, 9s=0d for a Book of Homilies and 15s=6d (77¹/₂p) for 'bindin the church bibill' (rebinding the bible). In 1710 they paid £3=10s=6d for a new pulpit cloth and there were regular payments of 2s=8d for the communion bread and wine. Another regular entry was for travel and subsistence for their visits to the local archdeacon's courts and to the bishop's visitations at Bedford. In 1788, they stayed at The Red Lion where their 15 dinners cost 15s=0d and liquors and ale 16s=10d. The minister's dinner cost 2s=6d.

The bells and their ropes frequently needed repair; bell ropes might cost 4s=0d, but they also had to pay 1s=0d for the 'shooting' or 'shouting' of the metal clappers. In 1710, just over £10 was paid to have a bell recast and transported back to Ravensden. From time to time, the bell-tower needed to be reinforced and the porch repaired.

However, it was the churchyard that most frequently needed attention. In 1762, stakes for the hedge were bought for 1s=0d and 6d paid to the workmen, with a further 6d for cleaning out the ditch. The following year, 10s=0d was paid for new bushes and stakes to replace part of the hedge and 5s=10d for hedging and ditching. The dead hedge was cut out and used as firewood for the poor cottagers. A lock for the gate cost 8d.

From time to time 1s=0d was spent on cleaning the church windows and 1s=6d on mending them. This was sometimes paid as bread and cheese. Washing the vicar's surplices cost 2s=0d. In 1738, the carpenter was paid 3s=7 $^1/_2$d to repair the stox (stocks).

The overseers who were responsible for the local poor were also responsible for helping travellers who came with a begging licence, but sometimes the Churchwardens assisted. Poor travellers looking for work, sailors returning home from voyages, the disabled and even prisoners on parole could get a licence to beg. Over the years, Ravensden guardians gave:
One shilling 'to a man with a letter' and three shillings to 'a seafaren man with a pass'.

In the days before insurance, families who suffered a real disaster, such as a fire, were also given a licence to appeal to the Sunday congregation. In 1732, the churchwardens paid 2s=0d for a man 'by loss of fire'.

However, the most surprising payments, which show up year after year, are those given for vermin. The payment was 2d a dozen for sparrows, 4d for a hedgehog, 1s=0d for a badger, 3s=0d for a fox and 6s=4d for a polecat. This was a sum comparable to a week's earned pay.

The Overseer's Accounts
There are some very detailed books in the archive; one runs from 1801-1831. In this, the overseer noted his collections and his expenses and also the income he received from the charity land.

In 1802 he collected four rates of one shilling in the pound and when that was not sufficient, a fifth of sixpence. This brought in £318=3s=9d, 31=10s being rent. His 'disbursements' (payments) were £303=8s=1$^1/_2$d, leaving £14=15s=7 $^1/_2$d to pass on to the following year.

His expenses had been:

> Regular small sums to families 'in need' or 'ill'
> Clothes and shoes - he paid the draper £9=6s=7d and bought 6 pairs of shoes
> Health care- 12s=0d for a truss, midwives and general nursing
> Funerals, including beer for the helpers

A lot of his outgoings were to support poor families by providing them with work to help other people on his list. There are regular entries such as - to the making of 2 frocks, 4 shirts and 3 petticoats. For these he supplied the sewers with cloth, thread and tape. Those who were poor but active, such as widows and mothers with small children, he provided more active work. There are constant payments for 'doing for' 'cleaning for' 'sitting nites'.

The evidence of this book is that the poor of Ravensden were well-cared for (by the standards of the day), the rates well-managed and the book well-kept. In 1802, when the population was approximately 220, the basic weekly payment, under the heading of 'those in need' was £1=16s=6d. Twenty-four years later, by which time the population had risen to around 260, the weekly list had only risen by two shillings. The breakdown of the latter sum was eleven payments of 1s=0d and others of up to 3s=6d. These small sums suggest that some were supplements for families where at least one member was in low-paid work. The 'desperate' poor were probably being cared for in the workhouse.

The population rose so sharply during the first decades of the 19th century that in parts of Bedfordshire, there was very high unemployment, leading to poverty and distress. In some villages, the overseers found it impossible to balance their books. Despite a particularly high raise in Ravensden, there is no evidence of breakdown.

The Parish Registers

These are also in the Record Office and reveal even more about life in the village.

Burials

Taking a random ten-year period in the 1770s and another forty years later, in the early 1800s, during which time the population probably rose by about 25%, the number of burials fell from just over 60 to around 45. During the first decade, the annual numbers varied from 3 to as high as 8; in the later decade, there was one year with no burials and several when there were only two or three.

One noticeable fact was the drop in child and infant deaths. In the 1780s, numerous baptismal entries were followed a few weeks or months later with the entry for an infant burial. During the period 1772-1782, nearly half the entries were in these two categories - 15 of them infants. There were far less in the latter period, although a few such burials did still occur.

Baptisms

With the higher level of population, it is not surprising that the number of baptisms rose, but it was only by about 10 over the decade and this number was artificially high because on one occasion, 4 brothers and sisters/baby up to 7 years were baptised on the same day.

Many of the names given are still fashionable, or back in fashion today. Elizabeth was probably the most popular name for a girl and also Sarah, but Mary, Hannah, Phoebe, Martha, Ruth and Fanny also occurred quite often. Thomas was probably the most popular name for boys and Richard, but there were entries for Edward, Samuel, Frederick, Robert and George. Old Testament names that have dropped from popular usage are Keziah, Elisha and Ezekial.

Marriages

On the inside cover of the first register was a list of prices charged for special services. Both the certificate and the banns cost 5s=0d, but the people who wished to get a special licence had to pay 10s=6d. Marriages were not annual events, although some years there were as many as four. In the majority of cases, both husband and wife came from Ravensden or the neighbouring villages. In the first sample, one young lady came from as far away as Sharnbrook and one was the daughter of the parish clerk from St Paul's, Bedford, but six of the men came from North Bedfordshire and two from just over the county border. On the later sample, the most distant partner came from Bromham.

The samples quoted above are not statistically sound, but the information arrived at paints a picture of rural family life in Ravensden. This was always very hard in villages where their livelihood depended on the success of the annual harvest. The service of Harvest Festival was, and still is, one of the key services of the year.

The Case is Altered

From time to time during the 18th century, the overseers noted expenses involved in the running of the parish workhouse. This was not a major expense and up to 1834, the house was used as a residential backup of what became known as 'out-relief'. It was cheaper and more humane if the overseer could pay a small weekly sum, backed up by heating, clothing and/or medical support and keep the needy person or family in their own home.

After 1834, the Poor Law Amendment Act did away with parish houses and brought in Poor Law Boards to administer Union Workhouses. This is the system that brought so much distress to the sick and aged and shame to the caring services. Large comfortless buildings were built in places such as Bedford and small local houses were sold and used for a variety of purposes. In Ravensden, the old thatched building was renovated and became a public house called The Case is Altered.

Thanks are Due to the Volunteers

The churchwardens, surveyors of the roads and overseers of the poor were elected and obliged to carry out these duties on an expenses-only basis. Sometimes a landowner, farmer or tradesman held the same position year after year. In most cases they changed every few years. The work was often difficult and unpopular; the Ravensden overseer who, having collected the four quarterly rates of 1s=0d in the pound, then had to ask for and collect another sixpenny rate, would have been extremely unpopular.

These officers, and others like them, carried the weight of the parish and social administration into the last half of the 19th century.

The Light Shines Out

On a fairly regular basis, the churchwardens paid out for repairs to the bells and bell-tower, probably because they were used much more in the past. Most parish, public and royal occasions were marked by a peel of bells. The wardens paid 5s=0d for beer for the ringers on such occasions as a coronation, 2s=6d, each November 5th and 1s=0d on many other public occasions.

Today the bells of All Saints ring out each Sunday and the sound is carried by the wind, down towards the A6 and the river. In years gone by, they must have formed a chorus with other church bells and carried their message even further.

In recent years, the parish has found an even better way to herald the message of Christmas. At the beginning of December, a churchwarden attaches a great cross to the tower, illuminated by light bulbs; this shines out every night leading up to Christmas. This great Christian symbol can be seen by motorists and others, even before they cross the county boundary into North Bedfordshire. When we see these lights and hear the bells, we should remember that All Saints Church has witnessed Christian worship for over eight hundred years.

ROUTE

The route meets the Kimbolton Road and follows a staggered crossing, still heading towards Thurleigh. This road passes Red Gate and Scald End farms, before it eventually comes to a T-junction with the converted Thurleigh windmill straight ahead. The route does not go into Thurleigh village, but turns left at the T-junction and travels along a short section of dual carriageway (intended originally to pass under a proposed aircraft taxiway); it will eventually come to another T-junction. Turn right at this junction and follow the road past the entrance to Thurleigh Airfield and Business Centre, before taking the left-hand turn to Bletsoe and the A6.

THURLEIGH

The sheriff only had about 60 acres in this village and he let that out to a tenant. The rest of the land was shared between three other main tenants, one of whom used 30 acres to support Solomon the priest. Before the Conquest, Bishop Wulfwy of Dorchester held this piece of land.

Like most churches, St Peter's has had many alterations and restorations but nevertheless, Thurleigh can boast of having one of Bedfordshire's few Anglo-Danish towers.[1] A major restoration in the mid 19th century provided the opportunity for an excavation that uncovered evidence of a small Saxon church and a later nave of about 1100AD.

The Royal Aircraft Establishment

The route associated with this chapter does not pass through the village but skirts the old airfield. The suffix 'leigh' comes from the Saxon word for a clearing and, as with many Bedfordshire villages, it is made up of a number of 'ends' - Cross End, Church End and Scald End, (where George Franklin provided a schoolhouse in 1618, replaced about 1840, with help from the Duke of Bedford) are still on the map today, but Backmore End disappeared in the 1950s, during the rebuilding of the airfield. By the time that it closed, the runway was nearly two miles long.

This was one of North Bedfordshire's six wartime airfields and was built for the RAF in 1941. However, in October 1942, it became the home of the American 306th Bombardment Group and the villagers became used to the nighttime roar of the B17 bombers. Not only the villagers but also the people of Bedford became very familiar with the camouflaged army lorries carrying airmen into the town. This is where they went to dance - at the Corn Exchange or the American Red Cross GI Club in Bromham Road.

1 Pevsner, N. Bedfordshire, Huntingdonshire and Peterborough

One of the great attractions at the dancehalls, for both the American airmen and the English girls, was the famous Glenn Miller and his band. It was from the adjoining Twinwoods Airfield that he flew out, heading for Paris, on the fateful journey of December 1944.

The 306 Bomb Group Historical Association

Connie Richard (née Stanton) was one of the teenage girls who danced with the Americans and was under the spell of Glenn Miller's music. By the time that she married Gordon, the war was over but even then, it was several years before they had a home of their own. Once they did, Connie's collection of memorabilia of the American Eighth Air Force began to grow. In 1962 both Connie and Gordon joined the American Eighth Air Force Historical Society in the States and about ten years later, they formed a similar society over here.

The 306 Bombardment Group Memorial

A great number of people, both in England and America, joined the society and they were instrumental in erecting this memorial. The stone is not on the route but stands on the Keysoe Road, just off the main village; it commemorates members of the bomber crews from both Thurleigh and Twinwoods who never made it back home. It was paid for by members of the Bomber Group and, on October 5th 1982, two hundred American ex-servicemen came to Keysoe Road for a Service of Dedication.

On each side of the stone, there is a flagpole and on the anniversary and memorial days, a Union Jack and a Stars and Stripes (rescued by Connie from the Red Cross GI Club) are flown. Members of the society and children from the Lower School lay flowers.[1]

The Third London Airport

The extension of the runway was made during the development of a research centre for the Royal Aircraft Establishment. In the late 1960s, a search was on for a third London Airport. The Roskill Commission considered four short-listed sites; two were in Essex plus Cublington, near the important Saxon church at Wing, and Thurleigh. A site large enough to relieve the pressure on the existing London airports would have caused serious damage to a number of surrounding villages and notices supporting Bedford Airport Resistance Association (BARA) sprang up. This threat passed and since then, several other ideas have been discussed.

1 Porter, S. 'On the American Patrol'. Bedfordshire County Life Magazine, Issue 5

BLETSOE

Following the Norman Conquest, Bletsoe was equally divided between the sheriff, Hugh de Beauchamp, and the Countess Judith. It seems likely that one tenant represented them both. Each owner had about 300 acres of arable land, woodland to support 100 pigs and some useful water meadows. There was one good, shared watermill.

ROUTE

Just before the junction with the A6, the church of St Mary's, Bletsoe is on the left.

The Norman sub-tenant, Osbert de Broilg and his descendants remained there for several generations and then, through a marriage contract, a daughter of Bletsoe passed it to the Pattishall family. In 1327, John of Pattishall bought a licence from the king to 'crenellate' his dwelling house. This was the year that King Edward II was murdered and because Edward III was under-age, England was ruled by a regency. The crenellation of the roof would make the house easier to defend in times of trouble. The last direct heir of the Beauchamps of Bedford Castle had died in 1265. However, they were not only related to the Beauchamps, Earls of Warwick, but also to several of Bedfordshire's leading families. In 1359, William de Beauchamp, who was distantly connected with the original Beauchamps, took over Bletsoe when it was inherited by his wife.

Margaret Beaufort, Duchess of Somerset

A later descendant, Margaret Beauchamp, inherited Bletsoe when she was only eleven and overnight became a most important heiress. No doubt, plans had already been made for her future marriage and she was at once married to Sir Oliver St John of Glamorganshire. He then became owner of her Bedfordshire and Cornish estates. He died in 1437, leaving Margaret with three daughters and two sons. Despite this growing family, Margaret was still very young when her second marriage was arranged in 1442. Her new husband, John Beaufort, Duke of Somerset, was nearly forty years old and in poor health. A baby daughter, Margaret, was born in the first year of this marriage. It is doubtful if her parents (or anyone else) realised that this Bedfordshire girl would, one day, be mother, grandmother and great-grandmother of kings or that she would later be recognised as somebody who had a great influence in the improvement of English education.

Sir John died in 1444, a year after his daughter's birth. The Court was staying at nearby Berkhamsted when King Henry VI heard about his death. He at once put the legal care of the baby and arrangements for her future into the hands of William de la Pole. Sometime before her seventh birthday, she went through a form of marriage with seven-year-old John de la Pole!

Despite all these political manoeuvres, her mother was able to arrange for the young Margaret to live much of her childhood with her stepbrothers and sisters at Bletsoe. While she was there, she shared the education provided for her stepbrothers.

At the time that Margaret was born, her father (grandson of John of Gaunt) was out of favour at court, but during the next ten years there were many changes. King Henry had become mentally ill and the throne was no longer secure. His son, Edward, was not born until October 1453, so at the start of that year, he had no heir. It was just possible that the husband of the young Margaret Beaufort might one day claim to be a contender for the throne. As the de Pole family was no longer in favour, Henry arranged for the childhood marriage to be dissolved. He then arranged for her to marry one of his half-brothers.

The Birth of the Future King Henry VII

Margaret's biographers[1] explain that the decision about who she should marry was left to the nine-year-old girl and that after a night of prayer, she chose Edmund Tudor, Duke of Richmond. They were married early in 1453 and just before her thirteenth birthday, the future King Henry VII was conceived! Edmund died of plague in Carmarthen on 1 November 1456 and baby Henry was born at his uncle's castle in Pembroke on 28 January 1457. The events leading up to his coronation in October 1485 are included in the biography of his mother.

The St John Family

Margaret Beaufort was a conscientious mother and was able to help her St John children find positions at court. For several centuries, the family played a leading role in both county and national affairs. They were still Bedfordshire's leading family when the Stuarts came to the English throne. King James I came into Bedfordshire in 1605 and on the nights of August 1st and 2nd, he and his household stayed at Thurleigh and the queen stayed at Bletsoe. They returned on several occasions and when the king himself stayed with the St John in 1624, James gave Oliver, 4th Lord St John, the title Earl of Bolingbroke. Nevertheless, when it became a question of king or parliament, the St John family felt obliged to support parliament. On 17 June 1642, the Commons ordered Sir

1 James, MK and Underwood, MG   The King's Mother

Beauchamp St John and Sir Oliver Luke to return home to organise the militia. At Edgehill, the first battle of the war, the Earl of Bolingbroke raised a regiment of soldiers and his son, Lord St John, commanded a troop of cavalry. The latter died from his wounds and the loss of his son, plus the horrors of the battle so aged the infirm earl that he took no further part in the fighting. Nevertheless, the family supported parliament in every way until it came to the question of regicide. Sir Oliver St John, who at that time held the position of Lord Chief Justice, returned to the country and did not sign King Charles' death warrant.

Slowly the country settled down, the Restoration occurred and life returned to normal. The family remained at Bletsoe into the 20th century and continued to play an active part in both county and national affairs. All that is left of the Bletsoe 'Castle' favoured by King James I is one range of the vast Tudor building and even this has been reduced to two storeys. It is privately owned.

The Church of St Mary

Described by Simon Houfe as a 'delightful thirteenth century church', St Mary's is another church that houses very important monuments. In the north transept (the crossing) is a memorial to Sir John St John and his family. He kneels with his sons kneeling behind him and he is faced by his wife and daughters. The facial details and costumes are particularly fine. Above their heads is an elaborate shield divided many times to show the arms of the different families to which the St Johns were connected. There is also a long Latin inscription (with translation), describing the family's connection with the Duchess of Beaufort and her life at Bletsoe.

A Modern Stained Glass Window

The four-hundredth anniversary of the Open Bible coincided with the death of Harry Cheetham, whose brother, Alfred Cheetham, had been the rector of St Mary's from 1936-1945. Harry Cheetham was a printer who founded the Broadwater Press in Welwyn Garden City; he died on 6 May 1938. It was therefore decided to erect a window that would not only commemorate the life of Harry Cheetham but also the fact that four hundred years previously, Thomas Cromwell had ordered that an English translation of the bible should be placed in every parish church.

It was Mr H Warren Wilson who designed the window that commemorates the lives of numerous people connected with the bible. These include St Jerome and the Vulgate Bible, (which he translated into Latin at the end of the 4th century), John Wycliffe, who, in the 14th century, began to translate the Bible into English; Gutenberg, who invented printing in the 15th century and produced the first printed Bible and William Caxton, who started the first English printing press in the second half of the century. Miles Coverdale also appears; in 1535 he produced the first complete English Bible. Many other men connected with different versions of the Bible are also represented, but it was Coverdale's version of 1538 that was distributed around the churches.

Norman Landholders Along the Second Part of the Route

Landholding in the villages involved in the latter part of this route follow a rather different pattern. The sheriff tended to have farms rather than villages or part-villages; in some villages he had no land at all. However, he and his tenants were well represented; he himself had a hunting park at Stagsden and Ranulf, 'Brother of Ilger', nephew of the previous Norman sheriff, held 600 acres at Pavenham.

Secular Tenants

Many of these villages were split up into small portions, packaged and given to senior Norman officers and other supporters of King William. Most of these men had no other interest in the county, eg Miles Crispin, whose castle was at Wallingford (Berks) and who was related to the new Abbot of Westminster, had an estate made up of 600 acres in Clapham, 30 acres in Thurleigh, 16 acres in Milton Ernest, plus 120 acres in Oakley which he rented from the countess. Four other men enjoyed similar estates: they put in tenants, received money from rents and no doubt, could make use of the scattered estates if they or their officials were travelling across the country.

Church Tenants

King William and his Norman advisors were great supporters of the church in Normandy. They brought bishops (and abbots) over to England to reform the church in this country. The Saxon Bishop Wulfwy had run the diocese, which included Bedfordshire, from Dorchester on Thames. This was because of the damage that the Danes carried out on the eastern side of England. He died c1070 and his Norman replacement, Bishop Remigius, moved the see to Lincoln. He was an active supporter of King William and had provided ships to help with the invasion.

Two Norman and two English bishops held land in Bedfordshire, three of them in this area. At Turvey, Odo, Bishop of Baxeux, King William's half-brother, held 120 acres and the Bishop of Coutance, a trusted friend of William, 480 acres and a mill. The Bishop of Lincoln held 150 acres and a small mill at Biddenham; the latter was used to support Ernwin the priest. Two 'Houses of Canons' (Minster Churches) were represented; St Paul's Church in the centre of Bedford held 90 acres at Biddenham and used it to support one of their canons. Five of the great Benedictine monasteries held land in Bedfordshire; eg the Abbot of Bury St Edmunds had 60 acres at Biddenham.

The Sheriff's Men

In every shire [county] the sheriff used small pieces of land to support, or as pensions for, his officials. To keep continuity within the shires, quite a few Saxon officials were kept on and allowed to keep their land. Osgeat of Bromham was a king's reeve who carried out much of the day-to-day administration for the sheriff. In addition to the 50 acres that he held in Bromham, he also had 60 acres at Turvey. A beadle of the king (an official who helped to keep order), had a few acres at Milton Ernest and Alwin the priest, about 20 acres at Turvey. Alwin was a Saxon but William allowed him to keep these acres provided that every Monday he performed mass for the souls of William and his queen.

MILTON ERNEST

As the route connected with this chapter passes through Milton Ernest, the A6 separates the clay plateau of North Bedfordshire from the slopes that fall westwards towards the Great Ouse Valley.

Back in the days of horse-drawn coaches, an increasing number of people built houses, inns and craft workshops on either side of the road that ran from London to Oakham. However, All Saints Church, the vicarage (built in 1694) and the manor house, farm cottages and the almshouses which were built in 1695, remain undisturbed nearby. There have been many changes but this area is still an attractive scene away from the busy main road, where farming continued as the main occupation.

ROUTE
Turn left onto the A6 and drive right through Milton Ernest.

The main roadside development did not occur until the 18th century. John Ogilby's map of 1675, marks the early road from London to Oakham as running through Oakley, Clapham and Odell; this was well to the west of Milton Ernest. However, a century later (1784) a pocket compendium map for travellers, drawn by George Augustus Walpole, marks the present road. The 1799 edition of Patterson's road book included a road (used by the hunting fraternity?) that crossed from Hitchin to Shefford and then on to Melton Mowbray. This ran via Bedford, Clapham and Milton Ernest. It took some time to come into operation, but a turnpike trust was formed in 1725, between Luton, Bedford and Rushden.

The presence of the roads contributed to the rapid increase in the village population. In 1671, before the development of what became the A6, it was still a small village of about two hundred people. The manor house had eight hearths, a little below average for Bedfordshire, but although more than half of the families managed with just one hearth, by far the majority escaped poverty. There was a smith who probably worked for the manor house and farmers, as well as the occasional travellers.

OAKLEY

It is not only in Woburn and its surrounding villages where one can see Bedford Estate houses. These 19th century cottages and farms were so well built and maintained that, if they come up for sale, they readily find buyers.

Bedford Estate Cottages

In 1757, Francis, 5th Duke of Bedford, bought the 17th century Oakley House and the estate that went with it. He then commissioned Henry Holland to modernise and adapt the house, so that it would be a suitable, independent home for the Russell heirs, before they inherited Woburn. Building on the interest that his predecessors had taken in agriculture, he started an experimental farm, a local agricultural society and what became the world-famous Woburn 'sheep shearings' (agricultural shows with an emphasis on all types of innovation). The family continued to take an interest in agriculture, both locally and nationally and the 7th Duke, another Francis, turned his attention to the housing of agricultural labourers. His son, William, was prevented from playing an active role in these matters but, through his cousin, Hastings, who became the 9th duke, the policy of cottage building continued.

Many years later (May 13 1896), Herbrand, the 11th Duke, made a speech at a meeting of the Thorney Unionist Association. This was delivered to an

ROUTE
Once south of the village, watch out, on the brow of a hill, for a right-hand turn to Oakley and Pavenham. Having entered Oakley village, continue across the small crossroads and the Bedford Estate cottages are on the right.

179

audience of landlords, tenant farmers and labourers and he aimed to cover questions affecting the welfare of all three. It attracted far more and far wider attention than he had thought possible and, as a result, he wrote the book 'The Story of a Great Estate'.* In this he states 'I know of no more satisfactory form of philanthropy possible for the owner of a great estate than the provision of good cottages'. He goes on to talk about good management and the importance of landowners keeping control of the cottages and not letting them out with the farms. This proved to be particularly important during the worst years of agricultural depression. The family accepted that the management of estate cottages was a branch of social welfare and would, at times, run at a loss. They could therefore, when necessary, lower cottage rents and keep up a high standard of repairs.

Duke Herbrand's Cottages

There are various features that identify the estate cottages; the most obvious being the ducal crown, the letter 'B' and the date. Another is the building materials of brick walls and slated or tiled roofs; the latter were chosen because they were more hygienic and healthy than wood and straw. However, the feature that is always mentioned is the absence of a front door. In every village the reason given is the same - the Duke did not like seeing the cottage women gossiping on their doorsteps! Where this story started and why ladies would want to gossip at their front doors is unknown.

This is a serious slur on the efficiency of the design of the estate cottages. In fact their design was greatly respected and passed round to other country houses. In his book, Duke Herbrand clearly explains the excellent reason why the estate did not allow front doors. 'If there are two doors to the dwelling there is a tendency, amounting in some cases to a practice, to leave one (door) unused.' He then goes on to point out the advantages of having only one outside door and one living room. Apart from the fact that two doors create draughts,** they also make possible a second, little-used room 'where china dogs, crochet antimacassars and unused tea-services are maintained in fusty seclusion. This idle parlour adds nothing to the comfort of the cottagers.'

He recommended dividing the ground floor space into a living room, kitchen, scullery and a spacious, airy, pantry. The upstairs should have two good-sized bedrooms; one for the parents and one for the girls. A third,

* *Published by John Murray of London 1897.*
** *The author grew up in a farm cottage with two doors and knows how true this is.*

smaller room must be provided for the boys. He also gave advice about washhouses, sanitary arrangements (buckets were best if the gardens were large enough for trenching), gardens and pigsties.

The Allotments
Over the centuries, the estate provided allotments in nearly every village in which they had an interest. However, Duke Herbrand pointed out the advantages of large gardens and the disadvantages of over-large allotments. He felt that the latter tempted cottagers to dabble in commercial growing and get into financial difficulties. He recommended $1/4$ acre plots, preferably as a cottage garden and felt that allotments of this size gave the labourer 'a profitable occupation for his leisure' as well as 'adding to his daily sustenance'.[1]

In 1867, George Cully visited Oakley on behalf of the Royal Commission into the Employment of Women, Young Persons and Children in Agriculture. He was genuinely interested in the well-being of labourers and their families and asked questions concerning all aspects of their welfare. When he asked to see the Oakley allotments, his guide explained 'You see, Sir, Oakley were a wild blackguard place and Mr Henley have done it to cure the place'! He spent some time in Oakley examining the cottages; when he made his report and listed the villages with the best and the worst cottages, Oakley appeared in both! The remaining timber-framed, thatched cottages, not on the Bedford Estate, were probably included in the latter and the new, brick-built ones in the former. He also made enquiries into the provision of education.

The Village School
Once again, estate villages gained an advantage. From early in the century, a handful of villages, including Oakley, had a small endowment to provide teaching for a few selected boys. Several of these were lost, or mismanaged and so of little value, but Oakley's was strengthened by the Duke of Bedford. A survey in 1800 recorded that it had a townhouse and 20 acres of land. The house was used as a schoolroom and £15, from the £25 rent gained from the land, was used to pay a schoolmaster 'who admits all such poor children of Oakley whose parents apply'.

In 1800, £15 per annum was a reasonable salary; many masters were on a lower salary and had an additional part-time or even full-time job. To prevent

1 Agar, N. The Bedfordshire Farm Worker in the 19th Century BHRS Vol 60

this at Oakley, the Duke of Bedford added another £5 per year to his salary. Because so few parents could spare their children from the odd jobs which helped to support the family, the trustees of the charity allowed him a further £2 a year to run a Sunday School. The trustees also reserved a further £2 for the school coal, (which, in many villages, the parents had to pay for) and a further £2 for repairs. In 1802, the Duke paid to have the townhouse converted to a proper schoolroom. Nevertheless, in 1818, when the vicar, Robert Mesham, reported that 'the poor have sufficient means of educating their children', only around 30 children from a population of 432 were attending the charity school. By 1833, the population had risen to 516; 39 boys were attending the weekday school and 51, the Sunday school. In addition, the Marchioness of Tavistock was supporting a school where 15 girls were being taught needlework and a mistress was being paid £4 per annum to run a Sunday School for 51 girls.

A government inspector visited Oakley in 1844 and reported that although there was an excellent schoolroom, the master was capable of improvement! This may be why, when the Church of England set up an enquiry, just over two years later, there were fewer girls attending during the week and far less boys and girls present on Sundays. These Sunday Schools taught bible study and the catechism but they also taught reading and writing. However, the Duke of Bedford, the Whitbread and the Howard families continued building proper schoolrooms and encouraging pupils to attend during the day. Before 1855 the Duke had paid for school buildings in eight Bedfordshire villages and contributed towards another seventy. At Oakley he had paid £480 for a boys school plus a house for the master. A dwelling house for the master would attract a better candidate.

In the years leading up to 1870, the government was working towards compulsory education. An enquiry was made to find out how much accommodation was available and how much more was needed. At Oakley, the new school only had room for 82 children. Until there was a desk for every child, compulsion was useless and the government ordered the setting up of local committees (or boards); these were to be empowered to borrow money and build a second or third school. In some villages, the Church of England was reluctant to give up their schools to a secular committee, but the Duke of Bedford encouraged this practice. Oakley Board School opened in 1878.

The Village

Oakley House, the estate farm and the Oakley Hunt provided employment in the village and the senior staff, who worked for the Bedford Estate, made it possible to support two or three shops.

At the very end of the 19th century, the Duke of Bedford used Oakley House and its estate as a home for his newly appointed Agent-in Chief, Rowland Protheroe. He was deeply involved in agriculture, entered politics and eventually became President of the Board of Agriculture. He was in his late forties when he came to Oakley and took an active part in village life. By the time that the Woburn Estate sold the village in 1920, it was considered a most desirable place in which to live.

TURVEY

This village is just off the route but there is so much to see that it is well worth a visit. Most of the villages and churches around this route are worth exploring on foot and this is recommended at Turvey, which is compact and built of stone.

All Saints Church

This church was described by Pevsner as 'very rewarding'. It stands proudly in the centre and has numerous features to attract the serious student, plus colour, decoration and effigies to attract every type of visitor.

England's Thousand Best Churches

When Simon Jenkins produced this well-reported book in 1999, it received criticism because of the numerous popular churches that had not been included in his personal thousand. In some communities, where the church has been included, there have been complaints of 'damning with faint praise' but at Turvey he gives a gives a detailed and complimentary description and quite rightly commends the guidebook.

ROUTE
When this road divides, the route takes the right-hand fork towards Bromham and Stevington. It crosses the attractive but very narrow, double Oakley Bridge, before turning right into Park Road, Stevington. The path to the windmill can be seen on the left. The road into Stevington village is long and winding but, just as you are approaching the entrance to the village, there is a good view of the windmill on your left. As you reach the centre of the village, with The Red Lion on your right and the cross straight ahead of you, turn left towards Stagsden and Bromham. (The Church of St Mary and the 'holy well' are down a hill to the right of the crossroads.)

ROUTE

This country road crosses the path known as the Stevington Country Walk (which leads back to the windmill) before approaching the A428. Turn left onto this main road (turn right if visiting Turvey) heading towards Bedford but watch for a second left-hand turn towards Bromham village.

The Village

Jenkins was not so kind when he wrote about the village. Depending on one's interpretation of the word 'smart', his introduction to Turvey can be described as sarcastic or even rude. 'Turvey (village) is smart Beds, smart houses, smart pubs, smart church.' There must be another word to describe its spruce, well-groomed and tidy appearance, without using a word that also infers that it is of fashionable appearance and inhabited by people seeking the latest fashion. Simon Houfe uses the adjective 'handsome', which is a far better description.

Throughout the centuries, Turvey was a 'closed' village; this means that there has nearly always been a resident lord of the manor, taking a personal interest in his village and the people who lived there. As a result, it has been passed down as a most attractive village, which the residents are anxious to conserve. The original manor house has long since gone but continuity of ownership is one of the factors that have contributed to the care of the village, church and people.

Following the Norman Conquest, part of Turvey was sublet to Arnulf of Ardres, whose descendants, before 1200, married into the Mordaunt family. They were soon one of Bedfordshire's leading families, helping the sheriff and, from time to time, representing the shire at parliament. Although, like many families, they lost money and position during the 15th century Wars of the Roses, in the 16th century, they held rewarding positions at court.

The Mordaunt Family Monuments

A secular brass in the Lady Chapel may be to an unknown member of the Mordaunt family who died just before 1500, but the three stone effigies commemorate known members of the family whose stories are linked with the history of England. The oldest is a tomb-chest of Purbeck marble, dated 1506. The figures are Sir John Mordaunt and his wife, Edith. This is the member of the family who chose to fight on, what became, the winning side at the Battle of Bosworth and so found favour with Henry VII. From then on, the family were in favour with the Tudor family and were able to extend their estate at Turvey by purchasing the land previously owned by St Neots Priory.

184

The second, far more elaborate, monument depicts the first Lord Mordaunt, who died in 1560, and his wife Elizabeth. He was amongst those who were knighted by Henry VIII, just before they left to meet the King of France, at the ceremony known as The Cloth of Gold. Then, in 1533, the year that Henry sent his wife, Catherine, to Ampthill during the annulment of their marriage at Dunstable Priory and his secret marriage to Anne Boleyn, Henry created him Baron Mordaunt of Turvey. The immediate result of this defiance was the break with Rome and Henry's self-appointment as head of the church in England. The majority of his subjects had absolutely no choice but to follow his example and leave the Church of Rome. Some welcomed the change; a very few, like the Abbot of Woburn, were brave enough to defy him but most of those who disagreed attended the new services and waited to see what would happen. The views of Lord Mordaunt are not known but he may have belonged to the group that was watching and waiting. He remained at court, officiating at Henry's wedding to Anne Boleyn and was there during the years that Edward VI introduced the Book of Common Prayer but his true beliefs showed through when Roman Catholic Queen Mary came to the throne. He was one of the first to arrive and welcome her and assure her that although he was too old to be of much practical help, he would pray for her health and safety. She died in 1558 and he lived on for four years into the reign of Protestant Queen Elizabeth.

His wife had brought the attractive house at Drayton (Northants) into the family and they lived there, using Turvey as a dower house; nevertheless, he was buried at Turvey. Whatever his religious beliefs, the 2nd Lord Mordaunt also managed to remain in favour. He died only eleven years after his father. His monument is dated 1571 and his alabaster effigy lies between and slightly higher than those of his two wives. This dilemma, whether to follow the Established Church and stay in favour, or stand up for their religious beliefs and be isolated, haunted the Mordaunt family for several generations.

The last, extremely handsome tomb chest is without effigies. It was designed for Lewis, the 3rd Lord Mordaunt, who died in 1601, two years before his queen. Elizabeth's policy on religion was to firmly support the Church of England but, provided they paid all their dues to their parish church and clergy and did nothing to convert others, Roman Catholics were allowed to worship within their own private chapels. However, Roman Catholic families would not get paid positions at court or in the county, also they were more likely to get requests for extra taxes. Unlike some members of his family, Lewis Mordaunt had firmly declared for the Church of England. He took part in the trials of

Mary Queen of Scots and Thomas Howard, Duke of Norfolk, but, following Lewis' death, his son, Henry, reverted to the Church of Rome. There were very few Roman Catholic families in Bedfordshire but Turvey is on the northwest border of the county and not far from the long-established Roman Catholic families of Buckinghamshire and Northamptonshire.

Gun Powder Plot

For confused reasons concerning the pope's support for Spain, which some people considered England's enemy, Roman Catholics were often regarded with suspicion - maybe money they sent to the pope would end up supporting England's enemies. Planning for the Gunpowder Plot of 1605 took place at nearby Gayhurst House. There was no evidence that Lord Henry had any part in the plot but he was arrested and put in the Tower of London. He was under forty years old but his stay in the Tower began to undermine his health. It is said that when he was eventually released, the church bells rang and the people of Turvey came out to meet him. However, the authorities didn't trust him or his wife. When he died in 1609, they stepped in and removed his eldest son and made sure that he was brought up as an Anglican. Some years later, in 1628, despite the fact that at Turvey his mother was providing accommodation for the pope's representative and his team of priests, King Charles I gave the young man the title Earl of Peterborough. He also allowed John's son, five-year-old Henry, to take the title Viscount.

A Troubled Time for the Mordaunt Family

The years went by and gradually the relationship between King Charles I and his parliament broke down. England was heading for a civil war. The Earl of Peterborough, who was sitting in the House of Lords, supported parliament and fought for them at Edgehill but when he died, in 1643, his sons raised a regiment to support King Charles. In May 1647, when King Charles was temporarily under house arrest at Great Lodge, Ampthill, the new earl took a great risk and rode over to swear his continued allegiance. More fighting broke out in 1648 and this time the earl was wounded, at a skirmish in Surrey. He escaped to Antwerp but during the following year, he decided to make his peace with parliament. He paid £5,000 to compensate for the trouble he had caused by his disloyalty and returned home to Turvey.[1] His brother, John, had escaped

1 A detailed inventory of his house taken by the Parliamentary Commissioners is included in BHRS Vol 65

from Surrey without being wounded and became increasingly troublesome, continually plotting against parliament. Also about this time, a group of Royalists from elsewhere were identified at a Turvey pub and were taken to Bedford for trial. An investigation proved that they were not actually plotting and they were released. Parliament had every reason to be suspicious of John Mordaunt. On 1 March 1659, he was included in a group of six men the future Charles II commissioned to represent him in England and when there were further uprisings, he tried to stir up a revolt in Surrey. While John was moving around in support of Charles, the second Earl remained quietly at Turvey. After the restoration of Charles II, he was made a Privy Councillor but once again, he became worried about religious matters. Roman Catholic King James II came to the throne in 1685 and the Earl reverted to the beliefs of his grandfather. Three years later, James was chased from the country and the Earl was lucky not to be imprisoned; he died in 1697. During the next century, the family regained favour and married into several of the country's leading families. They are buried in the family vault at All Saints Church. The fifth and last Earl had no heirs and sold the estate to Charles Higgins, who was already living at what became known as Turvey House.[1] A relative, John Higgins, built Turvey Abbey House in 1794.

Charles Languet Higgins and Turvey Village

Turvey 'Abbey' stands at the further end of the village. Charles Languet Higgins, the son of John Higgins, inherited the house from his uncle in 1846. 'Abbey' was a name that had been chosen for the house; it had never been a monastery. He was forty years old in 1846 and had studied both law and medicine. He used his skills to help the village people and set out to improve their health, houses and education. Between 1849 and 1851, he built forty-nine cottages and some shops; he had already provided a National School and a Reading Room. In 1852, he began the restoration of the church. Where it was necessary to rebuild, he used local stone and carefully preserved the memorials and architectural details. The red brick mausoleum that had been built for his family can still be seen in the churchyard today. He died in 1885, having done everything within his power to help the people of Turvey. More about this good man and his influence on the village can be found in Simon Houfe's book 'Bedfordshire'.

1 Kuhlicke, F.W. A Bedfordshire Armorial. Beds Mag Vol 6

Turvey Abbey

Until 1880, the only connection that Turvey had with religious houses was the portions of land that had been given to them before the Dissolution. In 1880, Abbey House was bought by a Benedictine Order that included monks and nuns. They have preserved the Jacobean house but, being careful to use the appropriate stone, have added several new buildings. It is a very active and respected House and welcomes visitors to conferences and retreats.

The Public Houses

There are several pubs in the parish; the Three Cranes, near the church and the Three Fyshes, near the bridge are important features of this historic village.

The Bridge and its Statues

There was a very early bridge at this point of the river but most of what can be seen today was built in 1795 and the 1820s. Standing on an island just near the bridge are two pieces of 18th century sculpture. There are many stories about these two unusual figures. It is said that Jonah was brought there in 1844 from Ashridge House and that his companion appeared in 1953[1].

BROMHAM

ROUTE
Drive through Bromham village and continue, with the park and St Leonard's Church lying back on your left.

The Normans divided Bromham into four parts. Once again, the sheriff kept control of the main riverside community but he let out 720 acres of land, a particularly valuable watermill and an eel fishery, to one of his tenants. The Countess Judith had a small estate, let out to her tenant, Hugh. Included in her rent-roll was a much smaller mill and eel fishery, but the commissioners recorded that it was not part of Bromham. In addition, 180 acres had been allotted to Count Eustace and a few acres to Osgeat, the reeve.

Over the years, these four parts of Bromham passed to various Northamptonshire families. Some time before 1500, a Henry Dyve of Northamptonshire married Elizabeth, daughter of Thomas Wilde of Bromham and from early in the 16th century, this new family was involved in county affairs.

1 Not Another Guide Book. Cameo Studies of North Bedfordshire. Book 1

Three Fyshes Turvey

Bromham Bridge

189

The Dyve Family

Henry Dyve had a son, John (1), who was knighted in 1510 and in the same year, became Sheriff of Bedfordshire and Buckinghamshire. Sir John's main estates were in Northamptonshire, where his son, William and daughter-in-law, Isabel, continued to live with their son, Lewis (1). In 1544, he also was made Sheriff of Bedfordshire and Buckinghamshire and soon began to buy up the three other Bromham estates.

By the time that he died in 1592, he was living at Bromham Hall and passed the whole village to his son, John (2), who was knighted in 1603. John (2) and his first wife also lived at Bromham Hall and when she died in 1598, she was buried at the church in the park. Within months, Sir John had remarried, this time to twenty-four-year-old Beatrice Walcot, of Walcot, Shropshire. The following year, on 3 November 1599, their first son, Lewis (2) was born and was baptised at Bromham Church on 25 November. Nine months later, a second boy was born, but died eighteen months later. One has only to look at the godparents who attended these two baptisms to see how well accepted the Dyve family was. The St John family of Bletsoe, the Botelers of Biddenham, the Mordaunts of Turvey and the Rattcliffes of Elstow were all represented.

Lewis (2) was not quite four when James I knighted his father and the magnificent memorial was erected in St Owen's Church. This commemorates the life of Sir Lewis (1), who had installed the family in this impressive estate. Sir John himself died four years later and on 19 December 1607, was also buried at St Owen's. While Lewis (2) was still a schoolboy, his mother married again and went to live with her new husband, Sir John Digby. Lewis attended Oxford University but spent his free time with his mother and stepfather in Madrid. On 19 April 1620, seven months before his twenty-first birthday, he was knighted by James I. He returned to live with his mother and stepfather (now Earl of Bristol) and was with them during the time that Prince Charles (later Charles I) came to stay for nine days at their Madrid house. Prince Charles had come with his advisors to discuss the possibilities of marriage with the Infanta. He travelled in disguise, referring to himself as 'Mr Smith'. On one occasion, the young Sir Lewis rode out in his coach, ahead of the royal party, to mislead and draw away part of the crowd.

Plans for the royal marriage fell through and Sir Lewis and his family returned to England. In 1624, just before his twenty-fifth birthday, he married a young Dorset widow, Howarda Strangeways. They settled at Melbury, where their first daughter, Beatrice, was born. A son was born in London three years later, but

190

died within a few days. Two more boys were born at Melbury; Francis, who was born in 1632, was named after his godfather, the Earl of Bedford, of Woburn Abbey and Lewis (3).

Sir Lewis' fortunes varied with those of his (Digby) stepfather and stepbrother and for some time he was out of favour at court and took an increasing interest in his Bedfordshire estates. The family was living at Bromham when a daughter, Jane, was born in 1639 and still there when she died a year later. They visited London but as Sir Lewis' stepbrother implicated him in plots against parliament, he was obliged to leave and join the travelling household of King Charles I. The division between King and parliament widened and at the end of April 1642, Sir Lewis sailed for The Hague. For some months he travelled together with various royalist supporters, returning to England and Bromham during the middle of July. From this it can be seen that Sir Lewis was a personal friend of King Charles, so it is not surprising that he was Bedfordshire's most prominent royalist.

Civil War Comes to Bromham

Sir Samuel Luke, of Wood End, Cople (who would later become leader of the parliamentary soldiers in this area) recognised that Sir Lewis Dyve was the most likely man to attempt to hold Bedfordshire for the king. On 25 July, he heard that Sir Lewis had been in Bedford, ordering the blacksmiths to produce 500 bullets and that he had been threatening those townspeople whom he suspected of supporting parliament. The following day, Sir Lewis received £1,000 to buy horses on behalf of the king and Sir Thomas Alston of Odel, who was High Sheriff of Bedfordshire, received a message from The House of Lords to arrest Sir Lewis and bring him to London. So, on 27 July, Sir Thomas, Sir Samuel and one or two others rode out to Bromham Park, where they met a local man near the gate, who told them that Sir Lewis was at home. When they came nearer to the house, a group of servants denied that Sir Lewis was within. One servant was sent in to fetch Sir Lewis but he returned and repeated that his master was away. Another messenger was sent in 'in the name of The House of Lords'. This brought Lady Dyve to the door, also insisting that her husband was away. Reluctantly, she allowed two or three men to enter the house, but they were stopped by a man holding a pistol. Time was wasted while the sheriff sent back to Bedford to fetch more men. Meanwhile, Sir Samuel Luke and Sir Thomas Alston waited at the front door. Suddenly they saw Sir Lewis, covered by a handful of armed men, preparing to escape out of the back door, towards the

191

River Ouse. Sir Luke rushed forward to prevent Sir Lewis leaving, but raising his gun, Sir Lewis announced that he was acting in the name of the king and would shoot anyone who tried to stop him. Luke bravely rushed towards the escaping man; Dyve fired and wounded one of the sheriff's men, before thrusting his sword through Luke's arm and also wounding his thigh. In the general confusion, Sir Lewis escaped; a pair of boots, which were until recently kept at Bromham Hall, are said to have been left on the bank as he swam across the river.

After the War

Throughout the Civil War, Sir Lewis was an active and loyal officer. He was captured and spent some time in the Tower of London, escaped and fled to the Continent. He was in Italy when Charles II, the Wentworths of Toddington and many other royalist supporters returned to London. For five weeks, he lay in bed, too ill to contemplate moving, even though he was longing to arrange a passage on a ship, out of Leghorn and 'congratulate his Majestie's happy restauration'.[1]

Some time passed before he was able to return to England and it seems likely that he spent most of his visit at his London house, in Henrietta Street, Covent Garden. Although he spent most of his remaining years abroad, Samuel Pepys saw him in London on 1 January 1668, watching men who were gambling for very high stakes. Pepys commented that 'Sir Lewis Dives who was here, and hath been a great gamester in his time....'

By 1668 his gambling days were over; it has been suggested that over nearly twenty years, his loyalty to the Crown caused him to lose something like £164,000. Not only did he lose rents of £481.4s.8d per year, for his estates at Bromham, Stevington and Sewell (near Houghton Regis) but also rents for his land in Northamptonshire, his London house and a small estate he had purchased in Somerset.

The Dyves were not one of the families who, at the end of the war, received great honours; Francis became a gentleman of the king's privy chamber and Lewis (3) became a captain while fighting in Ireland. They could not afford to buy back the family estate, nor could Sir Lewis, who eventually returned to his

1 A large number of letters and papers written and received by Sir Lewis and his family, both before the war and during his time in the Tower of London, have been published as BHRS Vol 27 & 38

small estate at Combehay, in Somerset. In an attempt to keep at least part of the estates in the family, Sir Lewis' father-in-law, Sir John Strangeways, in 1652, bought Bromham for £4,970.13s.5d. Four years later, Sir John died and eventually Bromham passed to Sir Lewis' heir, Francis. When Sir Lewis made his will on 12 April 1669, he referred to himself as 'Lewis Dive late of Bromham....' but asked to be buried at Combehay; he died five days later.

Later Members of the Dyve Family

Francis Dyve, who presented a new pulpit to Bromham Church, died, at the age of fifty-three, sixteen years after his father. He bequeathed Bromham to his brother, Captain Lewis Dyve, who was still living in Ireland, but he died the following year. His son, another Lewis, came to Bromham when he was twenty-three and lived there for eight years. In 1708, he sold the whole estate for £21,394.2s.6d.to Sir Thomas Trevor, Lord Chief Justice of the Common Plea; Queen Anne created Sir Thomas Baron Trevor of Bromham. The youngest of Sir Lewis' sons, a second John, had already died in 1692, but although the Dyve family had no further connection with Bromham, it is possible that the Charlotte Dyve who married Sir William Clayton of Sundon was a daughter of this John. She took her two nieces, Charlotte and Dorothy Dyve, to Queen Caroline's Court.

Bromham Bridge

This bridge, which divided the parishes of Bromham and Biddenham, was originally named after the latter village. It was a notoriously difficult piece of road for travellers and the flooded water meadows, on the Biddenham side, made it particularly difficult to provide a safe bridge. The account of annual events [Annals] kept by the canons of Dunstable Priory, recorded a tragedy which took place in 1281. Water and frost had weakened the piers that supported the bridge and one particularly severe frost, followed by the movement of the swollen river, caused the piers to crumble. A lady, who was standing on the bridge,

> **ROUTE**
> When this road comes up to the Bedford Road, the route turns left and crosses Bromham Bridge. (The entrance to the mill is on the left at the approach to the bridge.)

fell onto the broken ice, along with the crumbling stone and was carried away towards Bedford. It may be that some travellers were among the crowd, who stood helpless on the riverbank, because someone must have described her perilous journey to the canons. No-one could reach her and, as the flowing water piled the ice against Bedford Bridge, she disappeared under the water.

At that early period, there were no tollgates and no national scheme for the repair of bridges. Local landowners had a legal duty to repair bridges, but this did not provide for major capital expenditure. Gradually, bridge building and repairs became recognised as a charity and the responsibility for bridges, or sections of bridges was given to religious houses. They would be licensed to ask travellers for alms and used the money collected to keep the bridges in a good state of repair; any surplus amounts were used for other good causes. Difficult river crossings, which slowed travellers down, made them vulnerable to robbers, so, in 1295, Matthew of Dunstable founded a chapel on the bridge, dedicated to St Mary. Thirty years later, the Rev Simon de Wolston gave sections of the land on both sides of the bridge to convert this original place of worship into a formal chantry chapel, dedicated to 'Our Lady and St Kathryn'. The chaplain would continue to attract alms by praying for the safety of travellers, but would also sing mass each day for the souls of founder, Geoffrey Smyth and all the faithful departed.

Over the years, several people from Bromham and surrounding villages left bequests to help to keep the bridge in good repair. All appears to have been well until 1548, when the chantries were closed. At that time, Peter Weyver, a naturalised Frenchman, was the incumbent. The estate, owned by the chantry, from which the rents were valued at £7=15s=6d (£7.77$^{1}/_{2}$p, profit £7.30p). It was made up of seven houses of various sizes; two or three of which appear to have been smallholdings. There were also several pieces of water meadow and pasture. The chaplain, Peter Weyver, had access to a quarry pit and other stone was also available. We do not know what happened to Weyver; he was not qualified to become a parish priest and received a pension of £5 a year. The chapel itself must have been very simple; either the chaplain had hidden the church plate and vessels before the valuers arrived, or he was using his own. The only 'goodes and ornamentes' that they found were two bells.

It is thought that the chapel and/or chaplain's house, stood on the Bromham mill side of the bridge and that it was absorbed into the millkeeper's house. This was demolished in 1902. Any other buildings associated with the chantry were probably destroyed during the frequent bridge repairs and rebuilding.

After the closing of the chantry, the income went to the Crown and the bridge was soon in a bad state of repair. During the reign of Queen Mary, parishes were made directly responsible for roads and bridges. They did not take their responsibility very seriously and the bridge suffered. It was impossible for the people of two, small, rural villages to maintain such an important bridge.

It was still known as Biddenham Bridge when a survey was made in 1630 and it appears that Bromham had no responsibility. Biddenham parish was responsible for a double arch over the actual river, but the other three high arches and the twenty lower ones, over the Biddenham water meadows, were kept in repair by a county levy. A surviving plaque records that the county undertook major repairs in 1685. This plaque can sometimes be seen from the mill, as can small sections of this early bridge.

However, by the early 19th century, the bridge was no longer suitable, and so, during 1813-14, it was rebuilt, in two sections. At the time, it was considered a great improvement but, in less than one hundred years, a county council committee reported that it was 'quite impossible for two carts to pass.....and unsafe for a horseman, pedestrian or cyclist to pass a vehicle in motion...'

This was at the time that 'self-propelled vehicles' [motor cars and vans] were beginning to share the bridge with traditional, horse-drawn carts and coaches; the bridge had to be widened. Most of the arches that we see today were built in 1813-14, but the section over the river was built in 1902-3. The full account of repairs and reconstruction, which have taken place in the last two hundred years, are set out in the Bedfordshire Magazine, by Paul Tritton.[1]

Bromham Mill

The Dyve family house still stands today (privately owned) and their monuments are in St Owen's Church, which stands in the park. The watermill, which the first Sir Lewis Dyve bought in 1565, was partly rebuilt by his descendants; the date 1695 is carved on existing stonework. After Sir Lewis' descendant sold the estate in 1708, the new owner carried out more changes and, at the end of the 18th century, the tenant was prosecuted because improvements and extension caused 'so much motion and noise', that the wheels in motion frightened horses passing over the bridge. It was said that drivers of coaches and carriages were frightened to pass by. Presumably, he arrived at the Quarter Sessions prepared with a scheme to muffle the noise, because he was only fined one shilling! (The early Turnpike Trust was renewed in 1790 and it was important not to discourage travellers.) This is the watermill that, in 1086, was valued at £1 and 125 eels per year. In 1708, the tenant was paying £53=5s=4d (approx £53.27p).

When a very old iron wheel was removed in 1939, an eel trap was found, which, it was said, had once trapped 1½cwt of eels in one night! Unfortunately, this has since been demolished.

1 *Tritton, P. Beds Magazine Vol 20 No 153*

ROUTE

Once over the bridge, the route continues towards Bedford and, just as it meets the Biddenham signs, bears right to rejoin the A428.
By turning left onto this road, the route will return to Bedford but there is a signposted right-hand turn for Biddenham village.

So today's Bromham Mill is one of Bedfordshire's few remaining sites which have been in use since before 1066. Over the centuries, there have been different buildings and different sources of power, but, by 1973, the building was in a very bad state of repair. It was bought by Bedfordshire County Council, but before they could start to repair it, there was a serious fire. Since then, both the building and the waterwheel have been completely restored and visitors are welcome to watch it working.

Today, the working watermill houses a contemporary art and craft gallery, with a busy programme of events, workshops and summer exhibitions.

The Mid-Bedfordshire Scenic Route

**Ampthill • Maulden • (Haynes West End) • Haynes Church End
Ireland • (Old Warden) • (Ickwell) • (Moggerhanger)
Southill • (Stanford) • (Sandy) • Shefford • Chicksands • Clophill
Silsoe • (Wrest Park) • Flitton • (Harlington) • (Flitwick)
(Woburn) • (Aspley Guise) • (Houghton House) • Ampthill**

Introduction

This route is approximately 30 miles long and passes through some of the most beautiful scenery in Bedfordshire. It is a shortened version of the Scenic Route designed by Mid Beds District Council. The theme of the route is historic houses and at four places along this route, directions towards other important houses are pointed out.

The Historical Background of this route starts millions of years ago with the climatic changes that resulted in a belt of greensand running diagonally across Bedfordshire. This proved very suitable for monks who wanted sheep runs and rabbit warrens.

In the 12th to the 16th centuries, the area was dominated by two large Cistercian monasteries, Woburn and Warden, separated by a Gilbertine House at Chicksands. In addition, several other religious houses, including St Albans Abbey and Dunstable Priory, also owned land in this area.

After the Dissolution, these estates were mainly bought by London courtiers and/or businessmen who continued the policy of maintaining large private parks, backed up by attractive home farms and strictly controlled tenancies. Because of this, Mid Bedfordshire is particularly rich in attractive estate villages.

During the economic problems of the 18th and 19th centuries, the inhabitants of these villages were sheltered from the exceptional unemployment and abject poverty experienced in some parts of England. The main exception to this was Maulden, where the scattered hamlets were never gathered into the safety of one great estate. Because of this, a potted history of this non-estate village is included in the historical background.

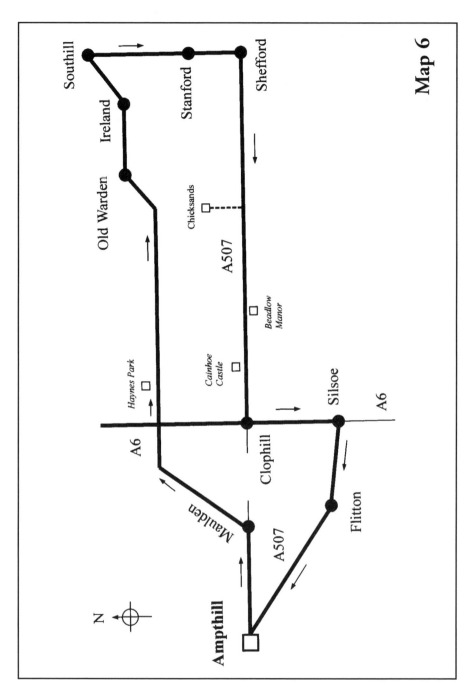

Map 6

This route is particularly rich in Historical Highlights. Starting in the attractive market town of Ampthill, with its Georgian buildings and antique shops, it passes through Maulden and heads for Haynes Park. This is not open to the public but there is an excellent view from the road. Ireland is not mentioned; it was once part of the 'inlands' of the Southill Estate. Scenes from Southill village can be found on calendars, as can those of Old Warden.

The Historical Highlights section illustrates how exceptionally rich this area is in historic houses. One by one, the secular history and quite often the monastic origins of these estates are discussed.

Because this is a much-shortened version of the actual Scenic Route, there are many important buildings that, under various circumstances, are open to the public, but not included in the route. However, they have been included in this section. The Scenic Route leaflet produced by the council and other individual leaflets also available at the TIC point out which of these houses and/or grounds do open to the public.

The area is also rich in other types of tourist attraction eg The Swiss Garden, Shuttleworth Collection and The Bird of Prey Centre at Old Warden, the RSPB Nature Reserve at Sandy and the amazing Stondon Transport Museum near Henlow. Variations of this route are also suitable for walkers and cyclists and both the written history and the highlights are an excellent introduction for newcomers and visitors to the county.

Historical Background

Along the Scenic Route, which has been signposted by Mid Beds District Council, there are many important historic houses*. These are set amongst miles of beautiful countryside. Some of this follows the traditional arable and hedgerow form of scenery, while some of it is more open, vegetable-growing country and, in addition to the magnificent parkland trees, there are areas of quite dense woodland. The reason for this beautiful scenery can be traced back over millions of years.

The Greensand Ridge
Around 100 million years ago a strong narrow channel of seawater swept across what we now know as Mid Bedfordshire and deposited a layer of sand on top of the existing clay. Changes, including the various Ice Ages, exposed a belt of this sand.

Leaflets available from all Tourist Information Centres

At the time of the last Ice Age, about 12,000 years ago, it is thought that the ridge was left bare and treeless but, over the next 4,000 years, the warmer, wetter climate encouraged the growth of thick forests. Nevertheless, some trees found the sandy soil too well-drained and this resulted in patches of heathland. There were also occasional, low-lying patches of water, such as at Flitwick, where there is still an area of peat left today.

Changes in the Scenery

During this period of lakes and forests, the people we describe as 'Mesolithic' were hunting boar and other wild animals in the forests and fishing and snaring wild birds around the lakes.

Increasingly, these hunters cut down small trees to build fires for warmth, cooking and protection. Because of their hunting and gathering lifestyle, they were constantly on the move and seldom cut mature trees. However, from around 4,000 BC, when farming skills were first introduced, an increasing amount of mature trees were felled for a wide variety of uses.

No doubt even more trees were used during the prosperous period when Roman officials ruled the country and when, during the 5th and 6th centuries, the Saxon farmers settled across Bedfordshire. They made clearings (leahs) in the woods, such as at Aspley (Guise)], where the aspen trees grew. It has been suggested that, in many areas, the woodland scenery of 1086 was similar to that of 1914, but this is not true in much of Mid Bedfordshire.

Different Woodland - Different Uses

The Norman, 'Domesday' tax assessment of 1086 recorded woodland in relation to the number of pigs that it could support. The fertile soils which covered part of the chalk around Luton supported 2000 pigs. On the other side of South Bedfordshire, at Leighton Buzzard, the trees on the sandy soil could only support 200. No pigs at all were recorded on the very large estate at Sandy, although there was a reference to 3 acres of woodland. One hundred and seventy pigs were supported under the deciduous trees on the north-west corner of Maulden and 300 on the clay to the south of Ampthill.

Until the light sandy soil was improved, arable farming remained very difficult. This meant that in the 11th and 12th centuries, many of the villages had a below-average population. Maybe this is why, in the 1220s, both Woburn and (Old) Warden were given to the Cistercian monks.

The Influence of the Religious Houses and Later Owners

Many other villages were absorbed into these two great estates and in between, Chicksands was given to the English order of Gilbertines. Part of Haynes was also given to the Gilbertines and Beaulieu (represented today by Beadlow Manor), was once the property of St Albans Abbey. Many more of the villages around the Scenic Route were owned by other religious houses and just to the north, Elstow and its environs belonged to a Benedictine nunnery.

These religious houses were surrounded by private grounds, gardens and courtyards; they also had a home farm and fish ponds. Much of the farming carried out to produce income, was the breeding and rearing of sheep. For privacy, their houses were built well away from the village centres and after the Dissolution, these monastic estates formed some of the great estates that we know today.

Although the descendants of these first secular owners may sometimes have cut down trees, they planted many more and developed much of today's beautiful scenery. King Henry VIII already owned Ampthill and its extensive park but following the Dissolution, his steward added much of the surrounding wood and scrubland. Parts of Flitwick, Steppingley and several other villages were drawn into the royal hunting preserves.

The Farming of Rabbits

Although hares are recorded as 'beasts of warren' in 1086, rabbits are not recorded until later. The Observers' Book of Wild Animals suggests that they arrived in England in the 12th century and there are written records concerning their management from the 13th century. They were then kept for the use of the king and for those landowners to whom he sold a licence. Tenant farmers could only catch rabbits on their own land if they had permission and poachers were very harshly treated. The rabbits were allowed to graze freely but to keep some control over them, the warrener tried to construct ditch and bank or stone-wall boundaries. They were kept for food and also for the warmth of their skins so they were fed hay in the winter and a supply of water was provided. Because the main concern was with the breeding stock and their young, sand (chalk in Dunstable) was piled into 'pillar mounds'. These were filled with artificial burrows so that if the cook demanded a number of young rabbits for the kitchen, they were easily extracted. The warrener's cottage usually stood out in the wood so that he could watch out for poachers and trap foxes and polecats.

Well before the Dissolution the monks were letting out their warrens; the Haynes warren (belonging to Chicksands Priory) was included in the Grange

Farm estate. Shefford warren was rented out separately; this rent included '40 couples or pairs of rabbits to be delivered at Christmas and the first day of Lent'.* After the Dissolution, Edward Peke paid well over £5 per year for four sections of the warren, plus 'the loppes (brushings)bushes, brome (broom?) and underwood'. Rowney warren was not included in the lease nor were the Great and Little vineyards. The Woburn warrens were valued at £5 and £7 per year.

On the royal estate of Ampthill 'Custodians' were paid to manage the warrens. There were two at Ampthill itself and one at Millbrook; they were each paid £4 per year. During the winter of 1542-43 they had produced 1624 coneys (rabbits) which were valued at 21s=0d per 100.

Living on the Greensand Ridge

After the Dissolution, when wealthy, secular owners took over the monastic estates, the rabbits, fish and animals within the parks were only for the benefit of the very rich. There were cottages and, by the standards of the day, quite good wages for the numerous people employed on the estates but it was a difficult area for tenant farmers to make a living. The comparative poverty of the farmers filtered down through the village communities and some suffered great distress. If the village was part of a big estate, help was usually available; if not, the only support came from Parish Relief. This was money collected from the better-off parishioners and those who were just managing and used to support the poor and sick. Therefore during years of extremely bad weather and disastrous harvests, very little help could be given to the poor because the farmers and tradesmen were themselves in trouble.

There was no national or county-based assistance and some villages, such as Maulden, suffered years of poverty. Part of that village was owned by the Houghton House estate but part of the parish was left to its own resources.

Help From the Great Estates

The chapter of this book concerning churches records the close relationship between the village church and the lord of the manor. Many examples of their patronage and parish assistance will be seen along this route eg schools, almshouses, farm workers' cottages and even village halls and sports facilities.

Village Schools

It was not until 1870 that the government passed the Board School Act which obliged every parish to build a school large enough to provide a seat for every

* By this date the monks were allowed to eat white meat during Lent

child in the parish. However, long before that date those landowners who saw the need for education, were providing financial help.

Charity day schools were very small and only available to the sons of farmers and the better-off traders but soon after 1800, a new form of education became more widely available. These first 'Sunday' schools were often in the estate villages; many in villages around the Scenic Route. At these, boys, girls and even some adults were taught reading and a little writing, based on the Bible and books of religious instruction. Then, one by one, the landowners began to provide teachers and if necessary, school rooms so that children could attend during the week. Many of these schools were linked to a Church of England charity - the 'National' Schools Association, a few were associated with the Non-conformist 'British' Schools charity.

Some of these schools can be identified along the route as parish halls, offices and even private dwellings. Other 19th century charity schools have been taken over, modernised and expanded by Bedfordshire County Council. They may be called 'Voluntary Aided' (VA) schools and the diocese may still have some influence on the running of them.

The Rural Industries

As the agricultural industry was so vulnerable to the weather and to political policies at Westminster, villagers needed a second form of income.

The Extraction of Minerals

Several villages along the route were saved from extreme distress by finding that they had a source of minerals that was in demand by industry. This route does not drop down as far as Heath and Reach, where sand and gravel are still being extracted today, nor to Leighton Buzzard where passengers on the railway can visit an industrial heritage and interpretive centre, but these are pointed out on other routes.

Not only were there many quarries for sand and gravel, but also patches of clay; because of this, many villagers were able to make bricks. When the route passes through Millbrook, it is on the edge of what was once one of the largest commercial brick-making businesses in Europe. Reclamation has resulted in some attractively restored countryside, several man-made lakes and the Forest Centre of the Marston Vale Millennium Country Park.*

A particularly rare and yet important mineral found along the route is Fuller's Earth. Originally it was in great demand for the cleaning of fleeces before the

* *Leaflets available from the Tourist Information Centres*

wool was prepared for spinning but today it is used in paint, chemicals and other modern industries. The seams at Woburn Sands have been worked for many centuries.

Roadside Villages

Clophill (which stood on what is now the crossing of the A6 and the A507) was well-placed to take advantage of passing travellers. It is typical of several similar villages along the route.

Within the parish of Clophill, Cainhoe Castle was deserted well before 1400 and Beaulieu, the very small priory belonging to Saint Albans Abbey, had been reduced to the status of a farm. In the centuries to follow, Clophill would have suffered very badly had it not been for the traffic passing between London and Oakham. Silsoe, sheltered by the Grey family of Wrest Park, provided accommodation for their house-guests as well as for travellers, but Clophill and other similar villages could also supply food, drink and other needs of passing travellers. What was probably just as important, was that the roads provided marketing opportunities for the villages' other local industries. Like their neighbours, the residents of Clophill grew vegetables both for the local towns and for the London market. They also made strawplait, which a dealer collected from The Flying Horse Inn, for the Luton hat trade. In later years, when there was an even greater demand for straw boaters, there was a small hat factory in the village and the local carrier took the finished hats into Luton.

Market Gardening

It is thought that this originated in the area of Sandy in the early years of the 17th century. It was already well-developed in the 18th century when there were references to the 'carret ground' and the 'rhedish (radish) ground'. It started on the alluvial-rich terraces of the River Ivel but as the demand grew, it became worthwhile to add large quantities of manure and straw to improve the lighter greensand. The coming of the turnpike system of road improvement (toll gates) in the early to mid 18th century made it possible to get vegetables to London much more quickly. The industry then spread over a wider area. Kent claims to be the 'Garden' of England but 'Orchard' would be a more accurate name. After the opening of the London to York railway in 1850, east Bedfordshire had a much stronger claim to the title 'Garden' of England.

Villages and the Railway

Although the first local railway was opened on 17 September, 1838, the stations at Linslade and Bletchley were over the county boundary.

The Branch Line to Bletchley

Eight years later a branch line was opened between Bletchley and Bedford (St Leonards) via Fenny Stratford, Woburn Sands, Ridgemont, Lidlington and Marston Morteyne. This linked the villages at the western end of the ridge with both London and Birmingham. The Duke of Bedford was influential concerning progress of this line and, using a silver spade and a wheelbarrow made from oak grown on the Bedford estate, the Duchess 'cut the first sod'. This was at the halfway point, at Husborne Crawley.

This railway line was very helpful to local industry; the Bedford to London horse-drawn coach took $4^{1}/_{2}$ hours and cost £1=1s, whereas the train did the same journey in $2^{1}/_{2}$ hours, for a quarter of the price. Eleven years after the opening of this line, the Mayor of Bedford pointed out that the traffic brought to the town had increased from 200 tons to 2,000 tons a month - and this did not include the 180 tons of coal.

The Midland Railway

After the opening of the Midland Railway in 1868, London could be reached even more quickly. Stations were built at Bedford (Midland Road), Ampthill and Harlington (also Leagrave and Luton) and two years later at Flitwick.

The Great Northern Railway

At the other end of Mid Bedfordshire's greensand, the vegetable growers benefited by the railway, which opened in 1850. This was built to link Huntingdon with London but was also used to transport fresh fruit and vegetables into Covent Garden. According to the Bedfordshire Times, the opening celebrations at Biggleswade began with the pealing of the church bells and ended with a grand dinner in the Town Hall for the local gentry. It was a public holiday and throughout the day the crowds were entertained by the Ampthill Brass Band. The original stations were Arlesey, Biggleswade and Sandy but seven years later, when a branch line went out to Potton, even more smallholders and growers had easy access.

Maulden - A Village on the Greensand Ridge

Over the centuries a great deal was done to improve the sandy soil and Maulden

205

is now an area of successful farms, and until recently, market gardens. The majority of residents live in attractive, modern or modernised houses and travel out of the village to their work, but in earlier centuries this was not possible. Many of the villages along the Scenic Route were partly sheltered from agricultural poverty by the presence of the great estates; others had a very hard time. Maulden, the first village along the Scenic Route, is one of the latter and some of its difficulties are entered below.

Early History

By the 11th century much of the original scrubland had been cleared and apart from the main village, there were several small settlements, including a watermill on a small tributary of the River Ivel, at what is now Hall End on the Clophill boundary. These 'Ends' may represent separate clearings which became divisions at the time of the Conquest, or they may represent later gifts to religious houses.

1066 and All That

When, following the successful Battle of Hastings, Bedfordshire was shared amongst King William's family, friends and key supporters, the people of Maulden found themselves with five different landlords. The sheriff kept a small farm for his own use and a second for one of his officials, Nigel of Albini from nearby Cainhoe, who later negotiated a further 25 acres. The two main landholders were Judith, niece of King William, and the Sheriff of Buckinghamshire. The latter's 360 acres included woodland capable of feeding about 50 pigs. It had a sub-tenant, Hugh de Bolbec of Whitchurch Castle (Bucks), who also held Woburn. This estate is commemorated by Bolbec Farm to the north-west of the village. It was a descendant of Hugh who founded the Cistercian Woburn Abbey but part of his Maulden estate was given to Warden Abbey.

Judith received the main 600 acre estate and then gave it to the Benedictine nunnery which she founded at Elstow. In addition to arable and woodland, this included the watermill and part of the water-meadows. The nuns appreciated the usefulness of this valuable estate; their bailiff farmed it carefully and improved its productivity. Over the years more portions of Maulden's land were also given to the Abbey. Warden Abbey's Grange Farm may originally have been run by lay brothers, but latterly the land was let out to tenants.

After the Dissolution of the Monastic Houses

Between 1535 and 1540 all monastic property passed into the hands of King Henry VIII. From Elstow's share of Maulden he received twenty-eight cottages, workshops and farmhouses, most of which must have been on the high ground along the present village road and its attractive turnings. By this time the watermill at Hall End was worth nearly 44 shillings (£2.20)] per year. The moats that were once clearly visible in the fields of north Maulden may represent the different Norman manors but it has been suggested that some were already deserted by the mid 16th century. This is because in 1542 the king's rent collector, John Brysco, reported that no profit was made from the 3 acre grove 'with the motes' at Limbershey in Maulden.*

In addition to the village, the church, most of the arable land, the meadow and the water-mills, the nuns had also owned all or most of Maulden Woods. No tenant was offered this piece of woodland; it was kept for the king. When his bailiff handed in the annual rents, he was allowed to keep back 13s=9d [approx. 69p] to repair a certain fence around this wood because ' there was great need.....that is for making 165 stakes at 1d each (under ¹/₂ p)'.

Gradually the king's stewards managed to sell and convert into cash much of the new, royal estates. During the next 100 years various parts of Maulden were sold and sold again. Then in 1635 the main village was sold to the Earl of Elgin of Houghton House.

The Civil War

No doubt the people of Maulden suffered, as did the rest of Bedfordshire, from high taxes and the compulsory levy of soldiers, horses and food. There is a family story that at the outbreak of the Civil War, Lord Elgin was preparing to ride across to Oxford to join King Charles, when his wife persuaded him not to do so. She had a premonition that Parliament was going to win and realised that if it did, the Royalists would lose their estates. He remained at home throughout the war but was always treated with suspicion by his Parliamentary neighbours. Nevertheless, his lands were not sequestered for the use of Parliament.

After the Dissolution, another local landowner, Edward Conquest, had managed to achieve the position of rent-collector and Custodian of the Royal Woods for part of the scattered Elstow estate, including part of Maulden. By the time of the civil war, his family owned land in Maulden village. Being both a

* *This sounds like a disused rabbit warren but, if so, Brysco would probably have mentioned it.*

Royalist and a Roman Catholic, Richard Conquest's land was sequestered; in other words his rents were collected and used by Parliament. William Pryor, one of his tenants who found himself in this same position, may also have held land at Maulden. Such tenants were sometimes charged twice for their rent, the Parliamentary rent collector calling during the day and the Royalist landowner's collector at night. The Toach family was Conquest's main tenant in their home village and one year, having handed over £110 rent to Parliament, Goodwife Toach (whose husband was away) woke to find Sir Richard himself standing by her bed with a cocked pistol. He threatened to destroy her whole family if she did not give him her rent. However the main Maulden 'delinquent' (enemy of parliament) was Thomas Cookson. When he was called before the parliamentary officers in 1646, to explain why his leased land in Maulden should not be sequestered, he made the following statement:

He had gone to Oxford during the Michaelmas term in 1643 to study 'physicke' but admitted that he had been caught up with the king's forces in Towcester and as a result had spent 10 weeks in the king's quarters at Oxford. However he claimed that 'he never did beare Armes against the Parliament'. He also assured the officers that he regularly attended communion in the Church of England ie he was not a Roman Catholic.

Nevertheless they voted to take over his lease 'for the use of the state'.[1]

The 17th Century

Early in the reign of King Charles II (c1662) a new tax was introduced; this was the Hearth Tax. The published tax for 1671 gives us the opportunity to compare the welfare of various Bedfordshire villages.[2] Those people who were suffering poverty were excused payment and this group made up nearly $^2/_5$ of Bedfordshire households but at Maulden, it was far less. This suggests that Maulden was slightly better off than many other villages. Further comparisons show that it was much better off than several of its neighbours.

The installation of proper chimneys that allowed for more than one hearth was comparatively new in Bedfordshire. Many Maulden households had only one hearth, representing a high proportion for mid Bedfordshire; however, the number in Haynes and Clophill were higher still. The earl's tenant or bailiff in the manor house had twelve hearths, compared with 55 at the earl's own great house at Houghton Conquest. Several of the Maulden farmhouses, both in and around the village, had 4, 5 or even 6 hearths and although much altered, some

1 BHRS Vol 49   2 BHRS Vol 16

of these still stand today. Looking forward to village life in the 18th century, it seems likely that the comparative prosperity may have been due to the start of the market-garden industry.

The 18th Century

Just when the demand for Maulden-grown vegetables occurred is not known but by 1671 some of the more prosperous cottagers had enclosed pieces of land and were probably using them to grow vegetables. By 1708 there are references to the sale of turnips, onions, carrots, beans and peas. These may have been sold in Bedford market or sent to London by carrier along what is now the A6.

The population began to grow but, like agriculture, market-gardening was dependent on the weather and the fickleness of the market. The Earl of Elgin and his son, Robert, Earl of Aylesbury, appear to have been conscientious landlords. They took a great deal of interest in St Mary's church, Maulden and had their mausoleum built in the churchyard*. In the previous century the Earl had bequeathed an investment of £100, the interest to be used for the poor people of Maulden. He also provided a building in which the ground floor was used as an almshouse and the upper floor as a schoolroom.

However, during the early 18th century, the family began to suffer financial distress and the Duke of Bedford had begun to buy up the occasional freehold cottage or piece of land. In 1738 he bought the manorial estate from the descendants of the Earl of Elgin. This was an enormous boost for the tenants because the Woburn estate offered its tenants advice and, at times, cheap (or even free) plants, shrubs and trees.

The people of Maulden enjoyed a close relationship with the more wealthy community at Ampthill, but as with any industry, some gardeners succeeded while others failed. However, even those who were successful at producing fruit and vegetables found it difficult to expand. They usually rented their enclosed plots of land but could not afford to buy them.

Towards the end of the century there was a great deal of rural poverty in Bedfordshire. Those villagers who worked for the Duke of Bedford were sheltered but amongst Maulden's growing population there were many poor people dependent on parish relief. The more the population grew, the lower the payments available. However, being so near to the township of Ampthill and the roads to both Bedford and London, they could gain some relief by making lace and straw plait.

This important mausoleum is currently being restored by Bedfordshire County Council

Although much of the land had been enclosed, many of the villagers still had strips of land on which to grow cereals and they also had grazing rights on the extensive common that they shared with Flitton. Even the right to cut turf for firing was a great help to poor families. When, in 1796, there was talk among the landowners of enclosing the remaining open fields and commons, the desperate people rose in revolt.

It was estimated that around two hundred people gathered in the village centre and were so 'disorderly' and their language 'so improper' that the local magistrate, the Rev Webster, of Meppershall, was sent for but he found it difficult to quieten them. Eventually, 'by moderation and fair speech' he prevented an outbreak of violence but the Enclosure Commissioners were frightened to carry out their survey without support from a military guard. The Rev Webster wrote to the War Office and requested that 30 or 40 soldiers might be quartered at Ampthill. The response was to send a troop of cavalry!

The 19th Century

The enclosure was eventually completed in 1803. Although a small area of common had been saved, many of the older cottages had lost their grazing rights and some of their free firing. Tenants of the new cottages were often without proper gardens. For work, many cottagers relied on casual, seasonal labour on the farms or gardens, eked out with equally seasonal work in the lace and strawplait industries. Cottagers who were direct tenants of the Duke of Bedford were much better off than their neighbours. He kept his old cottages in good repair and built two pairs of new ones. He also set an example in the neighbourhood by laying out numerous new allotments.

The Population Explosion

In 1671, the population of Maulden was estimated as 599 but by 1801 it had risen to 738. No speculative building would have been allowed in the part of the village controlled by the Duke of Bedford but elsewhere freeholders were delighted to sell odd pieces of their land to builders. In the next 17 years the population rose by more than a hundred.

Socially the village was divided; smallholders, gardeners and men in regular employment lived in relatively comfortable cottages but many others lived in some of the worst cottages in Bedfordshire. The local Overseer of the Poor collected poor rates from those who could afford to pay, wrote up his accounts and distributed the money to those who were in desperate need. A 'townhouse' sometimes called the 'workhouse' was supported from this money. In Maulden this appears to have been a row of cottages which were described in 1790 as being in such a dreadful state of repair that they were 'an offence to the common feeling of humanity'.

Although the overseer was backed by the local magistrate, he was not to be envied. He was constantly blamed for being too sympathetic (with other people's money) or of not being sympathetic enough. During the winter of 1814 he twice turned single men away from the workhouse and was reprimanded by Justice Samuel Whitbread, who made him admit them. One of these was desperately short of clothes and may have been a vagrant.

Mr Whitbread was no soft touch but he was a practical and humane magistrate. The year before, the overseer had refused help to an old lady whose lame husband was suspected of malingering. Mr Whitbread sent someone to check the details, sent the husband to Bedford hospital and ordered the overseer to support the old lady. This was all before the Poor Law Act of 1834 that brought an end to 'out relief' which had concentrated on keeping people in their own homes. The new Act enforced the sale of local buildings and the provision of 'Union' Workhouses. Maulden was in the Union of Ampthill and any individual or family needing support was obliged to go there as a resident. Once there, families were split up and lived on a diet of bread with gruel, bread with beef and potato soup or occasionally bread with small quantities of meat or cheese. Only the elderly were allowed very small quantities of butter, tea and sugar. In some parts of mid Bedfordshire this Act was followed by individual or organised outbreaks of violence. In May 1835 crowds gathered in the garden of the Union Workhouse, broke all the windows and did a great deal of damage. The riot continued for several days and was only disbanded by the arrival of members of the Metropolitan Police. The workhouse had to be entirely rebuilt.

No men from Maulden were arrested at the scene of the riot and the influence of the Woburn steward may have prevented trouble in the village, but nevertheless, several men were arrested for poaching. There were few charities available to help to support the people of Maulden. An Ampthill lady had provided for four poor Maulden women to receive a blue gown and a pair of shoes at Christmas and there was still the Earl of Elgin's almshouse and schoolroom.

The National School

The income from the earl of Elgin's bequest and from another much smaller one was used to teach five poor boys to read, write and cost accounts and five girls to read and do 'several kinds of work' (housework and plaiting?). In the 19th century the day school became even smaller but there was a Sunday School for 58 boys and girls. This was the position in 1818 when the rector reported that 'the poor are desirous of possessing sufficient means of education'. Unbelievably, between the survey of schools in 1818 and the next one in 1833 the population of Maulden had risen by nearly 50%. This was at the height of the agricultural depression when lace-making had become a very important economic factor. Although only 5 boys were attending the charity school, 36 boys and 60 girls were attending lace schools. The five boys were probably the sons of farmers and tradespeople because the poor needed all the money that the children could earn. Because they really were desirous of education, 50 boys and 80 girls were attending the church Sunday School; in addition, 50 boys and girls were attending a Baptist Sunday School and 20 boys and 24 girls went to one run by the Wesleyan Methodists.

By 1845 it was possible for a few children to attend a new day school in Ampthill but one was still needed in the village, particularly for infants; the problem was that, even if one was built, it would not be supported by the parents. Nevertheless, ten years later, the Duke of Bedford donated the site and materials of the old school plus £192 to start a new Church of England National School. When a school inspector visited Maulden in July 1851, (haymaking time?) there were only 28 children present. He thought that the school mistress was a 'respectable and conscientious young woman' and that the arrangements were quite good. However, he noted that 'out of a population of 1,400 only 20 (children) were in daily attendance'. He blamed 'the occupation of the parents' for this poor attendance. Numbers had, at times, been higher than this but they always fell sharply when there was fruit or vegetables to harvest or when help was needed with the haymaking. Despite the financial problems that were experienced in Maulden, the numbers gradually improved.

As the years went by there was an increasing demand for compulsory education but there was little point introducing such an Act unless there were sufficient school places. A date was set by which time every parish should supply enough places. If they failed to do so, the parishes would be obliged to elect a committee or 'board', borrow the money from the government and build a new 'Board' school. On March 3rd 1873 Maulden's National School was taken over by a Board.

The new National School had been built for 160 children but there was now need for another 117 places. It was decided to use the National School building for girls and infants and to build a new school for the boys. In some villages there were serious disputes concerning religious education but at Maulden there was a happy compromise. All the children were to study the Bible and the rector would provide instruction in the Catechism but, so as not to offend the Nonconformists, this was to be an optional class.

In the early years Board schools were allowed to make a small charge. At Maulden it was decided that there would be three levels of payment:
1. Farmers, tradesmen and gardeners with more than 3 acres - 3d per week
2. Journeymen, tradesmen and gardeners with less than 3 acres - 2d per week
3. Labourers' children would be charged 1^1/$_2$d per week for the first child but only 1d per week for any subsequent children.

The Nonconformist Movement

In a village which lacked the care of a residential Lord of the Manor and whose population included a number of small farmers, growers and tradesmen, Maulden was bound to have a strong 'non-conforming' group of worshippers. These would object to the form of service that was used in the parish church.

St Mary's Church

The name Maulden is said to come from a 'hill marked by a 'moel' (or cross) and later, when a stone church was built, a hilltop site was chosen. For many centuries, St Mary's has watched over the village and its people and today is still the much-loved parish church. Despite many alterations, the west tower and part of the wall, at the north-west end of the north aisle, remain from the church that watched over the people of Maulden during the troubled medieval period of its history.

No wealthy landowner or rector came forward to build on an ornate chantry chapel or to support a valuable relict or statue. When a survey was undertaken, prior to their closure in 1548, all that was found at Maulden was a very small piece of meadowland, which some forgotten benefactor had given to support a light. This rent was probably used to provide candles (maybe a small lamp) to be kept burning on the altar, representing a chain of ceaseless prayer, offered through Christ, on behalf of All Souls. This particular light is mentioned in both Maulden and Ampthill wills.

The only will that has been found giving real support to St Mary's is that of miller, John Samwell. When he made his will in April 1524, he requested burial in the churchyard of Our Blessed Lady of Maulden and asked his executors to give 2d (less than 1p) to the high altar, 20d (8p) to the torches (used for funeral processions), 20d for the bells and 12d (5p) to the All Souls light. The mill, mill-house and most of his land went to his eldest son, John; his younger son, Richard, received three houses at Water End and meadow by Clophill Bridge.   One of his executors received a house at More End, a paddock abutting 'the brack' (Brache) and a hempwik.*

Back in 1463, John Samwell junior (or his father), had negotiated an 80-year lease with Warden Abbey to work 'le Tyled myll' at Greenfield, together with water-meadows and 'lez dammes'. He still held this in 1542 and was also tenant of Limbersey, including the grove with the 'little motes'. In 1542, John Ellys was renting the watermill on the once Elstow Abbey estate at Maulden and Richard Samwell, a watermill at Marston, together with a house and a cottage 'once his father's'.

The Seventeenth Century

The Bruce family, from nearby Houghton House, held the manor from 1635 and during this century, had their mausoleum built beside the church.** No doubt they carried out some renovations on the church, but by the mid seventeenth century, the village was under the influence of John Bunyan and his friends at St John's Church, Bedford.

Neglect of parish churches and their furniture was a growing problem in Bedfordshire and during 1668-9, the archdeacon set up courts of enquiry at both Bedford and Ampthill. At nearby Pulloxhill, the steeple had fallen down and right across the area, parishioners were reported for refusing to pay their church rates. At Maulden it was recorded that St Mary's lacked both a Bible and a Book of Homilies.

Later Centuries

During the early 18th century, the Bruce family spent an increasing amount of time abroad and, in 1738, sold the manor to the Duke of Bedford. Conscientious clergy took an interest in the building and, with financial help from the parishioners, minor repairs were regularly carried out. Despite the large

*A labourer's daily wage of 4d gives some idea of values   ** This was rebuilt in 1858-9 and is currently being restored by Bedfordshire County Council

number of Non Conformists living in Maulden, the congregation grew and, in 1824, the galleries were enlarged. The rector and congregation still continued to keep up with the necessary repairs and a new organ was installed in 1833, paid for by subscriptions.

In March 1851, an Ecclesiastical Census was undertaken and the data collected proved that, despite the enlarged gallery, St Mary's was, at times, overfull. The total number of seats was 484 and the average number of adults and children attending the afternoon service was 410. Allowing for low congregations on cold wet afternoons, there must have been some summer Sundays (especially on feast days) when every seat was taken. This was probably why, in 1858, it was decided to carry out such a major restoration that it resulted in parts of the church being completely rebuilt. It was re-opened on 27 September 1859. The nineteenth century repairs and alterations, together with the numerous accounts and descriptions of the work are included in the four volume collection of such Victorian works, edited by Chris Pickford.[1]

The Congregational Meetings and John Bunyan

The first, registered Nonconformist meeting in Maulden was in 1672; this was at the house of widow, Sarah Tomkins. In answer to an enquiry in 1603, the incumbent at St Mary's had declared that he had no Nonconformists in his parish, which was the normal Bedfordshire reply.* At the next religious census in 1669, he reported that there were about twenty Quakers in Maulden, who sat silent and had no leader.[2] The followers of John Bunyan's message must have been successful in remaining unobserved.

John Bunyan Visits Maulden

As a boy, the young John Bunyan would have accompanied his father, the brazier, and his grandfather, the chapman (pedlar) as they walked the lanes and country roads of Bedfordshire. After the Civil War, he became a local tinker and would have visited Maulden on many occasions, mending small garden tools and agricultural implements. Once he became a speaker, on behalf of the group that met at St John's Church, he probably stayed on in the village, after work, to teach and preach.

While Oliver Cromwell was Protector of England, god-fearing and respected speakers were encouraged to preach, whether or not they were ordained, but

Only eleven were recorded in the whole county
1 Pickford, C. Bedfordshire Churches in the 19th Century. 2 Wigfield, WM BHRS Vol 20

with the arrival of King Charles II, in 1660, opinion changed. Even before the law had been changed, Bunyan was arrested while preaching in Harlington and spent nearly twelve years in Bedford gaol.

Although he would return to prison for a few months, in 1676, 1672 was a most important year for Bunyan and for his church. He was the newly elected minister of his group when, in March, King Charles issued a declaration, which made his and other nonconforming congregations safe from prosecution. It stated that those who 'doe not conforme to the Church of England could apply to licence their own meeting house'. In May, Bunyan applied for a licence to preach, a licence to use Josias Ruffhead's barn as a Bedford meeting house and also for another twenty-six licences on behalf of other, scattered groups. One of these was the house of Sarah Tomkins at Maulden. Right from the beginning, the Maulden Congregational meeting was part of what became Bunyan Meeting Freechurch, based at Bedford.

Nehemiah Coxe

The preacher licensed for Maulden was Nehemiah Coxe, who would soon become one of London's most respected Baptist Ministers. Coxe had been connected with the Bedford meeting for at least three years and was one of the seven who had been called to the work of the ministry at meetings 'usually maintained by this [Bedford] congregation.' He was supporting himself in Bedford as a shoemaker and had already had one spell in Bedford gaol for preaching before the Declaration. In 1673, the group at Hitchin requested that he should be released to work with them, but this does not seem to have happened. This may have been connected with a disagreement that he had with his Bedford friends. Although he did 'publickly make an acknowledgement of several miscaridges by him committed and declared his repentance......' not everyone was satisfied and the congregation at Hitchin asked for someone else to lead them.[1]

In 1675, Coxe left Bedford and became joint pastor at Petty France in London. His more famous father Benjamin Coxe had, before the war, been a vicar in the Church of England, where baptism took place soon after birth. At Dunstable and at Petty France, baptism had to be at an age when candidates were old enough to understand the commitment, whereas Bunyan and his friends were prepared to accept adults as full members if, having received

1 BHRS Vol 55. The Minutes of the First Independent Church - Now the Bunyan Meeting Edited by HG Tibbett

216

baptism as children, they refused a second baptism. Strict as they were concerning attendance and behaviour, they tried to avoid schisms and divisions.

There is a gap in the registry during the 18th century, but in 1798 a group of men got together and registered the house of William Barns. Other certificates survive for the 19th century, including a Baptist Meeting House at Duck End, Flitwick Road. The religious census of 1851 described the group as 'Independent Baptists'. As the Independent Bedford group included both Congregationalists and Baptists, this would explain the change in name. They had 610 seats in the chapel and at festivals, another 100 could be seated in the vestry. The average congregation, during the year 1850-51, had been 356 and their minister was William Charles Robinson. There is still a Baptist Church standing at Duck End and, to commemorate Sarah Tompkins' cottage, which was undoubtedly visited by John Bunyan, a nearby group of houses is called John Bunyan Close.

In this same 1851 census, there was what was described as a Wesleyan Methodist chapel 'commonly called Clophill Wesleyan Chapel being contiguous to Clophill'. The minister was Walter Coates from Ampthill. He also ministered to the Wesleyan Methodists at Steppingley. He noted that the group had been founded in 1814 and that there were 290 seats. The average evening attendance during 1850-51 had been 125. In 1854, William Henry Clarkson, superintendent in Bedford, registered this chapel as being on Bedford Road. The replacement chapel was built in the parish of Clophill. However, in 1861, Edward Bishop of Bedford registered a Primitive Methodist Chapel at the Broche (Brache), Maulden. This chapel is still there today.*

Maulden - An Independent Village

This brief account of life in Maulden, a village on the Greensand Ridge, not sheltered by the paternal protection of a great estate, illustrates the determined independence of its people. Century by century, they stood together and have made Maulden into the attractive and friendly village that it is today.

Village History via the Volumes of the Bedfordshire Historical Record Society

This short history is mainly taken from documents published by the invaluable Bedfordshire Historical Record Society. It is far from complete but it illustrates the wide range of information available from these books, many of which are still in print.

* *I am grateful to Eileen Brown for help with this section*

Historical Highlights/Route

CAINHOE CASTLE

ROUTE
Note, most of the time this route is following the signposted Scenic Route, but not on every occasion.

Cainhoe is not the first place along the Scenic Route but it has been put here for reasons that will become clear.

At the time when Ampthill was still a small village, Cainhoe Castle, just east of Clophill crossroads, was the centre of a valuable but scattered estate. Following the Battle of Hastings and the coronation of King William I, Nigel Albini (from Aubigny near Coutances) received a strip of about 6000 acres of land on either side of Clophill crossroads. He also received an even larger, scattered acreage a little further away. This became known as the 'Barony of Cainhoe'.

Nigel's father and one of his brothers had also helped William to gain the throne of England and, unlike many of Bedfordshire's new Norman landowners, they decided to build their castle within the county. They chose a site near the crossroads, on a spur of high ground that was protected on the north by a small stream. They used this stream to make one side of a moat and press-ganged local villagers into digging out a 40ft diversion to the stream to complete it. They then added a surrounding stockade or bank.

Part of Albini's rent to the king was to support 25 knights; some of these were given land on his Bedfordshire and Hertfordshire estates. The land leased to his senior officer, Nigel Wast, included Ampthill. Nothing is heard about his wife but Silsoe was set aside to support his concubine!

Many of the Norman families who supported King William had, like him, patronised religious houses in their home country. As the second and third generations began to regard England as their home country, they supported, or even founded, monasteries over here. One of Nigel's brothers, called Robert, was a monk back in Normandy. He came over to England to become Abbot of St Albans, where he was supported by generous gifts from his family. They were even more generous when Nigel's granddaughter became a nun at nearby Sopwell Priory. Around 1140 the family gave the abbey the site of what became Beaulieu Priory. This once stood near today's Top Farm, Beadlow.

At first all went well with the family and in 1198 a descendant was sheriff of Bedfordshire but twice the male line died out and on each occasion the estates were divided between three heiresses. Descendants of Nigel Albini remained in and around Cainhoe during much of the 14th century but by the end, the

218

Cainhoe Castle

White Hart Ampthill

castle had been replaced by a more modest house and the scattered estate had been divided so many times that the barony had come to an end. Nothing remains today of the castle or the manor house which replaced the original building. All that can be seen are the earthworks that run down to the hedge on the left-hand side of the road, between Clophill and Shefford. There is a very clear aerial photo of the site in Miss Godber's comprehensive book of Bedfordshire.[1]

AMPTHILL

The Albini family's tenant at Ampthill was Nicholas Poinz who, recognising its central position, opened a Thursday market. In 1242, Henry III conferred on Joan d'Albini the right to hold the market and also granted an annual fair from 21-23 July, the eve, feast and morrow of the saint, Mary Magdalene, patron saint of the village church. This was the turning point that started Ampthill on its way to becoming an important administrative centre.

Although there were some fertile areas of land, much of Ampthill's soil was sandy and only suitable for rough grazing or rabbit warrens. However, as a market centre it was an ideal place for small tradesmen, itinerant salesmen and workers to make their base. Then, sometime after 1415, Ampthill was sold to one of the heroes of the Battle of Agincourt.

ROUTE

Starting in the centre of Ampthill, the route leaves the town via Church Street, passing St Andrews Church, which is on the left. From then on, the A507 is clearly marked into Maulden and there are signs marking the Scenic Route.

Ampthill Castle

Sir John Cornwall was King Henry V's uncle and frequently represented him as both commander and diplomat. After the fighting was over he had the opportunity to amass a great deal of wealth. Back around 1400, he had married King Henry's widowed aunt, Princess Elizabeth of Lancaster; now he could afford to build a 'palace' to suit their style and status. His new house stood on the top of the hill in Ampthill Park, near where the crosses stand today and his estate included the 'great' park. Although it has always been referred to as a castle, a 16th century description mentions several towers which appear to have stood at the corners of a great four part house, built around a courtyard, plus a lesser house around a second courtyard.

1 Godber, J History of Bedfordshire

Sir John Cornwall remained in favour during the reign of King Henry VI. He had already been made a Knight of the Garter and in 1433 he was given the title Baron Fanhope of Fanhope (Herefordshire) and nine years later Baron Millbrook. His arms, surrounded by the Garter, can be seen, painted on glass, in Millbrook church.

The newly created Baron Millbrook died in less than a year of receiving the honour and was buried at the church of the Dominican Friars, Ludgate. Like many senior landowners of his day, he not only mixed with military leaders and diplomats but also with senior churchmen. During his time at the castle, Ampthill witnessed the comings and goings of many important people. They and their followers brought trade and business into the town. At the time of his death he was entertaining both the Archbishop of Canterbury and the Bishop of Lincoln; they were able to pray for his soul and supervise the reading of his will.

His wife had died in 1426 and in 1421 his only son had been killed fighting in France. During his remaining lonely years, Fanhope had taken a mistress and at the time of his death they had two young boys. In his will he provided for them financially and also left money to his chaplains and household servants. He had kept a very large staff and from the names of some of his soldiers we can tell that they came from all over England and also from parts of Wales and Ireland.

By now this was Bedfordshire's only remaining castle and there was some concern as to who should be allowed to purchase the influential estate. Discussions and disputes continued for some years and it was not until 1454 that the important house, park and land was sold to Lord Edmund Grey of Wrest Park.

The Grey Family at Ampthill

1455 was the year that the battle of St Albans opened the events that we now know as the Wars of the Roses. It may have been to gain his loyalty that King Henry VI allowed Lord Grey to add Ampthill and its great estate to his Wrest Park estate. As this included the villages of Silsoe and Flitton, it gave him great influence across the western side of Mid Bedfordshire. If loyalty were Henry's reason, he would soon be disappointed. At the Battle of Northampton in 1460, Lord Grey withheld his troops and gave the victory to the future Edward IV.

When in 1467, Edward married Elizabeth Woodville, whose previous husband, Sir John Grey, had been a cousin of the Bedfordshire Greys, the family were brought even closer to the throne. Edmund had already been created first Earl of Kent and from then on even more honours were given to him. In addition to his Bedfordshire estates, which included Blunham, and Harrold and his Welsh estates, he received income from several well-paid positions at court. He remained in favour throughout the short reign of King Richard III and died in 1490, five years into the reign of Henry VII.

The second Earl, Edmund's son, George, married the sister of King Edward's queen and continued in royal favour. He was at Ampthill Castle when he died in 1503. His son, Richard, also spent much time at court but was a quite different character to his father and grandfather. Already a heavy gambler, his debts continued to grow and within five years of inheriting, he was obliged to give up his entire interest in Ampthill. King Henry VII died in less than a year of receiving the castle and it was part of the royal estate that passed to the young Henry VIII. As he grew older, Henry made frequent visits to the castle and so another phase of Ampthill's history began.

King Henry VIII at Ampthill

Apart from his enjoyment of country life and sports, Henry had two other reasons for wanting to visit Ampthill - the clean, fresh air and the hunting park.

As was normal in the 16th century, he had little understanding of hygiene and sanitation but he had observed that the plague and other infections spread rapidly across London during late summer and autumn. Consequently, most summers, the royal family left London for the country. Sitting on its high position, Ampthill Castle was considered particularly healthy, so it is not surprising that Henry, some of his wives and all their children, became summer or autumn visitors. Henry also realised that people who had travelled through an infected town could carry disease. For this reason, all his visitors were obliged to spend a few days in quarantine in the village of Ampthill, before going up to the castle. This led to the development of several high-class inns and turned Ampthill into a successful tourist centre. Accommodation and services of this quality would be in demand even when there were no royal parties.

Henry's other reason for visiting Ampthill was the excellent hunting. Following the Dissolution of the Monasteries, thousands more acres of scrub and woodland were drawn into the hunting park, making it even more attractive. To keep these preserves well-stocked and in good condition required a large staff and brought more jobs into the area, as did the maintenance and management of the castle.

Catherine of Aragon's Last Visit to Ampthill

In the early years of their marriage, Henry took his wife Catherine with him when he travelled around the country. She still travelled with him, even after the birth of the future Queen Mary and the numerous miscarriages that ruined her health. Then the beautiful young Anne Boleyn came to court and things began to change. In 1532 it was Anne who accompanied the royal party to Ampthill. Whether or not Henry was hunting on horseback is not recorded but the ladies and the older gentlemen sat on a wooden stand while the huntsmen drove the frightened deer within reach of their bows and arrows!

Having convinced himself that Catherine's numerous miscarriages were due to God's displeasure concerning his marriage, Henry decided it must be annulled. Despite opposition from the Pope, he managed to convince Anne that legally he was single. During the early spring which followed their visit to Ampthill, they were secretly married. Anne was soon pregnant and Catherine was sent to Ampthill under house arrest. While she was there a conference was arranged at Dunstable Priory, to discuss the king's weighty matter. During her stay, Catherine was desperately worried about the proposed annulment. She flatly refused to attend the conference or to co-operate with the enquiry; when representatives visited her, she refused to see them. Her health was poor and a pin that had stuck in her foot had turned poisonous.[1]

It was not until July 3rd that she agreed to receive a deputation, headed by her chamberlain, Lord Mountjoy. She lay on a couch and gathered all her servants around her while the document was read out loud. She listened intently but when the title Princess Dowager was read out, she sent for a pen and crossed it out; she was, she said, 'the Queen and the King's true wife'. It may have been this understandable stubbornness, together with the risk that the king's enemies could have used her to start a revolt that caused Henry to send her further away. On 17th August she was removed to the Bishop of Lincoln's palace at Buckden. By the time that she died, in 1536, she had been moved on to Kimbolton Castle.

The End of Ampthill Castle

Henry VIII continued to visit the castle and in 1548, the young eleven-year-old King Edward VI was taken there for a hunting party. He was already very poorly and the royal physicians may have hoped that the Ampthill air would strengthen him. In fact, he became gradually weaker and died five years later. By

1 Evans, V. Proud Heritage.

this date the castle roofs were falling in and the stone walls on the point of collapse. Neither Queen Mary nor Queen Elizabeth took an interest in the building and the latter's officials took literally thousands of oak trees from the park for the use of the navy. Elizabeth's successor, King James, was most anxious to repair or even rebuild the castle but the project was too expensive even for a king.

Park House
In 1606 James agreed to abandon the castle and to enlarge what was then known as Park Lodge. It was already of a size and design suitable for the gentleman steward and to accommodate the overflow of royal parties.

MAULDEN

Maulden appears in the Historical Background of this chapter, as an example of a village without a major historic house.

HAYNES

Although at 1086 Sheriff Hugh de Beauchamp owned Haynes as one complete manor, it was later divided. When one of his descendants founded nearby Chicksands Priory, part of the land was given to help with its support. After the Dissolution of the Monasteries, that part of Haynes followed the secular ownership of Chicksands.

By the spring of 1537, when it was obvious that the end was near, the prior negotiated a 31-year lease of their Haynes land with a William Arderne. He was to pay £11=13=4d per year and also keep the chancel of Haynes church in good repair. Five months later, John Waller, a wheelwright from Haynes, signed a 31-year lease for the 'parsonage' (vicarage) farm. When the priory was finally closed, during October 1538, the leases were honoured and Arderne negotiated further leases. Richard Snowe, who bought the main Chicksands estate, also bought the land that the priory had held at Haynes. This estate became known as Haynes Grange; it continued as an outlier of Chicksands for several centuries. Within

ROUTE

Once in Maulden, watch for the Scenic Route sign, which points left up Brache Road towards Haynes West End. This road crosses the Greensand Ridge Walk as it winds north and east towards Haynes West End and the A6. (It passes Bolebec Farm and Limbersey Farm, mentioned in the history.) It is a long road, with a series of bends and skirts (but does not go through) Haynes West End village.

224

the Victoria and Albert Museum is a panelled room, known as the 'Haynes Grange Room'. It is thought that Inigo Jones designed this spectacular room that has a ceiling decorated with blue plaster pigeons. Little is known about its history until 1908, when Sir Algernon Osborn, of Chicksands, sold it to a dealer, after which it was installed in a house in Notting Hill. In 1928 it was again on the market and Professor AE Richardson (of Ampthill) made an appeal to purchase it for the nation. Within a few weeks £4000 was raised and it was presented to the Victoria and Albert Museum.[1]

Hawnes (Haynes) Park

This was first mentioned in 1313 and, together with the manor house and estate, remained for many years with different members of the Beauchamp family. Then, in 1488, Sir Reginald Bray, who had supported Henry Tudor at the Battle of Bosworth, bought the estate. Two years later, a grateful King Henry VII granted him Eaton (Bray) in South Bedfordshire. By 1564 the male line of the Bray family had died out and a newcomer to the county, Robert Newdigate, rented and then bought the Haynes estate. There is a brass in St Mary's Church, which stands beside the park gate, depicting an Anthony Newdegate, dated 1568. In 1622, his family sold the house to Sir Oliver Luke, of Wood End, Cople. Luke frequently represented the county, or the Borough of Bedford, at Parliament, but unlike their neighbours at Chicksands, Sir Oliver and his son, Samuel, were strong supporters of Parliament.

It was the Newdigate family who, at the end of the 16th century, built a house on the rising ground in the park. In 1605, Robert Newdigate entertained Queen Anne while King James was staying at Houghton House and on the Sunday accompanied the royal party to St Mary's Church. Little, if any, of this house remains today.

ROUTE
It eventually turns left towards Wilstead, continues on a still-winding road and finally meets the A6. At this point, the route turns left onto the A6, but at once watch for the sign pointing right towards Haynes Church End, as this is almost a staggered crossroads. Having crossed the A6, follow the Scenic Route for some distance and the road will pass (on the left) Haynes Park and St Mary's Church. (The route is now heading for Old Warden.) Once past the church, the narrow road continues towards the A600; at a small T-junction, turn away from North Wood End and Silver End to approach the A600.

1 George, Mary in Beds Mag Vol I

Sir George Carteret

As noted above, the Luke family had been active supporters of Parliament, but the next owner was a very active Royalist. At the outbreak of the civil war, Sir Philip Carteret was King Charles' Governor of Jersey, in the Channel Islands. The islanders were strong supporters of Parliament but Sir George put such Royalists as there were into key positions and the administration ran comparatively smoothly. After the collapse of Royalist support, in the south-west of England, he entertained the young Prince Charles at Elizabeth Castle. Charles and about three hundred of his officers and household stayed on the island for some time and Sir George helped the Royalist cause in many different ways. Following the execution of Charles I, Sir George instantly proclaimed the prince King Charles II. In return, the new king confirmed Sir George as his representative on the island. He held several other important roles; as a vice-admiral he robbed Parliamentary-owned ships and was registered as a pirate!

After the Restoration, he became treasurer of the Navy and was regularly visited by Samuel Pepys. Unlike many Royalists, his adventures during the war made him a very wealthy man. King Charles granted him land in America, where he founded New Jersey. In 1667, he decided to buy a country estate, which is when he purchased Hawnes. Sadly, five years later, his son was killed in the ship, the Royal James, fighting against the Dutch.

OLD WARDEN

The Cistercian Monastery

It was the Cistercian monks who originally preserved the beauty of this attractive wooded area. In the early 11th century Walter Espec, a descendant of the first Norman who owned (Old)* Warden, was working in Yorkshire for King Henry I. His base was at Helmsley Castle and he helped a group of Cistercian monks to settle nearby; this became known as Rievaulx Abbey. These monks were a 'reformed' order; they felt that many Benedictine monks had allowed society to intrude into their lives and had lost sight of the Rule of their founder. The Cistercians would only accept gifts of land in isolated places away from towns, main roads, and

ROUTE

Once at this busy junction, carefully cross onto the country road towards Old Warden and Southill. (The Scenic Route is heading for Old Warden but the main part of this route is heading for Southill.)

* A later addition to the name

226

even villages. A farm on the outskirts of Warden was an ideal situation, so Walter Espec gave them land on his Bedfordshire estate. In 1135, Rievaulx monks and their supporters began to clear an area of woodland ready for building. The house became known as 'St Mary de Sartis'; an assart was a newly cleared piece of woodland.

For many years they lived quietly and tried to concentrate on a life of work and prayer. However, as the years went by, in return for masses and prayers, they accepted more and more gifts of land, finally becoming owners of a great estate. Although their house was kept as quiet and peaceful as possible, around 1500 discipline broke down and so did their reputation. They were closed in 1537. The whole estate then passed to King Henry VIII, from him to the young Edward VI and so to Princess Elizabeth.

However, it was Robert Gostwick, the last steward of Warden Abbey, who was responsible for building the first secular manor house.

The 16th Century House
Sometime around 1546 Gostwick began to adapt the buildings into a house suitable for a gentleman of his position. When he died in 1561, the senior branch of the family, at Willington, appears to have had little interest in the property. It changed hands several times and began to deteriorate. Unlike Woburn, the monks of Old Warden had not owned the whole village. By 1700, the manor house in the village had risen in importance and the abbey-house was replaced by a nearby farm. Around 1790, most of the old buildings were taken down.

The Landmark Trust
Early in the 20th century, a local landowner converted the remaining building into a dovecote. However, the Landmark Trust, which renovates interesting historic buildings and uses them as holiday homes, bought the remaining buildings and immediate site. They managed to save a surprising amount of the Tudor brickwork, a length of crenellation, some stone window-frames and a spectacular twisted chimney.

Not only did they fully restore the building, but also managed to convert it into a comfortable, modernised house. This can be rented via the Trust's booking office.

The New Mansion House

Once upon a time there were corrody cottages (monastic almshouses) somewhere near the abbey gates but these disappeared and the main village expanded on its present site. In the 17th century, the Palmer family had a substantial manor house in the present park. They played their part in local affairs but, in 1696, they sold their interest in the village to bachelor Samuel Ongley.

The Ongley Family in Bedfordshire

Before coming to Bedfordshire, Samuel had made a fortune in the city and had travelled widely. His fortune came from his successful business as importer, wholesaler and linen draper. He was also a director of the East India Company. He and his heirs took an active part in county affairs. In 1776, one of his heirs was given an Irish title and became Lord Ongley.

The attractive and quite unique village that we see today is due to the 3rd Lord Ongley. He was only eleven when he inherited the estate but by the time that he had grown up he had become passionately interested in the style of gardening known as 'picturesque' and ownership of the estate and the village of Old Warden gave him the opportunity to try out his ideas.

On one side of his house he already had lawns, flowerbeds and shrubberies; there was also a walled garden and glasshouses. On the other side he had an extensive park. Wanting to try out the new, picturesque style of landscape gardening, he planned two entirely new schemes.

Old Warden Village

The lodge is where the park enters the village and most of the cottages were rebuilt. Paths and banks were planted with wild flowers and cottage-holders encouraged to grow a range of garden flowers. In this way the Ongleys and their guests could drive through a fairytale landscape on their way up to the mansion.

Although road widening has destroyed the banks of wild flowers that once lined the road, the actual cottages, pumps and well-covers can still be seen today. To quote Simon Houfe's important book, 'Bedfordshire', 'The 3rd Lord Ongley's enthusiasm spilled over into the village at his park gates' where the cottages, lodges, pumps and public buildings were designed 'in the cottage orné style'. Ongley's other scheme also survives for us to enjoy today.

The Swiss Garden

The main estate at Old Warden is in an area where the greensand meets an area of Oxford clay. In 1820, Lord Ongley obtained permission to move the road and take in an area of acid mire and a small lake; the latter was enlarged, streams diverted and water piped in from the greensand.* This lake is on the grassy area between the mansion garden and the boundary of the actual 'Swiss' garden. The latter is only about eight acres but includes shrubberies, ponds, groves, arbours and winding paths, which lead to, and often form, a series of intimate and tranquil vistas. 'The romantic mood of the garden is further heightened by the careful deposition of numerous built features such as the rock-garden, the well, the summerhouse..... (and) the grotto.....' The above is taken from a small part of a leaflet produced by Bedfordshire County Council. The word 'vistas' is of great importance because all these attractions, plus, at different times, displays of bulbs, roses, shrubs and autumn colours are arranged so that the whole garden is made up of a series of views.

The 3rd Lord Ongley was a bachelor but the romantic story concerning the history of the garden is woven round a possible Swiss fiancée. It is said that she was in the garden during heavy rain, that she sheltered under an oak tree, caught cold and died and that he had a 'Swiss' cottage built in her memory and a thatched roof put around one of the trees. There is a stone tablet nearby with a poem that he may have written, 'The Forgotten One'. It includes the verse:

> A shower in June, a summer shower
> Drove us beneath the shade;
> A beautiful and greenwood bower
> The spreading branches made;
> The rain drop shines upon the bough
> The passing rain - but where art thou?

The Shuttleworth Family

The 3rd Lord Ongley outlived his brothers and, as none of them had married, he decided to sell the estate. Before the date of the auction (26 February 1872) he was approached by the agent of Joseph Shuttleworth, a partner in the firm of Clayton and Shuttleworth. They were iron-founders who had been experimenting in steam-powered, agricultural machinery. The sale was completed towards the end of September, architect Henry Clutton was employed and within four years, the present, unusual house was completed.

This may have already been planned by the 2nd Lord Ongley

229

This family also played an active part in county affairs. Joseph died in 1883 but in 1889, his son, Colonel Frank Shuttleworth was an early member of Bedfordshire County Council.

The Second Mansion House

Frank Shuttleworth also took a great deal of interest in both the village and the estate; in 1904 he had the present village hall and reading room built.

This took place two years after his marriage to Dorothy Long, a local clergyman's daughter. He was already fifty-seven but she was considerably younger. Their son, Richard, was only four years old when, in 1913, his father died. Although Dorothy remarried and had a daughter, she continued to manage the family estate. In 1924 she was again widowed and from then on devoted her life to the education of her son, his estate and in preparing him to gradually take over control.

Richard Shuttleworth

The description by his biographer, TE Guttery, is of a popular and attractive young man, mad on motor racing and flying but one who accepted his responsibilities and was a County Councillor by the time that he was twenty-four. He originally chose a career in the army but changed his mind and applied for the RAF. This was more difficult than he thought and it was 1939 (the outbreak of war) before he was accepted. He was killed in a flying accident on the morning of 2 August 1940.

His mother, Mrs Dorothy Shuttleworth OBE, was devastated and, as his sole heir, decided to design a memorial to Richard, his father and grandfather and, at the same time, to use the estate to help other young men. She founded the Richard Ormonde Shuttleworth Remembrance Trust in his memory. It was to be an educational centre 'for the teaching of science and practice of aviation and of afforestation and agriculture'. It was, and still is, run by a Board of Trustees. Her original aim was a 'College for Youth' to train (male) school-leavers in the 'Science of Aviation, Agriculture and Forestry, both in research and practical work'. There have been many changes over the years but the mansion house and grounds have become the Shuttleworth College for Agriculture and Horticulture, and the home of the Bird of Prey and Conservation Cente. The Swiss Garden adjoins the mansion gardens and next to this is the world famous Shuttleworth Collection of Historic Aeroplanes and Vehicles. These are all regularly open to the public and, with St Leonard's church and the picturesque village, they make an excellent family day out.

The Shuttleworth Legacy

231

THE NORTHEAST LOOP

The Scenic Route continues north as far as Moggerhanger and then turns east, south and finally west before re-joining this route at Southill. It passes through beautiful areas of countryside and passes old houses, public houses, thatched cottages and old churches.

The leaflet 'The Scenic Route' points out items of particular interest such as: the Tourist Information centre at Sandy, the typical old English village of Ickwell with its beautiful cottages, green and the permanent maypole, (which is used once a year for a major May Day celebration), the clock on Northill Church, built by the Tompion family, the very rare, medieval packhorse bridge at Sutton, Jordan's mill and shop at Broom, home of the famous range of healthy, cereal products, the Lodge and RSPB Nature Reserve at Sandy.

Historic Houses

There are many attractive old houses around this part of the route. Three that are open, under different arrangements, are included below.

Ickwell Bury

The first recorded residents of this attractive site were representatives of the Knights Hospitallers, whose headquarters were at Melchbourne. All that remains of their occupation is the lake, which is thought to have been developed from their fishponds. The Harvey family replaced the Elizabethan house that was built in the park, at the end of the 17th century. They remained at Ickwell until 1925, when the house was sold and used as a boarding school. It was sold again twelve years later and this time left standing empty. Unfortunately, it was then burnt down; only the stables and the dovecote were saved. The former has a rare clock built by Thomas Tompion (born at adjoining Northill).

Col GH Wells, who commissioned AGS Butler to design the present house, that Pevsner describes as 'Free neo-Georgian', then purchased the estate. Following the death of both Col and Mrs Wells, it was bequeathed to Bedford School and the house remained empty for seven years. In 1978 it was leased to the Yoga for Health Foundation. This is a unique institution which each year entertains thousands of visitors. Some have an interest in yoga to help relieve the stresses and pain associated with ill-health, some to maintain good health and others to learn relaxation in the warm and caring environment, and beautiful grounds. Many of the visitors come from Bedfordshire and surrounding counties but there are a number who come from much further away, including countries all around the world. Anyone wanting to know more should contact the Foundation for its newsletter and other leaflets. Both the old and the new buildings are kept in a very good state of repair and members of the Foundation are restoring the gardens and the walk down to the lake.

Moggerhanger House

In 1777, the Moggerhanger estate came into the hands of Godfrey Thornton, who was a director of the Bank of England. He and his son entertained the landscape gardener, Humphrey Repton, who, during the 18th and early 19th centuries, was carrying out several commissions in Mid Bedfordshire. To design their new mansion house they chose Sir John Soane, who was the architect employed by the Bank of England. He visited them as early as 1791 and no doubt they discussed their plans, but the building actually took place between 1796 and 1811, incorporating ideas suggested by Humphrey Repton. The resulting Grecian-style house can be seen today.

In fact, we are extremely lucky to be able to see this magnificent example of Soane's work. It was already in need of major repairs when it was vacated in1985 and as it stood empty for ten years, it became derelict. Then, in 1955, it was purchased by the Centre for Contemporary Ministry (CCM). This registered charity is home to a number of national Christian organisations. These include the British Growth Association, the Family Matters Institute, who work with Parliament on matters relating to family breakdown and the bi-monthly magazine 'Prophecy Today'.

Moggerhanger House Preservation Trust

There is a separate charity, The Moggerhanger House Preservation Trust (MHPT) that is working to completely restore the building, inside and out and, in the future, to completely restore the grounds and gardens.

Volunteers are doing much of the work but professional researchers have been used to explore the original papers, letters and plans of both Soane and Repton. With help from both English Heritage and Mid Beds District Council, professional builders, skilled at restoration, have already carried out an amazing amount of structural work and internal decoration is well under way.

CCM co-ordinates all the different activities that take place at 'The Park' and the work of the Friends who come together to offer skilled and unskilled help. Enquiries are welcome concerning all aspects of The Park and there are regular

Moggerhanger House

Entrance to Ice House at Moggerhanger House

open Heritage Days. These open days are advertised in the local press and at Sandy Tourist Information Centre. In this way, as many people as possible can see the inside of the house and the exhibition that covers the research and stages of the restoration.

Sandy Lodge

This estate is closely connected with the family of Sir Robert Peel, Prime Minister from 1814 -1846, best known for the introduction of the Metropolitan Police Force. Although the Lodge has a Tudor appearance, it was actually built between 1869-77. Sir Robert and his family began to buy land in the area from about 1852, when there was a 'Swiss' cottage on the site of the present Lodge and this became the home of Sir Robert's third and fourth sons.

The former, Captain Sir William Peel RN, led an exciting life. He rose rapidly in the navy and travelled widely. He also took leave from the navy and became a renowned explorer. His second spell in the navy covered a period of the Crimean War and the Siege of Sebastopol. Following an act of extreme bravery, he was awarded the Victoria Cross in 1854. He bought another local estate, Sandy Place, which is now a school and had his own private railway built between Sandy and Potton. He called his first engine 'Shannon' after his ship.

The latter, Arthur Wellesley Peel, followed a political career and became Speaker of the House of Commons from 1884 - 1895. When he retired he was made Viscount Peel of Sandy. In 1862 he married Adelaide, the daughter of Sir William Stratford Dugdale, and in 1870 employed Henry Clutton to design the present house. The armorial bearings of both families can be seen over the front porch.

In 1934 Sir Malcolm Stewart bought The Lodge and his family owned the estate for many years. They took a great deal of interest in the pleasure gardens and built a swimming pool. Around 1960 the Royal Society for the Protection of Birds (RSPB) was looking for a suitable estate so that it could move out of London. It bought Sandy Lodge in 1961 and it became the Society headquarters. The gardens were retained, with some adaptations to attract birds, and the swimming pool is now a small lake. The reserve extends over 104 acres and walks are laid out across an undisturbed area of greensand.

The RSPB is one of the oldest and largest bird protection societies in the world; it runs a membership scheme and a Young Ornithologists' Club. For a small charge, non-members are welcome to enjoy the nature trails, which cross the formal gardens, past the lake and around the mature woodland, pine plantation and the birch and bracken slopes of the surviving heath.

ROUTE
When the road divides, follow the right-hand road signposted Ireland and Southill. Once past the Black Horse, follow the road round to the left towards Southill. Cross over the old railway bridge and you will soon see the signpost pointing left towards Southill. This route is heading for The White Horse at Southill. At The White Horse, the route connected with this book bears left, leaving The White Horse on the right and continues through the village. At the parish hall (on the right), it turns right onto the Stanford Road, heading towards Stanford and Shefford.

SOUTHILL

Several famous names are associated with this estate. Lord Justice Kelyng, who prevented John Bunyan's release from prison, lived here in the 17th century and George Byng, later created Viscount Torrington, in the 18th century. The house where he lived was near the church but by 1724 he was referring to newly-erected house, at some little distance from the old one pulled down.'[1] In 1777 Lancelot 'Capability' Brown completely redesigned the park and following a great deal of expenditure on this and other matters, the fourth Viscount was forced into bankruptcy.

The viscount's younger brother, John Byng, was obliged to live in London and worked in the Stamp Office. However, he loved Southill and each year he rode out of London, keeping a written account of his travels. As often as possible he stayed at The Sun Inn, Biggleswade and visited friends at Southill and round about.

The Whitbreads at Southill House

Samuel Whitbread bought the estate in 1795. In 1734 he had been apprenticed to a London Brewer and by 1766 had his own impressive business. He played an active part in the social welfare of Bedfordshire and in his will left £8,000 for the building and upkeep of a hospital at Bedford. His son, another Samuel, was a well-known Whig MP during the time of the agricultural depression; among other things, he worked for poor-law reform and free education. In 1795, he introduced an unsuccessful bill in the House of Commons that would have empowered judges to fix a minimum wage.

For many centuries, administration and welfare were dependent on the character of the men who owned these great country houses. Many of them

1 Bell P, 'Southill and the Byngs' in a collection of essays 'Southill and the Whitbreads', 1995 Within this collection there is a detailed description of this house and the later Whitbread house There are also essays covering the estate management and the interest that the Whitbread family took in the village, especially the church and schools

would try to help the families on their own estates; give food or clothes, build good cottages and support Sunday Schools. In the 19th century, some rich men went further and organised help on a regional or county basis. Whitbread was a leading member of committees that built Bedford Infirmary, asylum and gaol. He was known as 'The Driving Whitbread' because of his enthusiasm and hard work.

Many men sat on these prestigious committees but Whitbread was also involved in local affairs and was available to help people from all walks of life. Poor people from all over Bedfordshire walked through the park and poured out their troubles. He was overseer of the poor for Southill 1806-1815, hired teachers for local children and, when necessary, hired buildings for them. His notebooks for 1810-11 and 1813-14 are in the County Record Office and from these we can see how involved he was in community affairs. In his role as Justice of the Peace, he checked up on the Overseers of the Poor and made sure that they were honest and humane. He insisted workhouses should be kept up to standard and made practical suggestions about draining ground and drying floors. Applicants, refused help by their own overseer, could appeal to him. He ordered Houghton Regis overseer to fit an applicant out with winter clothes and pay him 4 shillings per week. He also checked on the Surveyors of the Roads and fined villages whose roads were not repaired. He took a personal interest and, if necessary, would arrange supplies of labour and materials, would check up on the weights of vehicles using the roads and advise about placing road signs and lopping trees.

Quite impartially, he negotiated between farmers and their workers, tradesmen and their apprentices. He even went so far as to make enquiries on behalf of a man who had lost trace of his brother in the army and passed on the good news when Lord Palmerston's office replied.

THE SOUTH EAST LOOP

The Scenic Route runs slightly to the east of Southill and drops south as far as Henlow before turning back on itself to Shefford, where it rejoins this route. The Scenic Route leaflet points out the unusual hedge-maze, set within an orchard on Hitchin Road, Shefford and also the Stondon

ROUTE

This route does not go into Stanford but, having passed The Green Man, turns right onto the B658, heading for Shefford. (The Scenic Route turns off to pass through Clifton and Henlow before rejoining this route at Shefford.) The route connected with this book is heading straight for Shefford and Clophill and joins the A507, towards Ampthill, by passing through the town of Shefford.

It passes the gates of
Chicksands Priory on
the right and Beadlow
Manor
(representing the site of
Beaulieu Priory) on the
left. The earthworks
marking the site of
Cainhoe Castle are on
the right, about a mile
west of the hotel, but
they are on a bad bend
and not easy to see
from a car.

Transport Museum, near Henlow. This houses one of the largest, private, transport collections in the country with more than 300 exhibits. On the forecourt of the building is a replica of Captain Cook's ship, 'Endeavour'.

CAMPTON
From Shefford, the Scenic Route drops down into the attractive old village of Campton. However, across the main road, A600, is a truly hidden, historic house.

Chicksands Priory
Payne de Beauchamp of Bedford and his wife, Countess Rohese, granted their manor of Chicksands to the nuns and canons of the Gilbertine Order. This was one of only nine such houses in England and housed both nuns and canons. Originally, there were large numbers of residents, but they fell into debt and some members were moved to other houses. When Chicksands closed, in 1539, there were only nine canons and eighteen nuns. The men and women lived in different buildings and were separated in church by a screen. There are several vague ghost stories connected with Chicksands, of which the most popular concerns a nun called Rosata. It is said that she became friends with one of the canons, that their friendship developed into a love affair and that Rosata became pregnant. It is also said that the guilty canon was executed and that poor Rosata was bricked up alive in the wall of the cloisters. Although more than 400 years have passed, Rosata has not been forgotten and the legend ends with the warning that on the 17th of each month, she walks in search of her lover. Although Rosata has not been seen, several ghostly and un-natural experiences have been reported.

The Priory was dissolved in 1539 and by the mid 16th century the Osborne family owned the estate. While Sir Charles Carteret was defending Jersey for the Royalists, Sir Peter Osborne was defending Guernsey. Towards the end of the war, Sir Peter's daughter, Dorothy, fell in love with William Temple, whose father was a friend and supporter of Oliver Cromwell. Vesper Hunter tells the story of their secret love affair and its happy ending; her account is illustrated by excerpts from the letters that Dorothy wrote during the many years that they were kept apart.[1] In one letter, swamped by loneliness due to their separation,

1 Hunter, V. *Pure Madness.*

she describes sitting on the local common and watching the village girls minding the cows. Sadly, she reflected that their complete happiness only lacked an understanding as to how happy they really were. Charles II made Sir Peter's son Baronet of Chicksands Priory; in 1740 their descendant, Sir Danvers Osborn(e)* remodelled part of the old monastic house and it was further changed in 1813. The estate remained in the Osborn family for over 300 years. The house still stands surrounded by lawns and overlooking the water; nearby there are 300-year-old Cedars of Lebanon. Medieval walls, pillars and floor tiles from the Priory are safely preserved inside what became the private house.

The Friends of Chicksands Priory

In 1936, the estate was leased to the RAF and in 1950, the USAF took over the base. The Americans continued to lease Chicksands until 1998. It then stood empty and there was concern about its future. 'The Friends of the Priory' is a private organisation whose aim is to increase interest in the Priory and to keep the building in a good state of repair. It has carried out research into the history of the Gilbertine Order and their stay at Chicksands as well as the Osborn(e) family and their house. The group was formed when the future of the house was at risk and for over twenty years has both restored the exterior of the building and the rooms, so that visitors can see them, as they were when the family was in residence.** In 1999, the estate was taken over by and the Ministry of the Environment completely restored the building. For details concerning possible visits, contact Sandy Tourist Information Office.

THE SECOND SOUTHERN LOOP

From Campton, the Scenic Route drops south through Meppershall, down to Shillington and back up through Gravenhurst to Beadlow - the site of Beaulieu Priory, mentioned above.

SILSOE

This village and the nearby village of Flitton were for hundreds of years owned by the Grey family.

> ### ROUTE
> At Clophill the route turns left onto the A6, heading for Silsoe. However, it soon leaves the main road and turns right into Silsoe village (Wrest Park is approached from the village, not the bypass.)

* *The spelling varies*
** *Roger Ward and the Friends of Chicksands Priory typify the aims highlighted in Chapter 3, Preservation of our Heritage*

Wrest Park

A gentleman called John Grey settled at Silsoe in the 13th century. He must have been a man of some importance, because in 1233, he became Sheriff of the county. His descendants bought more land in Bedfordshire and elsewhere. During the 'Wars of the Roses', Edmund, Lord Grey of Ruthin, supported the Lancastrian side, but during the Battle of Northampton changed sides to support the House of York*. In 1463, he was made the king's treasurer and in 1465, became the first Earl of Kent.

From their house in Silsoe, the Grey family had great influence in Bedfordshire until the 3rd Earl gambled away much of the family fortunes. His estates, including Wrest Park, were sold in 1506 to pay his debts. The new owner, Henry Wyatt, intended pulling down the house and selling off the timber, but Sir Henry Grey, heir to the estate, managed to buy it back. He lived quietly and the family fortunes revived. By 1603, a Henry Grey was Lord Lieutenant of Bedfordshire.

During the 17th century, more than one generation 'married' money and their estates in Bedfordshire grew again. The 11th Earl and his wife had the north front of the house rebuilt and in 1687 enlarged the park. They had a formal French garden laid out to the south of the house, with two great fountains. In 1710, the 12th Earl was made Duke of Kent and planned to completely rebuild the house but lost a great deal of money in the South Sea Bubble; so the old house remained. Nevertheless, he enlarged the gardens, made a great canal and at one end and Thomas Archer helped him design what is now called 'The Pavilion'. Between 1834-36, the second Earl de Grey had the whole house rebuilt in the French style.

Since the Duke of Kent's influence on the gardens, they have been altered by Lancelot 'Capability' Brown and then changed again by the second Earl de Grey, but many of the old trees, water gardens, statues and buildings remain. It is therefore a delightful garden to visit, with something unexpected around every corner. Some of the buildings are scheduled as Ancient Monuments. The family continued to live at Wrest Park for many more years, but in the early 20th century, it became the residence of the American Ambassador. During the First World War, it was used as a military hospital and then as offices.

In 1947, the Ministry of Public Buildings and Works acquired the estate, as a national monument and leased the house to the National Institute of Agricultural Engineering. It is now in the care of English Heritage. They

see under Ampthill.

Ickwellbury

Wrest Park

ROUTE

Once approaching the village centre, watch for the Scenic Route sign, which directs you right up Newbury Lane, heading for Flitton. Follow the Scenic Route signs through Wardhedges, into Flitton. The church of St John the Baptist, which includes the important Grey family mausoleum, is on the right.

From Flitton, the Scenic Route heads south to Flitwick but this route is heading back to Bedford. This can be done by heading north towards Maulden and then rejoining the A507 or by heading southwest to Flitwick and joining the A5120 via Ampthill.

maintain the elegant ground floor rooms and staircase and have restored the 18th century gardens to their original glory. Check dates but both of these are regularly open to the public.

FLITTON

Although the Grey family chose to build their manor house and handsome grounds, at Silsoe, they chose Flitton for their parish church and mausoleum. (Up to 1831 Silsoe was a chapel of ease within Flitton parish). Edmund, Lord Grey of Ruthin, rebuilt the church in the 15th century. The Welsh title was a reward for the family's assistance in helping to control the border counties and the later earldom for their support of Edward IV. The mausoleum was built around 1614 to house the family memorials and a hundred years later, it was enlarged by the Duke of Kent. Pevsner described this as 'one of the greatest storehouses of monuments in England.' It is made up of four small rooms and has chest and wall memorials covering many different styles. There are traditional figures with various 17th century costumes, a room of reclining, classical 18th century figures and, in the other two rooms, a variety of 18th and 19th century memorials, including the handsome figure of the Duke of Kent and his first wife. The mausoleum is also in the care of English Heritage and open by arrangement.

THE LONG, NARROW, WESTERN LOOP

From Flitton, the route connected with this chapter returns to Ampthill but the Scenic Route continues west to take in Woburn and its surrounding villages. There are many more historic houses along this part of the Scenic Route, some of which are mentioned in the following pages.

242

Flitton Church

Monuments at Flitton Church

243

SOME MORE HISTORIC HOUSES

Harlington

Before reaching Woburn, the Scenic Route drops down to this attractive village with its thatched cottages and a parade of timber-framed houses and the village pub. The small manor* house includes the unspoilt, 17th century room where John Bunyan appeared before the local magistrate. It is privately owned and not open to the public but is kept in a good state of repair.

The John Bunyan Connection

During the 1650s, Bedfordshire's renowned preacher and writer was able to travel around the country and preach quite openly. When, in 1660, Prince Charles was brought back to England to be crowned King Charles II, the stricter members of the Church of England began to persecute the non-conforming preachers. Even though he knew he was at risk, Bunyan accepted an invitation to preach at Harlington and was arrested. After questioning him, on and off for two days, Frances Wingate JP sent him from Harlington to Bedford gaol. Neither of them knew that he would remain there for more than ten years.

The Church of St Mary the Virgin

Sitting with Wingate and encouraging him to issue the commitment which sent Bunyan to gaol, was Dr Lindall. Soon afterwards he became vicar of Harlington church.

Today, Bunyan is greatly honoured in the village. The Grade I listed church has a stained glass window in his memory and an altar made from part of the oak tree under which, reputedly, he used to preach. A visit to the healthy young oak tree, which replaced the original one, is part of a package that can be arranged when parties visit the church.

Flitwick

As we have seen in previous pages, the cost, as well as the responsibility, of maintaining our historic houses is very high. The three houses on the northern loop are each supported by a different charity, while this and the next one are supported by hotels. On the Preservation Route, the elegant house and attractive grounds of Pendley Manor have also been used to make the nucleus of a country house hotel with all modern amenities.

*An honorary title for this important old building

244

Flitwick Manor Hotel

In 1800, Flitwick manor was inherited by a lady called Ann Hesse. Her second husband, George Brooks, was a director of a private bank, known as Dixon Brooks and Co (part of the Nat West). Their son, John Thomas Brooks, married in 1816 and received the manor as a wedding present. In his early twenties he moved out to Flitwick with his young wife and settled down to enjoy life as a country gentleman. He took his responsibilities seriously, helped in the administration of Mid Bedfordshire and took his turn as High Sheriff. On the other hand, he and his wife had a wide circle of friends and enjoyed a wonderful social life. The alterations and extensions that he made to the house, to bring it up to the standard he felt was suitable for his position are described in his diary. Horticulture and arboriculture were hobbies that he took seriously and he regularly visited shows in London and other parks and gardens. The alterations that he made to his own gardens and the trees that he planted are also mentioned in the diary.

The Brooks family continued to own this small, private estate until 1932. Between them they added even more trees and special features to the grounds. A later owner decided that it would make an ideal country hotel and managed to preserve the main reception rooms enjoyed by John Brooks and his family, also most of his magnificent mature trees and other garden features.

Woburn

From the village, the entrance to the abbey is via a long drive with great banks of rhododendrons, typical of the Greensand Ridge. At 1086, there were only abut twenty families living on the 1200-acre estate and in the 12th century, it followed a similar pattern to that of Old Warden.

The Abbey

In 1145, Hugh de Bolebec, whose main estate was at Whitchurch Castle (Bucks) but who was working in Yorkshire, gave Woburn to the Abbot of Fountains Abbey. The abbot sent Adam, his master mason, to study the layout of the land and the mason decided that it was an ideal site for a self-supporting monastery. Apart from the arable and the grazing for sheep, there were ponds suitable for fish and sandy banks for keeping rabbits.

As most of the villagers lived at Birchmore, even further away than Woburn village, they were assured of seclusion, so they laid out the gardens and orchards and employed masons to build the house. Originally the monks attended a midnight service and then other services every three hours. At many other houses, the main mass of the day was shared with the tenants and workers; however, for greater seclusion, the Cistercians at Woburn provided a parish church at Birchmore. The monks had complete control of this church and the curate lived at the abbey. In common with all the early Cistercians, they had very little contact with the outside world and probably provided accommodation for travellers up in the village.

Gradually the Cistercians were obliged to give up much of their seclusion and play an active role in the community. It was probably Abbot Hugh of Soulbury's family who, c1281, gave them Soulbury rectory and they soon owned three more churches and their land, plus scattered farms in several counties. They developed Woburn village, where they had a horse mill, blacksmith and numerous workshops; what may have been their original hostel became an inn called The Kings Head and there was another inn, known as The George. Gradually the people who lived at Birchmore moved to the present Woburn village, which, being on the main road from London to the Midlands (via Hockliffe), prospered. In 1242, the cellarer obtained a licence from Henry III for a weekly Friday market and an annual fair on the 14th September. The 'pitches' (cobbled area outside the present Town Hall) mark the site.

The Closing of the Abbey

The last abbot, Robert Hobbs, was an educated man, a member of the Luton Fraternity and popular in the neighbourhood. He provided a school for the sons of the local landowners and was able to persuade Francis Bryan, steward of King Henry's Ampthill estates, to become abbey steward. The king himself showed his approval and, in 1530, granted two more fairs, one in March and the other in July.

Hobbs must have been very shocked when Bryan's cousin, Anne Boleyn, caused the annulment of Henry's marriage to Catherine of Aragon. Bryan supported the king at the Dunstable enquiry of 1533 and went to Ampthill Castle to try to persuade Catherine to attend. Nevertheless, as far as Hobbs knew, he and Bryan remained friends. Matters came to a head during the following year when Thomas Cromwell sent out commissioners to obtain compulsory signatures confirming King Henry as head of the church in England. They were to supervise, or at least to order, the erasing of the Pope's name from all service books. Nearly all the monks in the country signed this oath; they had no choice. However, Woburn cannot have been the only house where privately opinions were divided. Hobbs' downfall was that he did not keep his views private. Too many people knew that he had copied the papers he had received from Rome, before he handed them over and that he advised crossing out the name of the Pope, not erasing it. The sub prior, the sexton and several other monks agreed with Hobbs, but the curate of the parish church, possibly encouraged by some of the younger monks, rode off to London and reported to Thomas Cromwell.

The commissioners returned; the monks were lined up and this time the three senior men were brave enough to refuse to sign. A trial took place at Woburn on the 14th June 1538. All three were found guilty of 'verbal treason' and were hung, according to legend, on an oak tree in the abbey grounds.

After the Dissolution
The abbey was dissolved, the monks departed and the estate and buildings passed to the king. The Receiver-General, John Williams, shared the leases of the Woburn estate with Sir Francis Bryan!

Saint Mary's Church
What had been the chapel of ease in Woburn village gradually became the main church, but it may have been well into the 17th century before the Birchmore church was finally destroyed and the stones used to build a church tower in the village. The 6th Duke paid Edward Blore to partly rebuild the tower in 1829-30 and the 8th Duke, in 1858, paid Henry Clutton to build the new St Mary's in Park Road. Standing just off Bedford Street today are the 'new' tower of 1830 (with some of the original old stones at its base) and the mortuary chapel, built in 1865, which replaced the first St Mary's Church.

The Woburn Heritage Centre
The mortuary chapel now houses the Woburn Heritage Centre and Tourist Information Point. It is a most useful place to visit as there is information about attractions, events and the local countryside, over a very wide area. It also has an informal museum depicting Woburn life over the centuries and changing exhibitions.

The Great Estate
At the time of the Dissolution, a West Country nobleman, John Russell, had become one of King Henry VIII's most trusted diplomats and was appointed as

one of sixteen counsellors to advise Henry's infant son. Henry granted him land to the value of £100 a year and soon after the coronation of Edward VI, John Russell received the lease of the abbey. Three years later, he was created the first Earl of Bedford.

He did not live in the abbey, so the buildings deteriorated but in 1572 Queen Elizabeth expressed a wish to visit Woburn and Francis, the second Earl, had to arrange for it to be quickly repaired, cleaned and furnished. From then on he took a personal interest in the estate and village; in 1582 he started a school for poor boys, which, in 1982, celebrated 300 years of continuous education.

Another Francis, soon to be the fourth Earl, had a large family and in 1625, when the plague was particularly severe in London, he moved his family to Woburn. He started to rebuild the old monastery as a private house, but during the unsettled period of the Civil War, he, like many of the other local estate owners, lost money. In November 1645, a large party of Royalist soldiers rode into Woburn village and set fire to several houses; the flames spread and seventeen or eighteen houses were lost.

The fifth Earl was in a very difficult position. He was a friend of King Charles I, who, in 1636, had stayed at Woburn but was also a great supporter of Parliament. At Edgehill, the opening battle of the Civil War, he commanded the cavalry, on the side of Parliament but in 1643 he tried to mediate with the king to prevent further bloodshed. However, his attempt failed and the fighting continued, so the Earl returned to Woburn and took no further part in the fighting.

Long after the Civil War was over and Charles II was on the throne, a group of young men set out to kidnap, maybe murder, the king and his brother, James (The Rye House Plot). The attempt failed and the conspirators were executed. The Earl's son, Lord William Russell, was implicated because he was a friend of the accused; despite the efforts of his wife, he also was executed. However, when William and Mary came to the throne, they accepted her evidence of his innocence. Parliament passed an Act whereby the judgement was reversed. In 1694 the elderly fifth Earl was, as recompense, given the title Duke of Bedford.[1]

The second Duke lived at Woburn and began the process of laying out the grounds and flower borders, paying men to travel abroad to bring back rare plants. He also improved the estate farms but unfortunately died of smallpox when he was only thirty-two.

---

1 Spavins, K and Applin, A The Book of Woburn.

The third Duke also died young and it was his brother, John, the fourth Duke, who had the house rebuilt and collected much of the furniture, which can be seen today. He was very interested in new methods of forestry and laid out the wood, now known as 'The Evergreens'. The head gardener was so worried that the duke's modern methods would destroy his own reputation that eventually, the Duke put up a roadside notice:
'This plantation has been thinned by John, Duke of Bedford, contrary to the advice and opinion of his gardener.'[1]

The fifth Duke had an even wider interest in agriculture. He founded a local agricultural society, started a 300-acre model farm and the world-famous 'sheep-shearings'. At this there were prizes for cattle, sheep and ploughing and anyone could demonstrate a new agricultural implement or talk about new farming methods. Later dukes helped to start the Smithfield Club and the Royal Agricultural Society and also to improve the standard of agriculture nationally. Locally, farmers were encouraged to take advantage of this modern information and were supplied with new types of stock, seeds and trees. At the farm they studied the use of different grasses for pasture and hay and followed this with experiments on feeding cattle. One of the results of their experiments, which was of great help to the farmers of Mid Bedfordshire, concerned fattening cattle. Traditionally, drovers brought cattle down from the north of England to be fattened on the grassland of South and Mid Bedfordshire. By draining the ground, improving the grassland and feeding turnips, the farmers of Mid Bedfordshire could carry far more livestock through the winter. Today, Woburn Abbey is still the centre of a large agricultural estate; as you approach the abbey, the farm buildings (which were built in c1780) are on your right. In some ways they were the innovators of the 'Stately Homes' business and they have done so much to improve standards and provide attractions which give whole families an entertaining day out. The present Duke first opened Woburn to the public on Good Friday, 1955. He set high standards and became the first president of the Thames and Chilterns Tourist Board.

His son, the Marquis of Tavistock has maintained these high standards and in the autumn of 1978 was invited by the British Tourist Authority to lead the US Heritage Mission to America. This was a fact-finding tour, examining American methods of presenting leisure, dealing with visitors and marketing. He has recently passed the responsibility of managing the estate to his son, Andrew, Lord Howland.

1 Herbrand, 11th Duke of Bedford, A Great Agricultural Estate

Aspley Guise

The Saxon settlement in the clearings where the aspen trees grow, was included in one of the very earliest surviving Bedfordshire documents. In a charter drawn up in 969AD, King Edgar granted his servant (actually a distant relative), Alfwold, the place called Aspley, with its fields, pastures, woods and fifteen husbandmen. The boundary of this estate includes fords and fens, streams and dykes, heaths and combes (small valleys), high woods and charcoal pits.[1]

Many Different Landowners

By 1066, a lady called Leofeva held Aspley, but following the Conquest, it was taken into the estate of the sheriff. There was a mill on the stream, meadow, arable and woodland.

There were at least twenty cottages and five families without land. Although it remained with the sheriff's family, it was sublet to Anselm of Gyse in 1267 and remained with his family for many years; the modern spelling is usually Guise. They were intermarried with the Beauchamp family and although they were often absentee owners, they held on to most of their estates into the mid 16th century. A John Guise was closely connected with the family of King Henry VII and the 16th century brass of a knight in St Botolph's Church is thought to commemorate his life. Details are no longer easy to see, but it was once possible to see a collar of S's, supporting the Tudor portcullis. (Opinions differ as to the date and identification of this knight.)

In 1540, the Guise family exchanged their Aspley estate for another in Gloucestershire. This was just at the time that officials were putting together the great royal estate, based at Ampthill Castle. The rent list of 1542 illustrates that, due to the absence of the Guise family, instead of one very large house, there were several which were above average size. This is borne out by 17th and 18th century records.

William Harding held the manor house, with a great deal of pasture, a rabbit warren, the claypits and fulling pits (Fullers earth). He was responsible for running the manor court and acting as the king's representative. His descendants stayed in Aspley for many years.

Thomas Pedder appears to have been the Guise family's tenant on one of the farms but after his death, Thomas Foster, who held the manor and the rectory farm at Salford, married Pedder's widow and took over Pedder's land at Aspley and Wavendon. Simon Fitz, tenant of the main (ex) Woburn Abbey sheep farm,

Village Scene Aspley Guise

Moore Place Hotel Aspley Guise

at Birchmore, appears to have had one large house and also several smaller ones in the village. Other houses and cottages were also listed individually and there was reference to the watermill.

The Story of Aspley Guise

This is the title of a book produced by Woburn Sands branch of the Workers' Educational Association in 1980. It is subtitled 'The Success of an English Village'. It is a very readable but also detailed assessment of the village as it was around 1851. Based on the census, it moves forward and backward to uncover the lives of the families who lived there at that time and also the growth of the village and the development of Woburn Sands.

Part One covers the gentry and straight away we find that at that time, there were still several important houses in the village.

In 1575, Edmund Harding, great-grandson of the above William, had built 'the handsome Tudor residence now known as Old House'. The family of Thomas Snagge of Marston Morteyne, (ancestor of John Snagge, the broadcaster), built nearby Aspley House in 1695. Pevsner describes this as 'a perfect specimen of its date'. Also nearby is Guise House, which was built in the early 18th century. By 1851, it was being used as a highly respected school for boys - The Classical Academy. This had been started c1720 and was fortunate to have a series of well-educated and well-respected masters. Also, unlike some 18th century schools, the boys were well fed and cared for. Because of this, the school not only attracted local boys, but also boys from distant countries.

The Moore Family of Moore Place

Sometime in the 1760s, a boy called Francis Moore arrived from Somerset. It is not known for how long he was a pupil at the school or whether he stayed on after the normal leaving age, but in 1766, while still described as a 'pupil', he married Susanna Sawell, the headmaster's daughter. Sawell not only owned Guise House and its small estate, but also around 100 acres of agricultural land and he continued to buy more. The young couple may have set up home in Aspley Guise with financial help from Moore's family, as they soon settled into the role of landed gentry. When Sawell died in 1770, they inherited both money and land and, in 1786, commissioned the building of an impressive house, right in the centre of the village. This became known as Moore Place.

For several generations, Aspley had been without a resident Lord of the Manor and much of the role had fallen on the respected How family. The

Richard How who was living in Aspley when the young Francis Moore began to take an interest in public affairs, was a bachelor. He was a Quaker who, having inherited some major debts, had moved out of the family house into a much smaller 'cottage'. Whether this affected his attitude, or whether the young Moore was tactless and rude, is not recorded, but for fourteen years Aspley became a divided village. This rivalry may be why Moore found it difficult to buy much more land in the village. However, he built up a very large, scattered estate, elsewhere in the district.

In particular he bought up much of Wavendon Heath, with its Fullers Earth claypits, rabbit warrens and woodland. He planted 500 acres with 51,376 Scotch Firs and, to quote The Story of Aspley Guise, 'completely transformed the environs of the village and gave the heath that air of Switzerland that was, in the following century, to attract both consumptives and Bedford merchants seeking a country retreat'. As a result of this, he won both national awards and public acclaim.

The Rev John Vaux Moore JP

When Francis died, his son, Captain John Patrick Moore RN, took over but he died in 1835 and the house passed to Francis' grandson, the Rev John Vaux Moore, Vicar of Ridgemont. In 1844, he managed to buy the Rectory of Aspley.

In 1851, he was living at Moore Place as a 57-year-old bachelor; his house was run by his cook, 27-year-old Mary Cattle, his housemaid, 19-year-old Elizabeth Ward and a 19-year-old footman, Edward Goodall. His immediate neighbours were a schoolmaster who had come from Huddersfield and other families who were financially independent. By this time, the rector was a wealthy man and employed a vicar to look after St Botolph's Church. He was very much one of England's sporting clergymen and the record that he has left behind confirms the best and worst qualities of his kind. He was criticised for neglecting his parishes by spending his winter following field sports and his summers boating and playing cricket but was conscientious about some aspects of parish life. By July 1850 he had supplied the ground and paid for the building of a proper school building and was already restoring the church.

In 1833 there were two well-supported Sunday Schools, one connected with St Botolph's and a much larger one run by the Methodists. One of the Quaker How family started a British day school with bible-based religious education and Moore started a National, prayer-book-based school. Visiting inspectors praised both schools.

In July 1850 Mr and Mrs Bickerstaff, who lived by the school, in Woburn Lane, were commended for their work, although Mrs Bickerstaff had poor health. They were replaced by a Mr and Mrs Ellen, who were given an even better report. At the church, the Rev Moore was responsible for rebuilding the south aisle and for several other major pieces of restoration.

Moore Place

The Rev John Vaux Moore died in 1864 and over the years, the elegant Georgian house changed hands several times. During the Second World War, it was used as the headquarters for the 6th Army Field Workshops RAOC; a corrugated iron building was erected in the grounds to provide a mess and cookhouse. By the end of the war it was in need of repair and much of the land had been sold. With so many other important houses in the area, Moore Place failed to attract a new owner who could restore it to its former glory and before long, it became a small private hotel, known as The Holt.

Moore Place Hotel

Although referred to above as Moore Place, this has not always been its name. In 1987, money was found to fully restore it and at the same time to convert it to a first class country house hotel. As the new owners intended to emphasise its previous role as a Georgian country house, Moore Place was the most suitable name.

It stands today as it has always done, right in the middle of the attractive village, with its Georgian facade looking across to what was once the market square.

The Henry VII Lodge

When talking about historic houses on this part of the Scenic Route, mention must be made of the small cottage, once known as Puzzle Gardens. This was built in 1810. At the request of the Duke of Bedford, Humphrey Repton designed a cottage to record various building styles of the period around 1500; he called it Aspley Wood Lodge. Today this is not always easy to see; it lies to the right of the A5130, just as the Woburn road is about to enter Woburn Sands. In 1851, it stood on an open piece of ground with a maze and a handsome tree-lined drive. The former was such a prominent feature that, at the time, it gave the cottage its name. The census records that the Woburn estate was using it as a home for one of its agricultural labourers, John Byway, who lived there with his wife Ann and their three children.

Ampthill

As the A418 leaves Ampthill, heading for Bedford, it passes Park House which was developed by King James I as a hunting lodge. This is now privately owned. On the right-hand-side, at the top of the hill, it passes the road leading to the ruins of Houghton House, which are now in the care of English Heritage.

Houghton House

Reputedly the inspiration for the 'House Beautiful' in Bunyan's Pilgrim's Progress, the remains of this early 17th century mansion still contain elements that justify the description, including work attributed to Inigo Jones.[1] It was built for Mary, Countess of Pembroke, sister of Sir Phillip Sydney. King James visited her there in September 1621, two months before she died. Soon afterwards, King James gave it to the Bruce family, who had supported him in Scotland and helped to make the arrangements for his arrival in England. In 1633, Thomas Bruce was given the Earldom of Elgin and in later years, his son was made Earl of Ailesbury and Viscount Bruce of Ampthill. King James visited them in 1624 and brought with him the future King Charles.

The family gradually obtained leases of all the royal interests in and around Ampthill and also of the ex-monastic estates in Bedfordshire. King Charles made Lord Bruce responsible for the preservation of game in Great Park and surrounding royal estates.[2]

The House Beautiful

John Bunyan, author of The Pilgrim's Progress, was born in 1628. By the time that he was old enough to accompany his grandfather, the chapman (a type of pedlar) or his father, who was a brazier, Houghton House was still very new and extremely impressive. Standing high on the hill (the 'Hill of Difficulty'), it could be seen for miles around and from the upstairs windows there were views of the Chiltern Hills (the 'Delectable Mountain'). There is no proof that Bunyan visited this house, but the household account books make clear that there were metal workers and salesmen among the regular visiting tradesmen.[3]

1 Foster, AJ Bunyan's Country
2 Underwood, A Ampthill, a Goodly Heritage
3 BHRS Vol 32 Domestic Expenses of a Nobleman's Household 1678 by the Earl of Cardigan.
Also EMH 5 Life in the Palace Beautiful by Evelyn Curtis

The Last Years

The Bruce Family remained in Bedfordshire for several generations but by 1700 the owner was living abroad. From then on the house was neglected and in 1738 it was sold to the Duke of Bedford. In 1764 it became the home of the fourth Duke's heir. Unfortunately, three years later, he died in a hunting accident and his inconsolable widow died soon afterwards.

In 1794 the Duke of Bedford had the roof removed and began to dismantle the empty building. Time and weather did more damage and there was concern for its safety. A hundred years later, representatives of the National Trust visited the attractive ruins but took no further action.

Houghton House Today

In 1923 a local farmer decided to clear the site. Sir Albert Richardson of Ampthill converted local opposition into a national campaign. The Bunyan connection was used to spearhead a long-drawn-out struggle. 1928 was the tercentenary of Bunyan's birth and this stirred even greater efforts; by December 1930 there was enough money to buy the ruins and the site on which they stood. Even then, £2000 was needed to repair the recent damage and to make the walls safe. This work was eventually undertaken by the Office of Works.[1] This beautiful site with its impressive ruins is now in the care of English Heritage. Enough details remain that, with help from the published 'Inventory of Furniture at Houghton House', we can visualise the position of the once elegant rooms.[2]

The Exceptional Number of Historic Houses Across Mid Bedfordshire

This chapter has pointed out what a wide selection of historic houses survive across Mid Bedfordshire. During the time that this book was being written, Lord Howland took over the management of Woburn Abbey and its estate. This is one family that has lived on its historic estate from the Dissolution of the Monasteries to the present day.

At least two of these buildings have, during the last fifty years, come near to collapse; several others have had a financial crisis. The positive message of this chapter is to point out the numerous ways that have been found by government

1 Houfe, Simon *Sir Albert Richardson, the Professor*
2 BHRS Vol 38 *by Evelyn Curtis*

departments, businesses, charities and private individuals to restore and maintain these important buildings. They have been helped by national organisations such as English Heritage, local authorities, such as Mid Beds District Council, and literally thousands of volunteer workers and fund-raisers. We owe a debt of gratitude to these conscientious and hard-working groups and individuals.

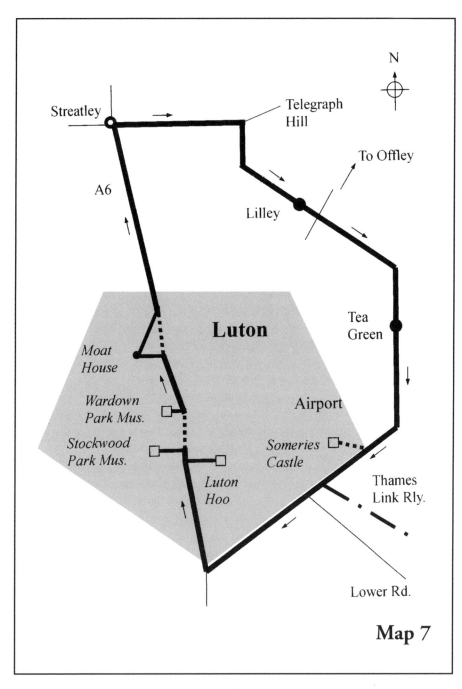

Streatley

Telegraph Hill

To Offley

A6

Lilley

Luton

Tea Green

Moat House

Wardown Park Mus.

Airport

Stockwood Park Mus.

Someries Castle

Luton Hoo

Thames Link Rly.

Lower Rd.

Map 7

CHAPTER 7 • *ROUTE 7*

Historic Houses of Luton

Luton - Wardown Museum • Luton - Old Moat House
(Putteridgebury) • Lilley • (Great Offley) • Tea Green
Someries Castle • Luton Hoo • Luton - Stockwood Park
Luton - St Mary's Church

Introduction

This Route is only about 15 miles long and is never far from St Mary's Church
in the centre of Luton. It starts at Luton Museum, in Wardown Park, which
houses one of Luton's greatest treasures - the register of the Fraternity of the holy
Trinity. The Historical Background to this route is based on this historic
register but, once out on the road, the Historical Highlights will pass a
surprising number of important historic buildings, including: one of
Bedfordshire's oldest secular buildings, now a restaurant, and two early 19th
century houses, both now used for conferences and adult education. It also
passes near the attractivley-landscaped ruins of the grand 15th century manor
house at Someries and a well-preserved mid 19th century manor house (which
has featured in several films) and is about to become a high-class hotel. It then
continues to Stockwood Park, where the stables and courtyard are currently used
as a craft centre and rural heritage museum. There are period, walled gardens
and a major collection of carriages and other horse-drawn vehicles. Back in the
town centre is the much altered Red Lion inn and the Grade I parish church of
St Mary.

Historical Background

The Fraternity of the Holy and Undivided Trinity and the Blessed Virgin Mary

In Luton Museum is the register of the town's 15th and 16th century Fraternity. This rare book reflects a wonderful view of Luton's past; its illuminations are respected in the international art world and the information that it holds is of great importance to local and family historians. This chapter uses the register as a way of tracing Luton's historic houses and sites.

It was quite common in the 15th century for people to leave a small bequest in their wills to provide for prayers or masses to be said after their death, to hasten the passage of their souls on their way to heaven.

Some examples are:

At Streatley someone left an acre of land, made up of strips in the open fields, the income to be used to have their name kept on the prayer roll.

At Kensworth two acres and at Lilley three acres were left to provide a lamp in each church. These were a symbol of ceaseless prayer offered through Christ or one of the saints.

At Redbourn a gentleman called Thomas Peacoke left an inn called The Swan, standing in the High Street, the rental of which was to pay for an annual 'obit' or obituary mass for the repose of his soul.

Rich country landowners might pay for the support of one or more priests, whose main work would be to pray for their souls and those of their families. He might also arrange for some charitable work to be carried out in his name. Such a one was William Dyve of Sewell who, in 1515, arranged payment for two priests to sing masses, one at his manor-house at Sewell and one to teach six poor children from Houghton Regis. In towns it became the accepted thing that the richer businessmen would pay for a priest to sing masses for the souls of the king and his family and of the members and their families and also to provide money for charitable purposes.

It was probably because of the arrival of the Rotherham family that the Luton Fraternity was founded in 1474. Lord John Rotherham (later Bishop of Lincoln), together with his brother who lived at Someries, the Vicar of St Mary's and other like-minded people, applied for the licence. Houses in Luton and land in the common fields were provided so that their rents could support 'two chaplens to syng within the parishe churche of Luton..... for the prosperous estate of Kyng Edward IVth and Queen Elizabeth his wyff and for the good

Pages from Luton Fraternity Register (F.L.M.)

estate of all the brothers and systers and all theyr benefactors.'[1] There is no evidence that they were involved in regular charitable works.

A beautifully-written register was kept of the members' names. After the closing of the fraternities in 1546, it appears to have passed, along with the manorial papers, to the various lords of the manor. In 1984 the Marquis of Bute, whose family were formerly lords of the manor, offered the manuscript register for sale and, after a great deal of effort on the part of the Friends of Luton Museum, it was eventually purchased on behalf of the museum. Each year the register opened with a royal dedication, then followed the titled members and respected country gentlemen and their families. These were followed by ecclesiastical members; not only were many local clergy enrolled but also the senior members of the local religious houses.

Over 6000 identifiable names are recorded in the surviving pages of the register. Although most of them came from in or around Luton, there were pockets of members from scattered places, some as far away as Boston in Lincolnshire and Kendal in Cumbria. These distant members may have been the families of married Luton girls or they may have been business associates. Each year prayers were asked for the souls of members recently deceased, while local land-owners who had died before the Fraternity was opened were made posthumous members.

The Fraternity Feasts

The society was partly religious and partly social; at some stage they built a Brotherhood House on the site of the present Red Lion Hotel on Market Hill. Each year the members held a great banquet and we can assume that there were regular meetings in between.

Account books have recently been bought by Bedfordshire County Council and are now in the Record Office. A predecessor of the present Lord Bute commissioned barrister-at-law, Henry Gough, to make a partial copy of the register and the account books. It was published in 1906 by Chiswick Press and there are copies in Luton Central Library and in Luton Museum Library. From this we can see that the great event in their year was the banquet or feast. Presumably it was held at the Brotherhood House, either inside or, certainly in the early years, outside, with an ornate cloth hanging behind the top table.

In 1527 a baker was paid 1s 6d (7$\frac{1}{2}$p) to bake bread and a brewer 4s 0d (20p) to brew, with 29 shillings-worth of malt. In addition they bought 7 barrels of

---

1 Brown, J.E. Chantry Certificates of Bedfordshire

beer at 1s 10d (9p) per barrel. The main courses were fish (trout and fresh salmon), poultry (91 geese at 3d (1^1/$_2$p) each, 64 capons at approximately 6d (2^1/$_2$p) each and 84 chickens, 84 rabbits and also joints of red meat. It is of interest that most of the rabbits were bought from the manorial warren at Toddington. Apart from spending over a pound on beef, 20 lambs were also bought at 1s 4d (6^3/$_4$p) each. Although pepper was still extremely expensive, 3lbs were bought for seasoning and it is interesting to compare the cost of one lamb with the 85p paid for one pound of pepper in 1990. The meat was cooked on a spit and two men were paid 4d (1^3/$_4$p) for 'watching of ye mette', while others were described as 'turner of spytt'. Vegetables were looked on with suspicion by the rich and do not feature among the ingredients.

Looking at the long list of sweet ingredients and bearing in mind that they bought a cream cloth, a jelly-bag, some calves' feet and gallons of milk, it looks as if in addition to several very large suet puddings stuffed with raisins and sultanas, they had a selection of what we would call milk jellies and egg custards. Milk, cream, eggs, honey and natural gelatine were probably heated and flavoured with mace (the outer covering of the nutmeg) and almonds. The final course was not of cheese and biscuits, but of dessert raisins, liquorice, prunes, almonds and sweetmeats. Unfortunately we do not know how many people sat down to enjoy this feast but there must have been at least 130 diners and probably many more.

A man called John Stevyns was paid to put up the trestle tables and lay out the cloths. Wood was cut (and hopefully planed) to make 14 forms at a total cost of 1s 6d (7^1/$_2$p). 11 dozen (132) 'sponys' (spoons) and 12 dozen (144) trenchers (wooden plates) were bought and 26 dozen (312) 'pewt' (pewter mugs) were hired. A man called Alyn, together with his wife, was paid 10d for washing up during and on the day following the banquet. Numerous 'haftelers' (ostlers) were paid 6d a day over a period of 4 days to cover the period of preparation and clearing up.

The banquet was quite formal. The master and the wardens had new liveries sent from London and they processed into the banqueting room behind an official carrying a banner. Two butlers supervised the serving of the meal and William Barne of Woburn arranged for musicians to entertain while the guests were eating. These included a group of minstrels and a harpist. On this occasion the cost of the Feast was £20.7s.0d but £39.2s.3d was collected from the members, so the day ended with a good profit.

Just as between 1536 and 1540 King Henry VIII closed the religious houses, so in 1546 his son Edward VI began to close the chantries and fraternities. Their property and land was transferred to the Crown and gradually sold. The registers ceased and if the annual banquets did continue, the account books have not been found. A colourful period of Luton's history had come to an abrupt end.

This route will link the estates of several of the more senior members of the Fraternity.

Historical Highlights/Route

LUTON

Early Manorial History

From some long time before the Norman Conquest until about the year 1275, Luton and its surrounding hamlets were one important royal or near-royal manor. When the inventory for the 'Domesday' tax report of 1086 was published, Luton was already a flourishing market town and, most unusually for the period, had a church supported by approximately 600 acres of land. The River Lea ran diagonally across the manor, supplying good fishing and no less than six watermills, contributing considerably to the prosperity of the Lord of the Manor. There was also plentiful arable land, water meadows, grazing on the Downs and ample mature woodland to support pigs and provide raw material with which to build houses.

Soon after 1275, following the disruptions caused by the battles that led to the signing of the Magna Carta and then Simon de Montfort's struggle to establish a parliament, the manor was divided between six heiresses. These were descendants of William Pembroke, Earl Marshall of England.* The Bury House, from which the king's steward had run the whole manor, (and which gave its name to 'Bury Park') was eventually allowed to deteriorate and was replaced by Bury Farm. New estates were established, many having their own manor houses. By the end of the 15th century, Someries 'Castle' had become the main manor house; the title was not bought by the owner of Luton Hoo until 1612.

The Early Church in Luton

The important background to Christian worship in Luton has been recorded in detail by the Rev. Henry Cobbe.[1] It may be as early as the 7th century that some

---

* Within a few years several of these shares had been subdivided
1 Cobbe, H. History of Luton Church

264

Saxon king gave a 600 acre farm and house to one of the newly-appointed bishops to help him establish Christian worship in and around the royal manor of Luton. A modern spelling for this estate would be Bishop's-cote (now Biscot). This was lost to the church during the time that Luton was on the very boundary of Danelaw. In the Domesday Book of 1086 the Saxon owner is recorded as Edwin Asgar and the spelling had become 'Bissopescote'. However, there was now a new church estate (later known as the 'Dallow Manor') and a new church, which Cobbe suggests had been built on the king's home or 'Bury' farm. He also suggests that Robert, Earl of Gloucester, illegitimate but much-loved son of King Henry I, had that building dismantled and a new church built on or near the present site.

The Population

The population of Luton and its hamlets at the time that the Fraternity was closed was approximately 1,500.[1] The commissioners pointed out what a large parish it was and that some of the parishioners had to travel three or four miles to church.

Throughout the 17th century there was a continued increase in population, so that by the time of the published Hearth Tax of 1671, it had risen to nearly 2,000. More than half of these lived in the township; Stopsley was the largest village with a population of approximately 200.[2] Still the increase continued and by the first census of 1801, the figure had comfortably passed 3,000.

However, as the straw-hat industry of the 19th century became more organized, young people flocked into the town. Year by year new streets were laid out and infill began to link the township with its villages. From under 8,000 in 1841, the population had passed 38,000 in 1901.[3]

The Parish Church of St. Mary

There was once a Saxon church in Luton but all that is known to survive is one corbel, a carving of a man's face, which is over the present south door. This is because it was partially rebuilt in the 13th century. From the 13th century to the Dissolution of the Monasteries, the church was owned by St Albans Abbey. A new church was started around 1131. The abbey made other alterations in the 14th century, as did various wealthy landowners. All this continual building has resulted in the largest parish church in Bedfordshire, with very fine pieces of

1 Brown, J.E. Chantry Certificates of Bedfordshire   2 BHRS Vol 16
3 Lunn, J. Beds Mag Vol 19

architectural design and with decoration from many different periods. It is worth visiting the church just to see the unique 14th century baptistry, which includes carvings of symbols representing the struggle between good and evil. Lovers of church decoration and architecture also have great respect for the carved stone of the Wenlock Screen.

The Wenlock Chapel was built in 1461, about the same date as the 4-seated sedilia that commemorates Abbot John Wheathampstead, of St. Albans. Within the Wenlock Chapel is the tomb of William Wenlock, who was Master of Farley Hospital from 1377 to 1391. Robert, Earl of Gloucester, and the families of Somery, Hoo, Wenlock, Rotherham, Crawley, Napier and Bute are all, in some way, connected to this church. The chantry of vicar Richard Bernard, who was Master of the Fraternity in 1478, is on the south side of the chancel.[1]

The Red Lion

In 1548 a survey and valuation was carried out of all chantries, fraternities and their sources of income. This was in preparation for their closure and transfer of their estates into the king's treasury. At that time the Luton Brotherhood House was let to a Thomas Perott for £7 11s 4d per year (approx £7.57p). Back in 1474, Thomas Perott senior was one of the founding members of the fraternity and they were the family with the greatest number of entries. On eighteen occasions a member of the Perott family held office and in 1476 a 'Thomas Perott of the Vyne' was one of the two wardens. Austin identified The Vyne as an inn, which in the 15th and 16th centuries was called The Vine or Vinecocks (Vinecotes).* It stood in Park Street, not far from the top of Market Hill.

The manor court rolls for Luton have survived for the years 1470-1559 and from these, at least three 'Thomas Perotts' can be identified. One held land in Biscot and Limbury and was a member of the jury when the surviving rolls started. Another was described as being 'at the end of the town' or 'at the foot of the hill'. The third, Thomas Perott of the Vine, appears repeatedly from 1533 onwards amongst a list of people fined for leaving piles of manure or firewood in the road outside their houses! From 1541 until his death in 1557 he was regularly a member of the jury who helped to run the Manor Court.[2]

We do not know for what purpose Perott was using the Brotherhood House nor when it was eventually purchased from the Crown. He was present at the

1 Rogers, K. The Stories and Secrets of Luton's Medieval Jewel
* 'Vinecotes' probably meant that it was a house licensed to sell alcohol
2 Luton Manor Court Rolls. Published by BCRO

Manor Court in April 1550 when a list was drawn up of Fraternity property recently purchased from the Crown. The list included a great deal of land together with three houses on or near the Market Hall but the Brotherhood House is not named.

Thomas Perott 'of the Vine' continued to attend the court but in 1559, when the death of a Roger Barbor was recorded, the latter was described as having been tenant of the Vinecotes. It is more than likely that Perott had opened the Brotherhood House as a high-class inn even before the Fraternity closed but whether it was he or a later owner who named it The Red Lion is not known. A deed of 1665 concerning two cottages near Market Hill refers to the nearby Brotherhood House as 'alias The Lyon'[1]

Wardown House

Wardown House is the beginning and end of our route but would have no connection with the Fraternity register if it had not become a museum. Nevertheless, as a historic house in its own right, it deserves a place here. The farm was once an outlier of Bramingham Manor so it was known as Bramingham 'Shott'. On July 2, 1868, it was bought by a Luton solicitor, Frank Chapman Scargill. He demolished the farmhouse and by 1877 had built the present building and had also commissioned the present lodges, stables, park and cricket ground. There were 16 bedrooms, a drawing room, dining room, 2 kitchens, a smoking room and a billiard room. Unusually for the 19th century, there were 3 bathrooms and 4 WCs. The inventory of 1897 gives a very good picture of a late 19th century country house. It includes a schoolroom, a laundry, dairy, apple room, boot room, game larder and a conservatory.

> ## ROUTE
> When the route leaves the museum car park, it is heading for the Moat House Restaurant. Turn left into the Old Bedford Road and immediately turn left onto Stockingstone Road. At the roundabout turn right to drive north up the A6 towards Bedford, but watch out for the first set of traffic lights, then turn left into Austin Road.

The next owner, BJH Forder, renamed the house 'Wardown', the name of his previous home in Hampshire. In June 1903 two local businessmen, Asher Hucklesby and Edwin Oakley, bought the estate on behalf of Luton Council, the park being opened to the public two years later. During the First World War it became a military hospital. In the 1920s a tearoom was opened on the ground floor and the museum was opened in 1931.

1 BCRO AD827

Wardown House - The Museum

The Old Moat House

The Moat House

This was built towards the end of the 14th century by the Bereford family and was typical of the new 'manor houses' that were built around Luton in the 14th and 15th centuries. Soon afterwards it was purchased by William Ackworth of Yorkshire; John Ackworth was a founder member of the Fraternity. This family rose socially and financially and by 1500, Thomas Ackworth was Master of the Stable to Elizabeth of York, Queen of Henry VII. During the 14th and 15th centuries the Ackworths held various positions at court, as soldiers, diplomats and civil servants, but in the 16th century they joined the professions and became lawyers, clergymen and members of the Merchant Tailors' Company. They then spent less time at the Moat House and in 1548 sold the manor to two fellow-members, one of whom was William Harper of Bedford. It changed hands several times and was owned for some time by the Wingate family of Harlington, who linked Biscot with nearby Limbury. In 1724 the combined manor was bought by John Crawley of Stockwood, who may have been responsible for its modernisation.

By the 19th century it had become a farmhouse and so it continued into living memory; for some years it stood empty, a fire destroyed most of the roof and it seemed likely that it would be pulled down. Local historians, together with South Bedfordshire Preservation Society, did everything possible to obtain a preservation order for the building. Eventually they were successful and Creasey Hotels bought the property and had it very carefully restored to be used as a bar and licensed restaurant. It is one of the oldest secular buildings in South Bedfordshire and we should be grateful to the present and earlier owners for their guardianship of this important part of our heritage.

> *ROUTE*
> At the next set of traffic lights turn right into Nunnery Lane. The Old Moat House is facing you.
> The route is now heading for the A6. With the Moat House facing you, bear left and at once turn right, so that it is now on your right. At the staggered crossroads, turn right into Bancroft Road (with a school on your right). Continue towards the A6, passing a shopping parade on your right (with the Warden Hills soon appearing ahead of you) and then another shopping parade on the left. Follow the signs for the A6 and then turn left towards Bedford. The route is now heading for Lilley.

PUTTERIDGEBURY

Although the route passes through what was part of the estate, the drive to the house is approached from the A505. This large estate which spread between

269

Luton, Lilley and Offley was, after the Norman Conquest, taken into the royal manor of Luton but the owner in 1556 attached it to his manor of Lilley. It is just beyond the Hertfordshire border, in the parish of Offley. Because of its valuable woodland, it was much in demand for hunting and later for shooting.

When the Fraternity first started, Putteridge estate was owned by Richard Lyster, solicitor to King Henry VII and Chief Justice of the King's Bench. In 1525 it was purchased by John Docwra, nephew to the Lord Prior of the Order of the Knights of St John of Jerusalem. For some reason neither of these families appear to have been made members.

There were several changes of ownership during the 18th century. It was in 1788 that John Sowerby, a self-made man from the City of London, bought the estate. This family remained at Putteridgebury into the 20th century. The important role that they performed in the life of Lilley, Stopsley and Luton has been recorded by James Dyer.[1] They still owned the house when it was destroyed by fire in 1808 and they then had a new Regency-style house built half a mile to the north of the old one.

However it was Thomas Meadows Clutterbuck and his wife Blanche who bought it in 1908 and were responsible for the present building. They had previously been tenants of Chequers, now the Prime Minister's country residence, and ordered the comparatively new Putteridgebury house to be taken down. Mrs Clutterbuck then employed Sir Ernest George and Yates to design and build a house very similar to Chequers. At the time the house was being designed, the young Edward Lutyens was one of Sir Ernest's pupils.

James Dyer points out the numerous representations of the rampant lion and other details from the family coat of arms, which can be seen in the house and in the grounds. The gardens and their associated buildings, which were originally laid out, around 1820, by the Scottish landscape designer, JC London, are also of historic importance. The estate is now owned by Luton University and used as a management college.

1 Dyer, J. The Stopsley Book

LILLEY

This village and its church are closely associated with Putteridgebury. The Silver Lion pub sign and the rampant lion crests, which can be seen on cottage walls and gateposts, were taken from the crests of the Clutterbuck family. During the years covered by the Fraternity register, more than a dozen families from Lilley were represented, some of them several times.[1]

The Church of St Peter

The present church was designed, in 1870, by Thomas Jekyll. He used mainly flint for the walls but retained one Norman redstone arch in the chancel.

GREAT OFFLEY

This village with its most interesting church and manor-house is just off the route. It is sometimes thought that its name comes from the fact that King Offa of Mercia (757-796) may have had a palace nearby. Unfortunately the life of King Offa is not very well recorded. It is known that c793 he founded the Bendictine monastery at St Albans and that the Abbey historian, Matthew Paris, stated that this was in response to a dream. One legend suggests that he was sleeping at his Offley palace when he had this dream. Eileen Roberts, who has carefully recorded the available information which concerns the building of the Abbey, points out that Paris mixes fact and fiction in a rather confusing way.[2]

One thing is certain. Offley has often attracted land-owners of wealth and importance. In 1066 Offley belonged to King Harold and after the Norman Conquest it was included in the personal estate of King William. It was later owned by the Ledger family of Ashby St Ledger and in the 1400s, Sir Thomas Hoo, of Luton Hoo, received it as part of his wife's dowry. Together with the rest of his Bedfordshire property, it eventually passed to the great-grandmother of Anne Boleyn. In 1475 Thomas, Baron Hoo and Hastings (d 1455) was entered as a deseased member.

In 1554 the estate was purchased by Sir John Spencer of Althorp Park, ancestor of both Winston Churchill and the late Princess Diana. A grand house,

ROUTE
Continue out of Luton with fields on either side, until, on your right, you pass a large pylon, then, just before the start of the dual carriageway, be prepared for a sign pointing right towards Lilley. Drive carefully along this narrow, and in parts, winding road, watching for signs pointing towards Lilley. Drive through the long village of Lilley, with the pond and then the church on your right.

1 Pinnock, Roy. *Between the Hills*
2 Roberts, E. *The Hill of the Martyr*

Offley Park House, was built c1600 by Sir John's fourth son, Richard. The male Spencer line at Offley ended with a bachelor, Sir John, who died in 1712 but the house remained with the female line. The Reverend Lynch Salisbury Burroughe began to make major alterations that resulted in the present house, known as Offley Park. The rebuilding was carried out by Sir Robert Smirks, the architect who designed the British Museum. Much of his grand design can still be seen as part of this important Regency house.

Offley Park

The Ackland family, who bought Offley Park in 1928, were very popular in the village but only lived there for 10 years and then leased it to the Froebel Educational Institute, which bought the estate in 1943. Several of their ex-students belong to the Old Students' Association. It became Offley Training College and for twenty-two years was a most respected local centre for teacher training. After this date there were several changes including a period as a successful Field Study Centre and as a residential college.

However, despite all these changes and essential alterations, the building has kept the general structure, dignity and elegance of a gentleman's country house. This meant that with public rooms ideal for conferences and wedding receptions and modernised bedrooms and bathrooms, Offley Park, with its elegant rooms, well-kept lawns and rose-gardens, is ready to welcome a new generation of visitors.

TEA GREEN (Stopsley)

Although this hamlet is in the county of Hertfordshire and in the parish of Offley, from its high position one can see down across Stopsley. Three Stopsley families were included in the group that originally bought the licence to found the Fraternity but little is known about either John Welle or William Bradley; Richard Stopisley was a founder member.

ROUTE
The route, which is heading for Tea Green, bears left out of the village and onto a bridge over the A505; it then continues along what is known as 'Lilley Bottom'. Drive between open fields and watch out for a partly hidden cross-roads, where you turn right towards Tea Green and Luton. The road is now even narrower! You will see a water tower on the hilltop. From this hilltop, by the White Horse, the route is heading, via Chiltern Green, to the B6533 (the Lower Harpenden Road).

The Stopsley Family

He may have been descended from the 'Alexander, son of Maurice of Stopsley', who was a respected man, chosen to help with the tax assessment of 1297. He was Lord of the Manor of Stopsley and, through his wife, also held land in Clapham, North Bedfordshire. The Stopsley family was related by marriage to Canon William Wenlock of Farley Hospital. When he died, in 1392, Canon Wenlock bequeathed money for a William of Stopsley to be sent to school. The last member was Agnes.

SOMERIES 'CASTLE'

The family which brought the name 'Somery' to Luton had died out in Bedfordshire long before the Fraternity was founded but later owners played a very important role.

The de Somery Family

At some time during the late 12th century a family with the surname of Somery came to Luton from Dudley Castle in Worcestershire. They built a large moated house on the outskirts of the town and lived there for several generations. However, when John de Somery died in 1321, the estate passed to his married sister and in Luton the family name died out. Although the family only survived locally for about 125 years, the second house built on the estate has commemorated their name ever since.

The First Castle

In 1926 Wilfred Fleet, steward of the Manor of Luton, made a survey of the earthworks which are all that remains of the original house. Austin recorded that the main building was approximately 111ft square and that it was surrounded by a ditch (dry moat), which at that date was still 3ft deep. There was also evidence of a narrow outer ditch. It is not known exactly when this house was built nor when it was dismantled in favour of the new manor house.

ROUTE
As the road divides, head first for Warden End and Luton, then towards Breachwood Green and Darley Hall and at a later junction, head for Breachwood Green and Kings Walden. The route enters Chiltern Green via a steep hill. At the bottom of the hill, turn right towards Chiltern Green and Petersgreen. The route soon comes to Dane Street cottages, which are on a dangerous bend. Follow the road to the left along a narrow tree-lined road. (If you want to visit Someries, watch for a small, unmarked turning to the right. This is opposite Chiltern Green House and is an optional, very rough road to Someries Castle.)

ROUTE
(Whichever route you take to Someries, drive very slowly and carefully, and be prepared to meet children, animals and farm machinery.) The main route continues down a steep hill, under a railway bridge and will cross the B653 and climb the hill on the other side of the road. (A slightly better route to Someries is to turn right instead of left and then watch for the sign pointing right towards Someries. Going this way, the road is slightly better, but you still have to go along the very pot-holed road to the left of Copt Hill Farm.)

The Mystery of Who Built the New 'Castle'?

After the death of John of Someries, the ownership of the property is less well recorded. However it is known that the brick-built ruins that still stand today were built by a different family. During the early 15th century, the Wenlock family from Much Wenlock in Shropshire was gradually buying up land in Luton. Dates are vague, but it is known that in 1433 Lord John Wenlock represented Bedfordshire in parliament. By 1438 he was described as being 'of Someries' and may have begun to build a new manor house, adjacent to or adjoining the old one.

It is also known that around 1472 Lord Thomas Rotherham, the future Archbishop of York, bought the estate, to provide a 'stately home' for his family near London. Finally, although it is known that around 1740 it was pulled down, by Sir John Napier of Luton Hoo, the mystery remains as to who actually built the 'castle'?

The Manor House at Someries

The remaining red brick walls are very important because they form part of one of the first brick buildings in England since the departure of the Romans.

In 1467 Sir John Wenlock, a soldier and diplomat, who was deeply involved in the Wars of the Roses, bought the main part of the Manor of Luton. This was an important move for the future history of Luton because he was adding it to the smaller part that he already owned. It is probable that he soon began to build Someries as his new manor house. However there are several pieces of conflicting evidence. Firstly Henry VIII's antiquary, John Leland, visited Bedfordshire (but not necessarily Luton); his comments concerning Someries are partly helpful and partly confusing. He was in no doubt that it was 'sumptuously begun by the Lord Wenlock' but suggested that he had not finished it. He made observations about 'the very large and fair' brick gatehouse and continued 'Part of the residence of the new Foundations be yet seen and part of the Old Place standeth yet'.

274

Pennant in his 'Journey from Chester 1782' was writing about a journey that he had made in the preceding year. He described Someries much as it is today with a gateway, part of a tower and 14 or 15 brick steps. He does not mention the chapel but it is possible that he did not visit the ruins himself but relied on hearsay. (He does not give a personal account of Luton Hoo either.) He quotes Leyland, that Lord Wenlock began but did not finish 'a house'. It is Pennant who records that Someries was pulled down by Sir John Napier 'about forty years ago'. From all this one can consider whether Lord Wenlock added the gatehouse, the chapel and some other rooms to the old Somery house; that his new house was never finished and that Leyland's 'Old Place' was the repaired or partly rebuilt 'Somery' building. This could explain why Sir John Napier did not pull down the chapel and the gatehouse, as they would be in much better condition than the rest. On the other hand, Leyland may have meant that the new house was begun by Lord Wenlock, perhaps in Totternhoe stone, and that the next owner, Archbishop Rotherham, ordered the building of the imposing chapel and gatehouse to be in red brick. As it was Lord Wenlock who had the beautiful chapel built in the parish church, he may not have needed a chapel at Someries; whereas alternatively, a bishop would have wanted a chapel in any house with which he was associated.

The Inventories

Davis, in his 'History of Luton' published in 1874, mentions an inventory of 1606, six years before Sir John Rotherham sold the Manor of Luton to Sir Robert Napier and one year after King James had visited Sir John at Someries. He mentions a 'Queen's' chamber and a 'le Grey's' chamber. In the 15th century, Thomas Rotherham married Catherine, daughter of Lord Anthony Grey. This Sir Thomas inherited Someries from the Archbishop and may well have built a suite of rooms for his wife. There was a room described as 'Miss Elizabeth's chamber' and another listed as 'Mr Cheney's chamber'. Thomas Cheyne (whose father owned Bramingham and other areas of Luton) married an Elizabeth Rotherham in 1546. Elizabeth was a popular name in the Rotherham family. Apart from these four, another seven chambers are mentioned, plus the great and little parlours, the servants' rooms and the kitchen quarters, so when King James made his visit in 1605, it was an impressive manor-house, probably built around a courtyard.

At a later date a third family lived for many years at Someries. In 1608 Elizabeth Rotherham married Francis Crawley, son of a local farmer and property owner, who had begun a successful career at the bar. During their stay a second inventory was drawn up; this was dated February 28th 1644. By this time Francis Crawley had been knighted and as an ardent Royalist had left Luton to join the king at Oxford. Prior to sequestration, Parliamentary officers always made an inventory and in addition to the earlier details, there was mention of the hall, with two tables and two forms and a dining-room, with a court cupboard (probably an elaborately carved sideboard) and a table with six well-made chairs and stools. One of the great bedrooms was still called 'The Queen's Chamber' but 'Miss Elizabeth's' had become known as 'My Lady's Chamber'. In total there were less individual chambers mentioned and some of these may have been converted into the hall and dining room.

The furniture listed was not a true record because some had already been removed. However, a good picture was drawn of a busy kitchen; it contained:

4 spits, 2 dripping pans, 1 jack (equipment for hanging the great pots), 12 pewter dishes, 3 little kettles and 3 skellets (various metal pots for boiling food), 1 iron pot and one brass pot.

As after the war Sir Francis' three sons all entered the professions, it is not surprising that the inventory ended with 'certain books in and around the house'.

Three Important Families at Someries

Sir John Wenlock spent most of his adult life at court or as a diplomat and soldier. He seldom lived at Luton but he married a local girl, widow Elizabeth Preston, the daughter of Sir John Drayton of Kempston. His family had been settled in the Luton area since the mid 14th century, his great-uncle being the Canon William Wenlock who, in 1391, was buried in the parish church. John inherited land in and around Luton and bought other pieces as they became available. During the reign of King Henry V, he served in France as a senior army officer and by 1440 he had joined the household of King Henry VI. In 1439 he was described as 'gentleman of London'. He took part in the negotiations that led to the marriage of King Henry and Margaret of Anjou and, in 1445, was amongst the large party that went to France for the proxy ceremony. By the time of her coronation on May 30th, he had become one of the Ushers of the Queen's Chamber. This was a position which gave him many chances of advancement, and he rose to become her Chamberlain. It may have been at that date that he received his knighthood. By the end of June 1448 he had become a Justice of the Peace in Bedfordshire. The years went by with Wenlock dividing his time between his administrative duties in Bedfordshire and his diplomatic duties in England and overseas. These were becoming exceedingly difficult because trouble was brewing between King Henry VI and his cousin, the Duke of York. In 1455, as part of his normal duties, he accompanied the king and queen when they set out on a journey north out of London. As they approached St Albans they learnt that the Duke of York and his supporters were also travelling towards St Albans, from another direction. This is how it came about that, on 22nd of May, Wenlock is recorded as fighting 'for' the king at the first Battle of St Albans. In fact the royal party was caught unprepared and many from that party were killed.[1] Wenlock was wounded, rescued from the market place in a cart and taken to recover at Someries.

When parliament met a few weeks later (1st July), there was an atmosphere of reconciliation. Wenlock had been appointed Speaker and it has been assumed that he had switched his support to the Duke's (Yorkist) cause. However, his biographer, JS Roskell, agrees that the appointment of a man associated with the king might have been seen as an attempt to avoid Yorkist domination of proceedings.[2] As in 1455 King Henry was suffering a period of mental confusion, of a type which had afflicted him previously, the Duke of York was made Protector but, when Henry recovered the following spring, he once again took control. Two years of uneasy peace followed and in May 1458, Wenlock with the Earl of Warwick and others went on a diplomatic mission to Burgundy. Whatever doubts he had about the Lancastrian cause, he was still sufficiently trusted to be included in the King's Council. At the Battle at Bloreheath (Staffs) on 23rd September 1459, Wenlock supported the Red Rose of York. The Yorkists were outnumbered and fled from the field. Wenlock (and his senior officer Earl Warwick) escaped to Calais, his position in parliament forfeit, his estates sequestered and with a reward offered for his capture. Nevertheless in June 1460 the party of exiles returned and while some defeated the king's army at Northampton, Wenlock stayed behind to arrest the Lancastrian officers based in the Tower of London.

The Duke of York was now in control of the country and Wenlock received high honours. The fighting continued despite the fact that the Duke of York was killed. In 1461 Wenlock was elected a Knight of the Garter. Together with the new young Edward of York, he immediately left London for Gloucestershire and

1 For local details of 'Politics and the Battle of St Albans 1455' see Bulletin of the Institute of Historical Research Vol XXXIII No 87 May 1960
2 BHRS Vol XXXVIII

therefore missed the attack that Henry's queen, Margaret of Anjou, made on St Albans on 17th February. They returned to London where Edward declared himself king.

Wenlock gave him his full support, both as a diplomat and as a soldier. His loyalty was rewarded and on 4th November 1461 he took up his seat in the House of Lords. He received several paid positions, including the lordship of Berkhamsted Castle and was able once more to take on administrative positions in Bedfordshire.

Then quite suddenly the news broke that Edward had secretly married Elizabeth Woodeville and that her relatives were taking over many positions previously held by traditional Yorkist supporters. Warwick and Wenlock left for Calais and spent the year 1470 in France. While they were there, the King of France persuaded them to support a Lancastrian, Margaret of Anjou, and they sailed with her to England. This ill-thought-out manoeuvre ended in disaster. Warwick was killed at the Battle of Barnet and Wenlock died in 1471, during the final battle at Tewkesbury.

Because Wenlock died fighting for the defeated Lancastrian party, his estates, including Someries, were at once forfeit to King Edward, whom he had deserted. Nevertheless, despite the disgrace, the committee who, three years later, founded the Luton Fraternity, entered Lord Wenlock as a posthumous member. The main sponsor of the Fraternity was the new owner of Someries.

Lord Thomas Rotherham

Although Lord Thomas Rotherham did not become Archbishop of York until 1480, by the time that he bought Someries he had already had a very successful career and had risen to become Bishop of Rochester. Coming from a humble family in Yorkshire, he had used his good education to become chaplain to the Earl of Oxford, where he was noticed by the future King Edward IV. This introduction, together with his own natural abilities, gave him the opportunity to rise very rapidly in the church, in diplomatic circles and in government. At one time he held the prestigious post of Lord Chancellor of England. During the so-called 'Wars of the Roses', he managed to stay neutral and was therefore in a position to buy the vacant Someries estate. His father had recently died and Someries became the home of his widowed mother and his brother John and family. They were both founder-members of the Fraternity. John's son, another Thomas, joined at a later date.

Compared with some other churchmen of his day, Rotherham was a devout man and he was very grateful for the education that had given him the chance of preferment. Preparing for his death, (which did not take place until 1500) he provided for his family and then left most of his great wealth to provide educational facilities. He paid to rebuild and re-endow Lincoln College, Oxford and in addition, endowed three schools in Rotherham. All of these were built in red brick. He recorded in his will that he believed it to have been God's grace that provided him and other youths with the good education which led to their successful careers and he explained that because of this he was founding the schools, to show his gratitude to his Saviour.

The direct line of the Rotherham family remained at Someries for several generations and they married into important Bedfordshire families, such as the Greys of Wrest Park and the St Johns of Bletsoe. In addition, John's younger son, George, rented Farley Farm from St Albans Abbey and started a second branch of the family. The direct male line died out and in 1611 Sir John Rotherham sold most of his land and, later, the title, Lord of the Manor, to Sir Robert Napier (see below). In 1608 his daughter Elizabeth had married their neighbour, Sir Francis Crawley. At first the young couple lived near the centre of Luton but in 1629 her father sold Someries to Sir Francis and his father. By the time of the Civil War the family was settled at Someries.

The Crawley Family were still comparatively small farmers and land dealers when the Fraternity was created. The respected Luton author, William Austin, in his book 'The Story of a Luton Family', has traced them back to their origins, firstly as farm workers, then as tenant farmers in the area of Crawley Green and continuing on to the present day. The family still owns land in Luton today.

During 1455 (the year that successful soldier and diplomat Lord Hoo died at his home in Sussex and Lord Wenlock was wounded at the Battle of St Albans), three men, called Robert, Thomas and William 'Crawlele', were tenants on the church land at Luton. They were therefore not of sufficiently high status to be founder members of the Fraternity. A 'William and Alice' were the first members to join, in 1479, at which time they were living at Dane Farm, on the Luton side of Tea Green.

During the 16th century the family became sufficiently wealthy to have sons who entered the professions and just as the Rotherham family was beginning to have financial difficulties, a Francis Crawley went to London to study law. He was very successful and in 1632 he became a judge. The family was strongly Royalist and at the out break of war Francis accompanied King Charles to Oxford, where he received a knighthood.

The three sons of Sir Francis were all Royalist supporters: the eldest, another

Francis, followed his father's profession, Thomas became a chaplain and later Rector of Barton and Robert became a doctor, practising, after the war ended, in Dunstable. Because the male members of the family were supporting the king, at home, Lady Crawley was kept under close observation, in case Someries became a centre for royalist spies. On at least one occasion she had to support parliamentary soldiers who were camped around the house.

When their mother died in 1658, her children wanted a traditional burial service using the Book of Common Prayer but at that time this was forbidden. The vicar, the Rev John Jessop, was torn between upsetting the church authorities by using the prayer-book or the family by using the modern Bible-based service which was then in use. However, the family outwitted him, slipping quietly into St Mary's Church where Thomas read the traditional service. Jessop reported the incident and was ordered to bring Thomas to personally explain his behaviour to Oliver Cromwell. However, the latter died before the meeting could take place.

The End of Someries 'Castle'

This luxurious country house had been started, if not finished, during the troubled years leading to a civil war. Many houses built at that time had a moat and/or a very strong gatehouse; this was not intended to withstand a siege but to keep out any undesirable strangers. The children of Francis appear to have neglected Someries. By the time that his grandson, John, felt the need of a country house, it was so old-fashioned and in need of repair, that when, around 1740, it was sold to Sir John Napier, of Luton Hoo, he decided to pull most of it down. Meanwhile John Crawley had commissioned the building of Stockwood House.

The ruins of Someries are well maintained by Bedfordshire County Council and stand in a pleasant area adjacent to Someries Farm. This is said to have been built with bricks taken from the old castle. Although there is no curator at the site and the approach road is very damaged, there is a carpark and visitors are welcome.

TEA GREEN

The Crawley Families

Despite the rural approach to Tea Green, if you look straight ahead you can see how close you are to Luton. The area, which is now under the airport flightpath, was once closely connected to the Crawley family, as were some of the farms that

Gateway Someries Castle

Stage Coach in Mossman Collection Stockwood Park

281

once lay to the left of Tea Green. The family was not of sufficiently high status to be founder members of the Fraternity. William and Alice were the first members to join in 1479. At that time they were living at Dane Farm, on the Luton side of the hamlet. The family continued to live in and around Stopsley but during the 17th century one branch moved to Someries.

ROUTE

The route turns left onto the B653 and then right, onto an unclassified road. It is heading for the A1081. (The road to Luton Hoo is signposted from this road.)

LUTON HOO

The house which stands today is not the comparatively new house with 60 hearths, which was recorded in the late 17th century, nor the one that was built for the Earl of Bute. Nevertheless, it is a Grade II listed building.

The Hoo Family

A family called Hoo arrived in the 13th century and built a large house in its own grounds, to the south east of Luton. By the end of the century they owned land in five counties and Sir Robert Hoo had twice been a Member of Parliament for Bedfordshire. In later years a Sir Thomas Hoo married Isabel St Leger who brought her husband large estates in Sussex. The best-known member of the family was a later Sir Thomas, who was knighted c1380; when he was honoured again in 1447, he took the title Baron Hoo and Hastings. His career in military and diplomatic affairs was not unlike that of his neighbour, Lord Wenlock, but being an older man he did not live to become involved in the Wars of the Roses. When he died on 13 February 1455, he was buried in Battle Abbey. He was entered in the Register, posthumously in 1475.

The Hoo estates were divided between his four daughters, the second of whom (Anna) married Geoffrey Boleyn. Her great granddaughter, Anne, married King Henry VIII and, for a short time, was Queen of England. Descendants of the Hoo family sold their Luton estate c1523 and soon after 1600 it became the home of wealthy London merchant, Robert Sandy.

The Napiers of Luton Hoo

The branch of the family which settled in Luton, in 1601, were the junior branch of a Scottish family, the Napiers of Merchiston. Senior members of the family arrived in England with James I but Robert's father, Alexander, travelled south to Exeter during the reign of Henry VIII. Once settled, he took the name Sandy, which may originally have been a nickname. However, as they were so

282

distant from the main line of the family, his children took it as a surname. Alexander's eldest son, Robert 'Sandy', was born in 1560. As an adult he travelled to London where he made a fortune in the City. He was a member of the Grocers' Company and expanded his business by trading with Turkey.

His mother, Ann Birchley, was from Hertfordshire, which may explain why he chose to buy a country estate on the Hertfordshire/Bedfordshire borders. At first he continued to spend a great deal of his time in London. He may have been presented to King James in London or maybe when the king visited Someries; certainly James was impressed by his wealth and made a point of visiting Luton Hoo during his progress of 1611. As Robert Sandy he became High Sheriff of Bedfordshire in 1611 but the following year, when he received first a knighthood and then a baronetcy, he took the title Sir Robert Napier. His eldest son, Robert, inherited his title and his second son, Richard, was knighted in 1647.

As has been noted above, Luton at this time was made up of a number of small manors or estates. In 1612 Sir Robert began the process of re-uniting these and once he had the manorial title, Luton Hoo became the main manor house of Luton.* During the next hundred years he and his successors bought up more and more of the small estates and farms.

Sir Robert also spent a considerable amount of money rebuilding the manor house and in 1623 bought a licence to enclose 300 acres of parkland. These together formed the estate and social position that, in 1637, the first Lord Napier passed to his son. The estate remained with the Napier family until the death of the last baronet in 1748. For a few years it passed between distant members of the family, but in 1762 it was sold to John Stuart, 3rd Earl of Bute.

The Earl of Bute

As a young married man living at Kenwood House, Bute was introduced, at Epsom racecourse, to Frederick, Prince of Wales. They became friends and Bute frequently visited the prince and his wife Augusta. For a time he acted as tutor to their son, the future King George III. When Frederick died and George became Prince of Wales, Bute stayed on as his advisor. George was crowned in 1760 and in less than two years made Bute his Prime Minister. He was never happy in this position and turned to his newly acquired garden at Luton Hoo for consolation.

'Manor' is a legal, not geographic term. It suggests one large, but perhaps scattered estate under the control of one owner and/or his steward

He had been born and grew up on the Isle of Bute, where he had taken a great deal of interest in plant growing and landscape gardening. He continued this interest at Kenwood, and later persuaded Princess Augusta to develop what we now know as the Royal Botanic Gardens at Kew. Over the years, various shrubs and plants were named after him.

Earl Bute at Luton Hoo

At Luton Hoo, Bute commissioned Lancelot (Capability) Brown to redesign both the park and gardens. Having increased the area of the park to 1500 acres, Bute then went on to dam the River Lea, thus creating a lake covering 60 acres.

He invited Robert Adams to design and rebuild a highly ornate house, but there were several problems during the building stage and, following a fire in 1771, a compromise was made. Part of the house was rebuilt using Adams' design and part of the old building was retained and refaced. When Dr Johnson visited 10 years later, he was most complimentary. He described the library as 'splendid' and commented on the dignity of the rooms and the number of pictures in the house. Another visitor reported that there was a screen beside each fireplace, listing the pictures and their artists on view in the room. There were 30,000 books in the library, which was considered second only to Blenheim and the other rooms were equally grand. Then in 1843 disaster struck; a fire started and could not be controlled. Although some books and paintings were saved, the building and many of the contents were lost.

After the fire the Bute family left Luton and in 1848, the estate was bought by John Shaw, a wealthy solicitor who had recently been mayor of Liverpool. He rebuilt the house, making use of surviving walls and, where possible, following the original plan. In 1903 the house and estate were sold once again.

Sir Julius Wernher

Sir Julius had emigrated to South Africa in 1871 where he became responsible for modernising the process of diamond mining. He was one of only five life governors of the De Beers company and was created a baronet in 1905. He collected furniture, pictures, tapestries, medieval ivories, Limoges enamels and many other items. Alice Sedgwick Manciewicz, Sir Julius' wife, collected English porcelain, especially Chelsea, Bow and Worcester. After major alterations were made to the house, their combined collections were transferred to Luton Hoo.

During the last war the house became the headquarters of the Eastern Command. Sir Julius had died in 1912, but his wife lived on until 1945. In

1919, Lady Wernher remarried; her second husband was the late Lord Ludlow, which is why there is sometimes confusion concerning her name. Sir Harold Wernher (son of Sir Julius and Lady Alice) married Lady Anastasia (Zia) Mikhailovna de Torby, elder daughter of the late Grand Duke Michael of Russia. He added English furniture to the family collection. Lady Zia brought her Carl Faberge collection and portraits of the Russian Imperial family. Sir Harold died in 1973, followed by Lady Zia in 1977; the estate then passed to their grandson and his wife, Mr and Mrs Nicholas Phillips. For many years the house and collection were open to the public and in recent years the house has been used in several films, the best-known probably being 'Four Weddings and a Funeral'.

Unfortunately, following the death of Nicholas Phillips in 1991, the estate debts were such that it was eventually put up for sale. The collection is now on show to the public at The Rangers' House, Chesterfield Walk, Blackheath and the house is likely to become a five-star hotel.

Stockwood Park

This is the estate that was laid out by John Crawley when he decided to return to Luton in the 1730s; it was completed by 1740 and became an elegant country residence. There were two storeys of public and private rooms, a basement for storage, an attic where the servants slept. In the 1870s, there were a governess, 2 nurses and a nursemaid, a butler, a housekeeper, 2 footmen, 4 housemaids, a kitchen-maid, a scullery-maid, a laundress and 3 laundry-maids, a gardener, 2 under-gardeners and 2 grooms. After the 2nd World War, Lieutenant Colonel and Mrs Ross Skinner sold the house and grounds to Luton Town Council. During the war and continuing until 1958 the house was used as a hospital, causing the house to deteriorate. It was demolished in 1964, leaving the stable court and walled gardens to be most successfully adapted to house Stockwood Craft Museum and period gardens. Today, the beautiful walled gardens are used to illustrate different periods of gardening and there is a café. Adjacent is the Mossman Collection of carriages and horse-drawn vehicles.

ROUTE
If visiting Stockwood Park, watch for the signs and turn left into Cutenhoe Road, right into London Road and watch for the sign pointing up Whitehill Avenue towards the park.
The route down to St Mary's Church, (see the beginning of this section for historical background) The Red Lion and the centre of Luton is clearly marked from both the A1081 and from Stockwood Park.

For St Mary's Church and The Red Lion Inn see the beginning of this section.

General Index

Religious Houses (see also Monasticism)
Augustinian Canons 10, 11, 27, 40, 45, 105
Ashridge 11, 42, 44-47, 53, 55, 56, 58, 82, 116
Bushmead 11
Caldwell 11, 145, 154
*Dunstable 11, 15-17, 25, 27-29, 45, 67, 71, 73-75, 105, 106, 116-120, 128, 142-145, 185,
193, 223*
Newnham 11, 105, 143-145, 154, 164, 165
Benedictine Monasteries 3-5, 41, 105, 178, 188
Beaulieu Priory 201, 204, 218
Redbourn Priory 21, 22
*St Albans Abbey 5, 7, 12-23, 25, 29, 31, 32, 34-36, 41, 52, 77, 92, 106, 108, 114, 119, 141,
146, 201, 218, 265, 266, 271, 279,*
Grovebury Priory (Abbey of Fontevrault) 108, 109
Cistercian Monks 10, 226, 227, 245, 246
Warden Abbey 10, 142, 152, 153, 164, 200, 206, 226-228
Woburn Abbey 10, 116, 200, 206, 245-247, 250
Cluniac Monks 10
Dominican Friaries 59, 221
Dunstable 73, 74, 91
Kings Langley 59, 60
Gilbertine Priories
Chicksands 200, 201, 224, 238, 239
Knights Hospitallers 232
Roads and their Repair 157, 195
Rural Industries 203
Lace 87, 148, 209, 210
Market Gardens 204-206, 209
Mineral Extraction 203, 204, 250, 253
Straw Hats 84, 87, 97, 148, 204, 209-211, 265
Russell Family - Dukes of Bedford 59, 126, 148, 154, 155, 165, 172, 179-183, 205, 209, 210,
212, 214, 247-249, 256
Schools 22, 51, 68, 70, 110, 147, 148, 158-161, 172, 181, 182, 187, 202, 203, 209, 212, 213,
237, 248, 252-254, 260,
Ship Tax 93-95
Straw Hats (see Rural Industries)
Tompion, T 232
Wall Paintings 37, 40, 53, 55, 72, 87, 88, 121, 122
Whitbread Family 147-149, 157, 182, 211, 236, 237
Workhouses (see Parish Relief)

Places Index

Aldbury 42, 46, 81, 82, 99

Ampthill 185, 186, 200-202, 205, 209-214, 217, 218, 220-225, 246, 250, 255, 256

Arlesey 205

Ashridge Forest 41, 42, 45, 99, 100

Ashridge House 42, 45, 47-51, 53, 100, 113, 116, 188

Ashridge College (see Monasteries)

Aspley Guise 200, 250-254

Aston Clinton 75

Aylesbury 87-90, 95, 96, 130

Barnet 17, 278

Barton 280

Batford 32, 33

Beadlow (see also Religious Houses) 239

Bedford 92, 105, 136-138, 140-146, 150, 154, 156, 157, 162, 164, 167, 172-174, 178, 187, 191, 193, 205, 209, 211, 214-217, 237, 253, 269

Berkhamsted 41-45, 47, 115, 130, 174

Biddenham 178, 179, 190, 193, 195

Biggleswade 156, 205, 236

Billington 112

Bletchley 200, 205

Bletsoe 94, 174, 190, 279

Blunham 156, 157, 222

Bovingdon 56

Boxmoor 56

Bromham 150, 170, 178, 188, 190-196, 202, 207-209, 212, 214, 225

Broom 232

Buckingham 86

Caddington 24, 29-31

Campton 238, 239

Cardington 144-147, 151, 157

Chalfont St Peter 73

Chalgrave 104, 106, 120-122, 124

Chicksands (see also Religious Houses) 201, 224, 225, 238, 239

Clapham 177-180, 273

Clophill and Cainhoe 137, 204, 206, 208, 214, 217, 218, 220

Colmworth 11, 121, 156

Cople 149-151, 191, 225

Cublington 173

Dunstable (see also Religious Houses) 16, 17, 21, 25, 27-29, 41, 45, 67-74, 84, 91, 105, 113, 117-120, 138, 142-144, 194, 201, 216, 246, 280

Downs 25, 75, 76

Inns 17, 27, 28, 68, 71-74

Swan Jewel 91-93

290

Churches Index

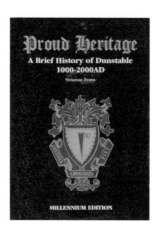

PROUD HERITAGE
A Brief History of Dunstable 1000-2000AD
Vivienne Evans

Dunstable was founded by a king, had a palace, a very important Augustian Priory and until 1600 was visited by nearly every king and queen of England. Sited on the crossroads less than forty miles from London, Oxford and Cambridge, Dunstable has been involved in many national events. Its populace has had to face economic and religious upheavals, but time after time Dunstablians pulled together, changed direction and won through to another successful era. Devoting a chapter to each of the ten centuries of the millennium, this book first sets the national and county scene in order to make more comprehensible the purely Dunstable events. Included in this book are stories about the Priory Church, Priory House, Kingsbury, Grove House, the Sugar Loaf and other inns, Ashton St Peter and other schools, Middle Row, Edward Street and other roads, the straw-hat industry and the growth of the town.

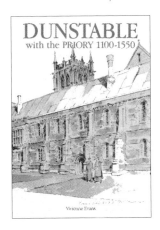

DUNSTABLE with the PRIORY 1100-1550
Vivienne Evans

This is the dramatic story of Henry 1's busy and influential town with its royal palace, Augustinian Priory, Dominican Friary and thriving businesses around a major crossroads. Its rapid rise to success sees it linked to many famous national issues such as Magna Carta, the Eleanor Crosses, the Peasants' Revolt, the annulment of Henry V111's marriage and the dissolution of the monasteries.

DUNSTABLE in TRANSITION 1550-1700
Vivienne Evans

The residents of Dunstable needed all their resourcefulness to rebuild the town's success without the Augustinian Priory.

Though disrupted by civil war, the developing coaching industry soon filled Dunstable with inns, as some new visitors brought wealth and importance to counterbalance other travellers who posed problems of poverty and disease.

The age's religious upheavals found a microcosm in Dunstable. The majority stayed worshipping at the Priory Church, but some left for America and others met in secret until reform led to the acceptance of Quakers and Baptists.

Scandal punctuated this period of turmoil - the baptism of a sheep at church, the hounding of a suspected witch and the predations of notorious highwaymen. All elements of Dunstable in a volatile, transitional phase.

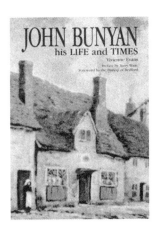

JOHN BUNYAN
His Life and Times
Vivienne Evans

Born to a humble family in the parish of Elstow near Bedford, John Bunyan (1628-1688) became one of the world's most widely read Christian writers - The Pilgrim's Progress eventually being translated into over two hundred languages. This lively book traces the events of his life with its spiritual turmoil and long imprisonment, as well as discussing many of his writings. Clearly seeing Bunyan as a product of his time and place, it also explains the intriguing social, political and religious background of the turbulent seventeenth century.

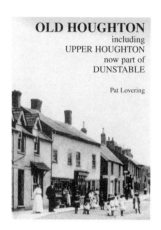

OLD HOUGHTON
including UPPER HOUGHTON now part of DUNSTABLE
Pat Lovering

Old Houghton is a pictorial record of the town, which captures the changing appearance over the last 100 years or so. In this book you can glimpse the past and see the quaint charm of a Bedfordshire village as Houghton Regis was until the late 1950s. It is fascinating to see the Village Pond, the Old Pound Tree and the High Street at the turn of the century. This book shows the importance of recapturing some of Houghton's recent past before it is completely forgotten.

The Book Castle

STREETS AHEAD
An Illustrated Guide to the Street Names of Dunstable
Richard Walden

Over the past 150 years Dunstable has expanded from a small rural market town with limited development beyond the four main streets, to a modern urban town of 35,000 inhabitants and over 300 individual streets.

The names of many of those streets have been carefully chosen for some specific reason. Dunstable's modern housing estates in particular have been spared the all too common anonymity of poets, painters, authors and birds found in most other town. In Dunstable, developers and the local Council have taken great care to select names, which record elements of the town's unique historical past and some of the characters and events, which helped to shape the local community.

Streets Ahead is extensively illustrated with hundreds of photographs and copies of original documents, many of which have never been published before. The content of this work also makes it a fascinating record of the town's recent history.

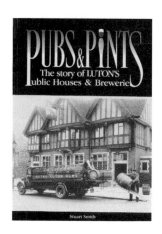

PUBS AND PINTS
The Story of Luton's Public Houses and Breweries
Stuart Smith

Whilst the town of Luton is well documented in other ways, this profusely illustrated book is the first comprehensive history of its important brewing industry and retail beer outlets-linked, staple trades in the area for over five hundred years.

The development of the modern public house from the early taverns and coaching inns closely followed that of the breweries, with the final decades of the last century seen as the high point in the number of houses licensed to sell beers for consumption on or off the premises. Since then the total has declined with the loss of around 40% during the last one hundred years, most of these losses occurring in the period from 1950 to 1970.

Although written documentation dealing with the early breweries and public houses is extremely sparse, it is the intention of this book to try to record the history of each brewery and public house that has had a bearing on the social and drinking pastimes of Lutonians over the last one hundred and fifty years. Similarly a special feature of the book is the vast range of three hundred representative photographs- many old, rare and unusual.

THE CHANGING FACE OF LUTON
Stephen Bunker, Robin Holgate & Marian Nichols

"The Changing Face of Luton" traces the fortunes of the settlement and economy of the town from the earliest recorded arrival of people in the area to the present day. It looks at different aspects of Luton and its development rather than giving a straight chronological account of its history.

Luton's roots go back a very long way, yet in less than 200 years it has changed from a small market town to today's busy industrial and commercial centre. This transformation is described, helped by a range of excellent photographs, thereby answering many of the questions frequently asked, and perhaps raising more, about this intriguing town.

The three authors from Luton Museum are all experts in local history, archaeology and industry.

CHANGES IN OUR LANDSCAPE:
Aspects of Bedfordshire, Buckinghamshire and the Chilterns 1947-1992
Eric Meadows

In the post-War years, this once quiet rural backwater between Oxford and Cambridge has undergone growth and change - and the expert camera of Eric Meadows has captured it all...

An enormous variety of landscape, natural and man-made, from yesteryear and today - open downs and rolling farmland, woods and commons, ancient earthworks, lakes and moats, vanished elms. Quarries, nature reserves and landscape gardens. Many building styles- churches of all periods, stately homes and town dwellings, rural pubs, gatehouses and bridges. Secluded villages contrast their timeless lifestyle with the bustle of modern developing towns and their industries.

Distilled from a huge collection of 25,000 photographs, this book offers the author's personal selection of over 350 that best display the area's most attractive features and its notable changes over 50 years. The author's detailed captions and notes complete a valuable local history.

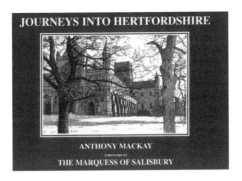

JOURNEYS INTO HERTFORDSHIRE
Anthony Mackay

A superb collection of ink drawings revealing an intriguing historic heritage and capturing the spirit of England's rural heartland, ranging widely over cottages and stately homes, over bridges, churches and mills, over sandy woods, chalk downs and watery river valleys.

Every corner of Hertfordshire has been explored in the search for material, and, although the choice of subjects is essentially a personal one, the resulting collection represents a unique record of the environment today.

The notes and maps, which accompany the drawings, lend depth to the books, and will assist others on their own journeys around the counties.

Anthony Mackay's pen-and-ink drawings are of outstanding quality. An architectural graduate, he is equally at home depicting landscapes and buildings. The medium he uses is better able to show both depth and detail than any photograph.

FAMILY WALKS
Chilterns - North
Nick Moon

This book is one of a series of two, which provide a comprehensive coverage of walks throughout the whole of the Chiltern area. The walks included vary in length from 1.7 to 5.5 miles, but are mainly in the 3 to 5 mile range, which is ideal for families with children, less experienced walkers or short winter afternoons.

Each walk text gives details of nearby places of interest and is accompanied by a specially drawn map of the route, which also indicates local pubs and a skeleton road network.

The author, Nick Moon, has lived in or regularly visited the Chilterns all his life and has for 25 years, been an active member of the Chiltern Society's Rights of Way Group, which seeks to protect and improve the area's footpath and bridleway network.

The
Book
Castle

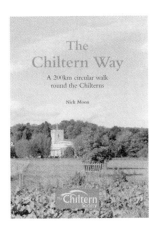

THE CHILTERN WAY
A Guide to this new 133-mile Circular Long Distance Path through Bedfordshire, Buckinghamshire, Hertfordshire & Oxfordshire
Nick Moon

The Chiltern Way has been established by the Chiltern Society to mark the Millennium by providing walkers in the twenty-first century with a new way of exploring the diverse, beautiful countryside which all four Chiltern counties have to offer. Based on the idea of the late Jimmy Parson' Chiltern Hundred but expanded to cover the whole Chilterns, the route has been designed by the author and is being signposted, waymarked and improved by the Society's Rights of Way Group in preparation for the Way's formal launch in October 2000.

In addition to a description of the route and points of interest along the way, this guide includes 29 specially drawn maps of the route indicating local pubs, car parks, railway stations and a skeleton road network and details are provided of the Ordnance Survey and Chiltern Society maps covering the route.

.

CHILTERN WALKS
Hertfordshire, Bedfordshire and North Buckinghamshire
Nick Moon

This book is one in a series of three, which provide a comprehensive coverage of walks throughout the whole of the Chiltern area (as defined by the Chiltern Society). The walks included vary in length from 2.3 to 10.8 miles, but are mainly in the 5-to-7-mile range poplar for half-day walks, although suggestions of possible combinations of walks are given for those preferring a full day's walk. Each walk text gives details of nearby places of interest and is accompanied by a specially drawn map of the route, which also indicates local pubs and a skeletal road network.

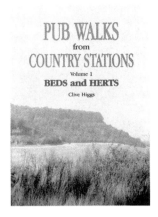

PUB WALKS FROM COUNTRY STATIONS:
Volume 1 Beds and Herts
Clive Higgs

This book is the first of two, both containing fourteen circular country rambles, each starting and finishing at a railway station and incorporating a pub-stop at a mid-way point. Volume 2 covers Buckinghamshire and Oxfordshire.

Volume 1 has 5 walks in Bedfordshire starting from Sandy, Biggleswade, Harlington, Flitwick and Linslade. Together with 9 walks in Hertfordshire starting from Watford, Kings Langley, Boxmoor, Berkhamsted, Tring, Stanstead St.Margaret's, Watton-at-Stone, Bricket Wood and Harpenden.
The shortest walk is a distance of 4miles and the longest 7 and a half miles.

JOURNEYS INTO BUCKINGHAMSHIRE
Anthony Mackay

A superb collection of ink drawings revealing an intriguing historic heritage and capturing the spirit of England's rural heartland, ranging widely over cottages and stately homes, over bridges, churches and mills, over sandy woods, chalk downs and watery river valleys.

Every corner of Buckinghamshire has been explored in the search for material, and, although the choice of subjects is essentially a personal one, the resulting collection represents a unique record of the environment today.

The notes and maps, which accompany the drawings, lend depth to the books, and will assist others on their own journeys around the counties.

Anthony Mackay's pen-and-ink drawings are of outstanding quality. An architectural graduate, he is equally at home depicting landscapes and buildings. The medium he uses is better able to show both depth and detail than any photograph.